PSYCHOLOGY
AS A PROFESSION

Pergamon Titles of Related Interest

Goldstein/Krasner   MODERN APPLIED PSYCHOLOGY

Nietzel/Dillehay   PSYCHOLOGICAL CONSULTATION IN THE COURTROOM

Romanczyk   CLINICAL UTILIZATION OF MICROCOMPUTER TECHNOLOGY

Walker   CLINICAL PRACTICE OF PSYCHOLOGY:
A Guide for Mental Health Professionals

Related Journal

CLINICAL PSYCHOLOGY REVIEW*

*Free sample copies available upon request

PSYCHOLOGY PRACTITIONER GUIDEBOOKS

EDITORS

Arnold P. Goldstein, Syracuse University
Leonard Krasner, Stanford University and SUNY at Stony Brook
Sol L. Garfield, Washington University

PSYCHOLOGY AS A PROFESSION
Foundations of Practice

WALTER B. PRYZWANSKY,
University of North Carolina, Chapel Hill

ROBERT N. WENDT,
University of Toledo

PERGAMON PRESS

New York · Oxford · Beijing · Frankfurt
São Paulo · Sydney · Tokyo · Toronto

U.S.A.	Pergamon Press, Maxwell House, Fairview Park, Elmsford, New York 10523, U.S.A.
U.K	Pergamon Press, Headington Hill Hall, Oxford OX3 0BW, England
PEOPLE'S REPUBLIC OF CHINA	Pergamon Press, Room 4037, Qianmen Hotel, Beijing, People's Republic of China
FEDERAL REPUBLIC OF GERMANY	Pergamon Press, Hammerweg 6, D-6242 Kronberg, Federal Republic of Germany
BRAZIL	Pergamon Editora, Rua Eça de Queiros, 346, CEP 04011, Paraiso, São Paulo, Brazil
AUSTRALIA	Pergamon Press Australia, P.O. Box 544, Potts Point, N.S.W. 2011, Australia
JAPAN	Pergamon Press, 8th Floor, Matsuoka Central Building, 1-7-1 Nishishinjuku, Shinjuku-ku, Tokyo 160, Japan
CANADA	Pergamon Press Canada, Suite No. 271, 253 College Street, Toronto, Ontario, Canada M5T 1R5

First edition 1987

Library of Congress Cataloging in Publication Data
Pryzwansky, Walter B., 1939–
Psychology as a profession.
(Psychology practitioner guidebooks)
Includes bibliographies.
1. Psychology—Practice. 2. Clinical psychology—
Practice. I. Wendt, Robert N. II. Title. III. Series.
[DNLM: 1. Professional Practice. 2. Psychology.
BF 75 P973p]
BF75.P73   1987   150'.23'73   86–25502
ISBN 0-08-033129-7 Hardcover
ISBN 0-08-033128-9 Flexicover

Printed in Great Britain by A. Wheaton & Co. Ltd., Exeter

Dedicated to
Kathy Barthalmus Pryzwansky
and to
Dianne, Beth, and Dave

Contents

Preface

The application of psychological knowledge to personal, interpersonal, and societal problems has grown dramatically within the last 40 years. Concurrently, the psychology discipline has moved significantly from being primarily an exclusively academic/scientific discipline to more and more of an applied profession, with a burgeoning increase in applied psychology specialties. Led by the clinical psychology subfield, other specialties, including counseling and industrial/organizational and school psychology, have established themselves, followed by the forensic, neuropsychological, and applied development areas. As a result, not only have professional psychologists emerged as a force in the industrial, health service, mental health, and educational settings, but psychology now produces more PhDs than the "hard" science areas. This shift to a "blended" field also has created numerous internal changes.

The growth of psychology as a profession has resulted in developments in accreditation of training program procedures, credentialing, and development of professional practice guidelines. At the same time, pressures for establishing and/or enhancing regulatory systems of this profession, as well as other professions, have resulted in the significant impact of external forces on professional psychology. These influences have been found in the legislative, legal, and service domains.

This book, therefore, addresses the history and current evolution of professional psychology content. The authors felt a need for a reference text to which applied psychologists could turn for current information, as well as a context in which to place professional needs or questions they faced. Often, in order to obtain such information, personal research on a topic had to be done, and frequently, the time and/or the sources of information were not readily available. For example, just keeping up to date with the activities of the American Psychological Association over the past 10 years almost always meant a commitment of some length to involvement in the organization. In other instances, the only exposure to topics was through professional seminars in graduate schools or professional workshops; here again, the quality of the content depended on a host of variables, not the least of which was the priority and relevance placed on the content. This book, then, is designed for both audiences, the practitioner and the graduate student. At the very least, it should serve as a handy reference book for the professional library. Also, it can provide the background for interpreting the current developments in the field. And finally, we hope it will be the impetus for future in-depth readings in the professional areas critical to the practicing psychologist.

There have been many people who have helped nurture this idea, which grew out of an APA symposium and the authors' experiences with that organization. Jerry Frank was supportive of the idea from the beginning; if not for him we might have treated it like all those other good ideas. Lyda Beemer and Sue Martin shepherded us and the manuscript through its many drafts. Jane Trexler did her usual precise and prompt typing of the chapters. Graduate students in W.B.P.'s Professional Seminar in School Psychology were enthusiastic, but candid in commenting on drafts, for which we will always be grateful. Carol Vatz helped out in so many ways and always with a smile. She assisted Carol Duncan in preparing the latter's materials on Health Maintenance Organizations; they represent the best of graduate students. Finally, our families tolerated us, and for that understanding we are grateful.

Chapter 1
Introduction

The self-confidence that professionals display is either a pretense or a mark of self-delusion. If a little learning is a dangerous thing, then most of us must live with virtually ubiquitous danger, for most of us do have a little, and the great learning of men of knowledge is still paltry, and still dangerous. (Moore, 1970, p. 243)

PSYCHOLOGY AS A PROFESSION

Most writers typically cite 1879 as the year psychology emerged as a separate and distinct discipline; the "new" field seemed to shed its cocoon of biology and emerge from that discipline, as well as the discipline of philosophy, to stand on its own. This same year marks the birth of modern psychology, because it was then that Wilham Wundt founded the first psychological laboratory labeled as such in Leipzig, Germany. While the biological roots of psychology remain evident in basic general psychology texts and in the research of some psychologists, the discipline's uniqueness has obviously been established. In the beginning, psychology as a science was characterized by the bulk of psychologists being employed in institutions of higher learning, performing teaching and research responsibilities.

It was not long after the emergence of psychology that psychologists began to apply their knowledge base in settings other than academia. Lightner Witmer established the first psychological clinic for the treatment of children's educational problems in 1896, an attempt to reaffirm the worth of the new discipline to society (Napoli, 1981). Witmer is also credited with coining the term *clinical psychology*. In a few years, the Binet Intelligence Test was being used to make school placement decisions for children. Another application appeared when government officials used psychologists to assist in the selection of armed services recruits during World War I. Napoli (1981) identified the first three applied areas of psychology to be clinical, educational, and industrial, with the specific emergence of *school psychology* associated with Arnold Gesell,

1

who was given the official title of school psychologist in 1915 by the Connecticut State Board of Education (Fagan & Delugach, 1985). That title, however, seemed to find its greatest use as a differentiation from psychology's other specialties following World War II, during the mental health movement.

Thus, from almost its beginnings, the new discipline was embraced by some who saw its potential as a science and advocated its emphasis be directed toward the development of new knowledge; and others whose prime interest was in the application of the knowledge to practical problems, that is, the scientists (researchers) and the practitioners (professionals). Napoli (1981) has noted that the first constitution of the American Psychological Association (APA) in 1894 defined its purpose as "the advancement of Psychology as a science" and limited its membership to those who were "engaged in this work." Napoli notes that with that charge began the immediate clarification of terms which seems to have never ended, as we shall see in chapter 6 of this book. For example, in spite of the existence of an APA, a Society of Experimental Psychologists was organized in the 1920s, while the establishment of yet another organization, the American Association of Clinical Psychologists, was considered in 1917. Manifestations of such tension should not be surprising when one considers that the basic researcher as well as the applied practitioner lay claim to the same title, "psychologist"; yet, their training and objectives of employment reflect very significant differences. Contrast this situation with the one between medicine and biology or chemistry, and the nature of the circumstances become more understandable. On the other hand, some have argued that the bifurcation of psychology is unnecessary and somewhat overstated. For example, the Boulder Conference, which will be discussed in chapter 2, recommended a scientist-practitioner model of training and practice for clinical psychology in 1949. The basic premise of that model is that the applied psychologist (i.e., practitioner, professional) is well-grounded in the scientific knowledge base of the parent discipline and contributes to that knowledge base as well. The scientist's investigations can be described as basic research versus the applied research of the applied psychologist, although that distinction could also be challenged.

Yet, in spite of the struggles noted here, psychologists could claim to be unique in that they were the only occupational group with academic origins (Napoli, 1981). Furthermore, it is difficult (and perhaps meaningless) to pinpoint the beginning of psychology as a profession versus psychology as a science. The early interest and efforts wherein the new science was applied have already been noted. However, if the common features of most definitions of a profession were to be used, the question of when psychology became professionalized would be more difficult.

Most definitions of a profession include the following: the existence of a formal organization, systematic training, a code of ethics, regulation of its members, and a body of knowledge. Some of the organizational history pertinent to this discussion has already been mentioned. In addition, it should be noted that in 1937, when the New York State Association of Consulting Psychologists reorganized itself into the Association of Consulting Psychologists (ACP), it was concerned with professional issues on a national level and, in particular, licensing and ethics. Consequently, we can assume, at the very least, that by this time (i.e., 1937) the profession of psychology had truly been developed. We will be returning to the definitional features of a profession to discuss them in greater detail (see chapter 2), but would like to turn to a consideration of two critical identifiers of a profession in this chapter: need and autonomous responsibility.

It has been argued (Dörken & Rodgers, 1976) that if psychology is to be a profession, the profession and the public it serves must be able to identify the unique field of need that is being served rather than considering a validated body of knowledge as its primary defining parameter. Fox, Barclay, and Rodgers (1982) argue that professional psychology be considered "that profession which is concerned with enhancing the effectiveness of human functioning" (p. 307). They do not intend to define the "field of need" in a monopolistic way in the sense that psychology is the only profession that will deal with problems of illness. Rather, they note that it is "the only profession that consistently focuses its efforts in solving problems through alterations in patterns of behavioral coping" (p. 308). The ultimate concern of professional psychologists is "all problems involving human coping skills and human coping effectiveness" (p. 308). It would seem safe to say that the majority of society's members would agree with this conceptualization, regardless of the differences in nuances of this question.

It can also be assumed that the professional will deal with the entire field of need, "even when effective solutions to the problems presented are uncertain" (Dörken & Rodgers, 1976, p. 290). Dörken and Rodgers argue that the responsibility for making decisions regarding problems wherein the solution(s) is less than apparent and the knowledge base wanting is what truly defines a profession. They go on to argue "that where a body of knowledge is adequately validated and adequately comprehensive to serve a field of need, then experts in that knowledge are basically technicians rather than professionals" (p. 289). In fact, they further point out that psychology's commitment to validated procedures and scientifically researched approaches can be construed as a commitment to a technology rather than a profession. Such an orientation leads to the technician serving and contributing to the informational needs of other professionals. Indeed, it has been pointed out that the contributions of psychology to education, law, and medicine can be of this highly specific type. This decision regarding emphasis also affects, then, the degree of independence assumed by the practitioner.

The professional autonomy issue has been addressed formally by organizations serving psychology. The American Psychological Association published its first official position on relations with other professions in 1954 (APA, 1954). It asserted that APA had full responsibility for overseeing the evolution of professional psychology while staking the claim of an autonomous profession for psychology, except where social responsibility is a factor. It further defined contributions to the social good as excluding nonfunctional constraints or restrictions, such as pressure from more established professional groups (Saccuzzo & Kaplan, 1984). However, the most controversial statement in the 1954 report was one that approved of psychologists conducting psychotherapy only in "genuine collaborations" with physicians. This position had actually been one of the recommendations of the Boulder Training Conference (Raimy, 1950). Four years later (APA, 1958) this restriction was removed and replaced with the notion of psychologists conducting independent psychotherapy when appropriate. Furthermore, legal support for psychologists who were challenged for engaging in such a practice was pledged by APA. The most current affirmation of the principle of autonomous functioning appears in the APA *Ethical Principles of Psychologists* (1981) (see Appendix), as well as the *Standards* (1977) and *Specialty Guidelines* (1981) (see chapter 3).

Finally in 1951, the executive secretary of the APA reviewed the obligations of psychology as a profession (Sanford, 1951). In an attempt to promote its development, he proposed 16 principles/criteria for consideration. Sanford's list was as follows:

1. A good profession is one that is motivated by a sense of social responsibility.
2. A good profession is one sufficiently perceptive of its place in society to guide continually its practices and policies so they confirm to the best and changing interests of that society.
3. A good profession is one that is continually on guard lest it represent itself as able to render services that are beyond its demonstrable competence.
4. A good profession is one that is continually seeking to find its unique pattern of competence and that concentrates its efforts on the rendering of the unique service based on its pattern of competencies.
5. A good profession is one that devotes relatively little of its energy to "guild" functions, to the building of its own in-group strength, relatively much of its energy to the serving of its social function.

6. The good profession is one that engages in rational and non-invidi-
   ous relations with other professions having related or overlapping
   competencies and common purposes.
7. A good profession is one that devotes a proportion of its energies to
   the discovery of new knowledge.
8. The good profession is one in which there are good channels of
   communication between the discoverers of knowledge and the ap-
   pliers of knowledge.
9. The good profession is one in which its discoverers of knowledge are
   not relegated to positions of second-rate status.
10. The good profession is one that is free of non-functional entrance
    requirements.
11. The good profession is one in which preparatory training is validly
    related to the ultimate function of the members of the profession.
12. A good profession is one in which the material benefits accruing to
    its members are proportional to social contributions.
13. The good profession is one whose members are socially and finan-
    cially accessible to the public.
14. The good profession has a code of ethics designed primarily to pro-
    tect the client and only secondarily to protect the members of the
    profession.
15. A good profession is one that facilitates the continuing education and
    training of all its members.
16. A good profession is one that is continually concerned with the
    validity of its techniques and procedures. (pp. 668–670)

Berstein and Nietzel (1980) used this list to retrospectively assess the
progress made by psychology toward the professional goal set by Sanford and came away with a positive conclusion. For example, criteria 3, 4,
13, and 14 are concerned with ethical behavior, and the *Ethical Principles
of Psychologists* (APA, 1981) are noteworthy in this respect. Training standards are dealt with in criteria 10, 11, and 15. Chapter 2 of this book
spells out the standards and validation procedures psychology currently
employs to insure the development and improvement in training programs. While continuing professional education remains the least monitored area, mechanisms are in place to enhance professionals' efforts in
this area. Over the past few years psychology has reached out to other
helping professions in a constructive way, and professional liaisons and
collaborative efforts have resulted (e.g., Millon, 1983). The remaining
criteria deal with the profession's responsibilities to society (1, 2, 5, and
12) and the promotion of the science and "applied science" of psychology (7, 8, 9, and 16). We examined the latter point to a degree when the
dual nature of psychology—science and profession—was discussed. This
last area remains a challenge and test of the success of the final outcome

of the applied psychologist's quest. Finally, psychologists seem sensitized to their social responsibility, partly because the field of psychology
has the advantage of being relatively young and thus can learn from the
struggles of other, older professions. But also, by the very nature of the
discipline and the values it espouses, psychology has always ap-
proached its objectives with social responsibility in mind. While it remains for others outside the discipline to make that judgment because of
their potential objectivity, the current standards and literature of the
psychology profession might be considered positive in this regard.

PROFESSIONAL TRAINING

Peterson (1985) concludes that over the past 20 years professional
schools and the professional doctorate have become established in
American psychology. However, Fox, Barclay, and Rodgers (1982) found
that three impediments stood in the way of the growth and development
of professional psychology. They noted the lack of a single agreed-upon
definition of the profession and its scope. With respect to the education
of professionals they identified two troublesome features: (a) training
settings that were so uncontrolled and variable that uniformity of training was lacking and professional identity hard to establish; and (b) practicum experiences that take place in service delivery systems controlled
by professionals other than psychologists. Finally, the absence of a credential by which the practitioner can be unambiguously defined was
also noted as a problem plaguing the profession of psychology.

It is important to complete this section with a description of some
recent developments related to graduate training in psychology (i.e., to
include both research-oriented and applied programs). For the past few
years, a number of groups within the field have been calling for a national conference on training to consider an effort similar to Flexner's (1915)
work at the turn of the century, which revolutionized medical education.
The last conference on graduate education in psychology was held in
1958 and was known as the Miami Beach Conference (Roe, Gustad,
Moore, Ross, & Skodak, 1959). By contrast, a number of conferences
have specifically addressed only professionally oriented training. Most
notable was the Shakow report (1947), wherein the need for psychological assessment and therapy in Veterans Administration hospitals led to
recommendations for a graduate training in clinical psychology. The emphasis on the scientific and professional areas of functioning was first
given recognition in this report. The Boulder Conference (Raimy, 1950)
specifically addressed training of clinical psychologists, as did the Chicago Conference (Hoch, Ross, & Wender, 1966), which stressed alternative
training models to the scientist-practitioner model. A conference focus-

ing on school psychologists' training was also held at this time (Cutts, 1955), along with a conference held at Stanford University that emphasized the need for community mental health programs (Strother, 1956). The Vail Conference (Korman, 1976) was notable for its endorsement of the professional degree in psychology (PsyD) and was followed by a conference to address several issues related to the practitioner model of training programs (Watson, Caddy, Johnson, & Rimm, 1981).

As a result, the APA Education and Training Board directed its Committee on Graduate Education and Training to consider such a possibility. At their planning meeting, they noted that at least three philosophical issues undergird all education and training concerns. Those issues include: "1) continuity and change in education; 2) independence and responsiveness to society; and 3) diversity and homogeneity of values and of professional activities or functions" (Brickman, 1985). Furthermore, 12 topic areas emerged that the committee felt needed to be fully discussed and reviewed by the field prior to a national conference (they recommended a time frame of 2 years for such discussion to take place). These 12 topic areas or issues, arranged into categories in Table 1.1, represent a comprehensive list of considerations that the profession faces in tackling the goal, considering the future shape and direction of gradu-

Table 1.1 Issues in Graduate Education

I. Professional Role Issues
   1. Is the primary mission of the department to train a practitioner-investigator-educator or is some level of integration expected among the three roles?
II. Educational Content and Process Issues
   2. Should there be a core curriculum or should the curriculum be individualized?
   3. What should the structure and content be at the undergraduate, graduate, and postgraduate level?
   4. Do we train generalists or specialists?
   5. Where should graduates operate on the technological transfer continuum, i.e., moving knowledge from the basic or applied research stage to practical application?
   6. How should psychology grow—increased specialization based on societal needs?
III. Educational Milieu Support System Issues
   7. What are the implications of the institutional and organizational setting for graduate education, e.g., should it be done in Departments of Psychology or free standing institutions?
   8. How diffuse or centralized should program quality control be allowed to exist?
   9. What role should societal and financial support play in training?
   10. How do we (Psychology) apply what instructional methods we have developed to our own educational programs?
IV. Student Issues
   11. How should recruitment and retention policies and procedures be arranged to achieve our objectives?
   12. How is effective socialization to be realized?

Data from: Brickman, L. B. (Ed.) (1985). *Issues and concerns: Graduate education in psychology.* Washington, DC: American Psychological Association.

ate training in psychology. Subsequently, a national invitational conference to address issues of graduate education in psychology has been
scheduled to occur in June 1987.

Recent Trends in Graduate School Enrollment

Some related trends should be stated from recent manpower surveys.
Stapp, Fulcher, and Wicherski (1984) point out that the number of psychology doctorates awarded to women has risen from 17.5% of the total
in 1960 to 47.5% in 1983, and that the women who received these degrees are likely to be employed part-time. In 1981–1982 doctoral graduate
psychology classes, 7.8% of the students were members of ethnic minorities and 96% were U.S. citizens. Regarding the type of degree earned,
91.7% of 1981–1982 of doctoral candidates in graduate psychology received PhD degrees, 2.4% EdD degrees, and 5.8% PsyDs. In 1982 there
were 44 programs with a sole emphasis on training the practitioner, and
4,992 students were enrolled in these programs (Caddy & La Pointe,
1984). Twenty-four of these programs were in freestanding schools with
27 programs leading to the PsyD degree. These authors conclude that
academic employment opportunities may improve in the future, although a period of relative stability in employment opportunities continues to exist—only 2% of the 1981–1982 class reported that they were
seeking employment. More than half (57.6%) of these respondents were
located in the same geographic areas (New England, South Atlantic,
etc.) in which they received their degrees. About 70% of the respondents
trained in the Middle Atlantic and Pacific regions stayed in those regions
after graduation.

While some have argued that the odds of being accepted into a graduate program in psychology are relatively favorable (Korn, 1984), others
analyzing the same data conclude that the situation is less optimistic
(Nichols, 1985; Werner, 1985). Hovancik (1985) combines data from several sources to present the number of applications, acceptances, and
enrollments for graduate programs in psychology by 10 subfields along
with candidate/acceptance ratios; his conclusion is also less favorable
than Korn's (e.g., 5% vs. 61% of applicants to APA-approved clinical
programs will be accepted).

Recent Trends in Employment

Since 1975 the American Psychological Association has been conducting annual surveys of doctoral recipients in psychology, and their data
suggest a picture of professional psychology's development. While the
major employer of doctoral psychologists in the period from 1930 to 1944

was a college or university (64%) and still remained high (50%) in 1950 (Webb, 1962), those figures dropped dramatically to 32.7% in 1975 and 26.2% in 1982 (Stapp et al., 1984). By contrast, 17.1% of the 1981–1982 doctoral graduates now work in hospitals, 15.6% in clinics, and 7.3% in other human service settings. Erdwin's and Buffardi's (1983) survey of recent graduates from master's programs in psychology found that nearly all of them were employed in the field or were continuing with graduate training. Among the larger psychological subfields, which are applied areas,

> 55.6% of the school psychology respondents have full-time positions in schools and other educational settings, 57.1% of the industrial/organizational psychology respondents are employed in business, government and other settings; and 51.3% of the clinical psychology doctoral recipients have full-time positions in hospitals and clinics. (Stapp et al., 1984, p. 1415)

Finally, it is also interesting to note that the subfields of clinical, counseling, industrial/organizational, and school psychology graduated 1,873 of the 2,993 psychology doctorates in the years 1981 and 1982; clinical psychology clearly graduated the most students ($N = 1,234$). A trend toward a dramatic increase in the numbers of professional psychologists has continued to grow since 1979 while doctorates in research subfields of psychology (e.g., experimental, social) have declined (Stapp et al., 1984). The increasing emphasis on nonacademic career roles and applied research has led to speculation that significant expansion in this aspect of the psychological discipline may continue and increase its influence in society (Pion & Lipsey, 1984).

Faculty

Given the number of graduates in the applied areas of psychology, it should not be surprising that when the clinical, counseling, and school psychology specialists are considered as a group, they constitute approximately one-third of U.S. faculty in graduate departments of psychology (Pion, Bramblett, Wicherski, & Stapp, 1985). One out of every five Canadian faculty members are in these areas. The largest percentage are in clinical psychology (23.2% in the U.S. and 19.9% in Canada). The major research specialities are experimental, developmental, and social psychology. Among the general characteristics of faculty members reported by Pion et al. (1985) were that 25% are women (20.7% in Canada), and 5% in the United States are members of ethnic minorities—black, Hispanic, Asian, or Native American (3.4% in Canada). The 1984–1985 starting salary for assistant professors was $22,000 ($27,050 in Canada, based on Canadian dollars and on a 12 month basis) in doctoral departments and $20,000 in U.S. masters' departments.

PSYCHOLOGY AS AN
INTERNATIONAL DISCIPLINE

In the beginning years, scientific psychology was formulated in Europe, particularly in Germany. The influence of European-trained psychologists was pervasive in America prior to World War I, and American psychologists continued to study abroad following this period. In the 1930s, the influx of European psychologists to the United States continued to have an impact on theoretical approaches, methods, and tools. However, as Sexton and Misiak (1984) point out, "the volume and significance of American contributions to psychology steadily grew, and as American psychology eventually outdistanced other countries in productivity, the history of psychology was actually being made in the United States, particularly after 1930" (p. 1026). Such growth and success, however, had its negative side effects in isolating American psychology from developments in other countries (Russell, 1984; Sexton & Misiak, 1984). While psychology in the United States will most likely continue to have its impact on the field in the years to come, significant developments of a theoretical and applied nature can be expected in the international community. As a case in point, Sexton and Misiak (1984) note that several applied specialities have been researched and practiced in a number of European countries before becoming popular in America. Those areas include clinical neuropsychology (France, Italy, Russia); the study of defectology, similar to but broader than the American psychology of the handicapped (Eastern Europe); and a topic of interest for decades in Europe, sports psychology.

It seems almost trite to observe that our world is shrinking, after the many reminders of the past decade. Yet, at times we fail to appreciate the international implications of that fact for the expansion of knowledge in other countries. We are fast approaching a time when an international perspective will be required in psychology in a way that is obvious in the political and social contexts. Psychology is truly becoming international in scope and perspective. While the number of psychologists per million persons is highest in North America (424), Western Europe is next with 322, Australia–New Zealand follows with 235, and Latin America with 120 (Russell, 1984).

PLAN OF THE BOOK

The purpose of this book is to collate and present information regarding the foundation areas of practice in the psychology profession. This material should be helpful to those aspiring to join the ranks of psychologists who apply the scientific psychological knowledge base to human need, as well as the seasoned practitioner. The information is as current as can be put together for a growing, dynamic profession and, in some instances, considers developments and trends in terms of what *might be*. The intent, then, is to prepare a text as well as a reference tool that can be used at all stages of professional development.

"Foundations of practice," as a phrase in the title of this book, is meant to encompass the essential components that define professionals in general. As noted earlier, generally these components include the established credentials of the field, standards of training and practice, formal organizations, and professional ethics. Consequently, chapters have been written that present the existing positions, standards, and/or documents with which all applied psychologists should be familiar. Given the diversity of subfields in psychology that can be considered applied, some readers, no doubt, will wish more or less emphasis was placed on a topic or issue. Again, when judged from the purpose of the book, we hope the reflected balance will be acceptable.

The initial section of each chapter, then, contains a summary of relevant information from existing documents and the general literature. Again, it is not intended that an exhaustive review be presented, but rather a careful compilation of basic content. The choice and emphasis of each chapter topic is spelled out. It is hoped that content will reflect what is needed to be known by all applied psychologists. The next section of each chapter, *Issues*, will highlight some of the major considerations related to the topic(s) as noted in the different perspectives of this field. Rather than promote a point of view, the authors have taken the position that professionals first need to be well-informed on the various positions that pertain to an issue, so that they can contribute to the dialogue at all levels of the profession functioning—local, state, regional, and national. These discussions of issues can at the very least alert the reader to the complexity of the matter at hand and stimulate discussion while serving as the basis for further, in-depth reading. In fact, the final section of each chapter will present a Suggested Readings list, to aid the reader in considering topics in an in-depth manner. These readings should begin that process, and include both articles and texts from the field.

Finally, it is important to note that the reader is encouraged to read the original sources referred to in this text and to follow up on other presented content. This advice is particularly important when pursuing membership in organizations or applying for a professional credential. For one reason alone, the fact that changes are taking place rapidly in the field because psychology is in a growth period, certain information or criteria may change. Second, the Zeitgeist may be quite different from when the book was written, so that other issues or topics need more emphasis. Finally, it is impossible (not to say a formula for dull reading) to include every qualification or detail related to applications. Material in this book is intended only as an introduction. If we have sensitized readers to the important aspects of their professional lives, and even made them think about becoming involved in its development, then we have reached our objective.

SUGGESTED READINGS

History and Issues

The historian Donald Napoli (1981) presents a comprehensive treatment of the emergence of applied psychology from 1890 to the present. The story of repeated attempts of applied psychologists to organize themselves, the threats from within and outside this young discipline, and the varying public demand for expert assistance in adjustment are chronicled in an objective manner by someone other than a psychologist.

The *Professional Psychologist's Handbook* (Sales, 1983) is a comprehensive reference book, which all applied psychologists should know about because of its potential use at one point or another. In spite of the fact that some of the material may be somewhat dated because chapters were written in 1979, and the price may be overwhelming to some, excellent treatment of many of the topics and issues treated in this text can be followed up in the *Handbook*.

Mary McHugh's (1976) book *Psychology and the New Woman* is a "choosing careers and lifestyles" book that considers the nature of experiences in all of the psychology subfields from a woman's perspective.

Kimble (1984) examines the dichotomy between humanistic and scientific beliefs of psychologists. He collected data from undergraduates, division officers of the APA, and members of selected divisions of the APA, regarding their attitude on a six-item inventory. Differences between groups of psychologists in their humanistic or scientific orientation are discussed.

By tracing his involvement in psychology for over 50 years, Crawford (1985) expounds upon the growth and change of psychology. He includes philosophical and technological changes, and the effect of these on professional training. In all ares, Crawford views psychology as responding to a complex society where many influencing factors are operating simultaneously.

Cattell (1983) reviews the "duel" between psychiatry and psychology in terms of qualifications to provide services. He proposes future directions for both professions. Much of the article is devoted to presenting a quantitative systems approach that he feels is the direction psychology is heading.

International Psychology

The topic of international psychology received special treatment in the September 1984 issue of the *American Psychologist* (*39* [9], 996–1042). Five articles deal with various facets of the topic, but their authors are in general agreement that U.S. psychology suffers from insularity. Russell's article is particularly interesting in that he examines factors that shape the growth of the discipline in a society. There is also an annotated bibliography of international materials for developmental and social psychology. Readers may also want to consider Ruben Ardila's (1982) article on "International Psychology," which appears in an earlier issue of *American Psychologist*. Ardila presents a worldwide perspective on psychology, including important developments in Western and Communist countries. International associations, journals, and congresses are described.

Graduate Training

According to Boll (1985), a combination of forces seems to be leading to a watershed period in psychology's education and training. He identifies and briefly reviews those developments, as he calls for active involvement of psychologists in related discussions.

Frank (1984) critiques the viability of the Boulder model using a number of publications, and McConnell (1984) explicates the rationale underlying the Doctor of Psychology model.

While there is a trend toward an increase in minority doctorate graduates in psychology, there are some signs that underscore the fear it may not continue (Isaac, 1985). Isaac has argued that a plan for retention of the minority student is as important as any recruitment strategy and outlines some efforts directed toward both objectives.

Finally, by their own admission, Fox, Kovacs, and Graham (1985) present 20 "controversial and revolutionary" proposals for how professional psychologists are trained and credentialed. Their comprehensive ideas reject the freestanding professional school call for a generic doctoral degree rather than one that is specialty-oriented, and carry that idea over to licensure. Their proposals touch on many of the issues presented in this book.

Reference Texts of Interest to Specific Subfields of the Profession

Clinical Psychology
1. Hersen, M., Kazdin, A. E., Bellack, A. S. (Eds.). (1983). *The clinical psychology handbook*. New York: Pergamon Press.

2. Saccuzzo, D. P., & Kaplan, R. M. (1984). *Clinical psychology.* Boston: Allyn & Bacon.

Counseling Psychology
1. Brown, S. D., & Lent, R. W. (Eds.). (1984). *The handbook of counseling psychology.* New York: John Wiley.

Health Psychology
1. Dörken, H. and Associates (1976). *The professional psychologist today.* San Francisco: Jossey-Bass.
2. Millon, T., Green, C., & Meagher, R. (Eds.). (1982). *The handbook of clinical health psychology.* New York: Plenum.

Industrial/Organizational Psychology
1. Dunnette, M. D. (Ed.). (1983). *The handbook of industrial and organizational psychology.* New York: John Wiley.

School Psychology
1. Reynolds, C. R., & Gutkin, T. B. (Eds.). (1982). *The handbook of school psychology.* New York: John Wiley.

REFERENCES

American Psychological Association. (1954). *Psychology and its relations with other professions.* Washington, DC: Author.
American Psychological Association. (1958). Committee on relations with psychiatry, 1958 Annual Report. *American Psychologist, 13,* 761–763.
American Psychological Association. (1977). Standards for providers of psychological services. *American Psychologist, 32,* 495–505.
American Psychological Association. (1981). *Ethical principles of psychologists* (rev. ed.). Washington, DC: Author.
American Psychological Association. (1981). Specialty guidelines for the delivery of services. *American Psychologist, 36,* 639–681.
Ardila, R. (1982). International psychology. *American Psychologist, 37,* 323–329.
Berstein, D. A., & Nietzel, M. T. (1980). *Introduction to clinical psychology.* New York: McGraw-Hill.
Boll, T. J. (1985). Graduate training in psychology: Time for a change? *American Psychologist, 40,* 1029–1030.
Brickman, L. B. (Ed.). (1985). *Issues and concerns: Graduate education in psychology.* Washington, DC: American Psychological Association.
Caddy, G. R., & La Pointe, L. L. (1984). The training of professional psychologists. In G. S. Tryon (Ed.), *Professional practice of psychology* (pp. 3–49). Norwood, NJ: Ablex.
Cattell, R. B. (1983). Let's end the duel. *The American Psychologist, 38,* 769–776.

Crawford, M. F. (1985). Psychology, technology and professional service. *The American Psychologist, 40,* 415–422.

Cutts, N. E. (1955). *School psychologists at mid-century.* Washington, DC: American Psychological Association.

Dörken, H., & Rodgers, D. A. (1976). Issues facing professional psychology. In Dörken, H. and Associates, *The professional psychologist today* (pp. 264–292). San Francisco: Jossey-Bass.

Erdwins, C. J., & Buffardi, L. C. (1983). Employment of recent MAs in psychology: A middle rung on the career ladder. *Professional Psychology: Research and Practice, 14,* 112–117.

Fagan, T. K., & Delugach, F. J. (1985). Literary origins of the term school psychologist. In L. K. Grimley (Ed.), *Historical perspectives on school psychology* (pp. 14–21). Terre Haute, IN: School of Education, Indiana State University.

Flexner, A. B. (1915). Is social work a profession? In *Proceedings of the National Conference of Charities and Corrections.* Baltimore, MD: Social Work.

Fox, R. E., Barclay, A. G., & Rodgers, D. A. (1982). The foundations of professional psychology. *American Psychologist, 37,* 306–312.

Fox, R. E., Kovacs, A. L., & Graham, S. R. (1985). Proposals for a revolution in the preparation and regulation of professional psychologists. *American Psychologist, 40,* 1042–1050.

Frank, G. (1984). The Boulder model: History, rationale and critique. *Professional Psychology: Research and Practice, 15,* 417–435.

Hoch, E. L., Ross, A. O., & Wender, C. L. (1966). *Professional preparation of clinical psychologists.* Washington, DC: American Psychological Association.

Hovancik, J. R. (1985). Comment: Acceptance in Ph.D. programs in psychology: The new odds are at odds with the laws of probability. *American Psychologist, 40,* 852–853.

Isaac, P. D. (1985). Comment: Recruitment of minority students into graduate programs in psychology. *American Psychologist, 40,* 472–475.

Kimble, G. A. (1984). Psychology's two cultures. *The American Psychologist, 39,* 833–839.

Korman, M. (Ed.). (1976). *Levels and patterns of professional training in psychology.* Washington, DC: American Psychological Association.

Korn, J. H. (1984). Comment: New odds on acceptance into Ph.D. programs in psychology. *American Psychologist, 39,* 179–180.

McConnell, S. C. (1984). Doctor of psychology degree: From hibernation to reality. *Professional Psychology: Research and Practice, 15,* 362–370.

McHugh, M. (1976). *Psychology and the new woman.* New York: Franklin Watts.

Millon, T. (1983). The DSM III: An insider's perspective. *American Psychologist, 38,* 804–814.

Moore, W. E. (1970). *The professions: Roles and rules.* New York: Russell Sage Foundation.

Napoli, D. S. (1981). *Architects of adjustment: The history of the psychological profession in the United States.* Port Washington, NY: Kennikat Press.

Nichols, D. P. (1985). Comment: Odd news in acceptance into Ph.D. programs in psychology. *American Psychologist, 40,* 854–855.

Peterson, D. R. (1985). Twenty years of practitioner training in psychology. *American Psychologist, 40,* 441–551.

Pion, G. M., Bramblett, P., Wicherski, M., & Stapp, J. (1985). *Summary Report of the 1984–85 Survey of Graduate Departments of Psychology.* Washington, DC: American Psychological Association.

Pion, G. M., & Lipsey, M. W. (1984). Psychology and society: The challenge of change. *American Psychologist, 39,* 739–754.

Raimy, V. C. (Ed.). (1950). *Training in clinical psychology.* Englewood Cliffs, NJ: Prentice-Hall.

Roe, A., Gustad, J. W., Moore, B. W., Ross, S., & Skodak, M. (Eds.). (1959). *Graduate education in psychology*. Washington, DC: American Psychological Association.

Russell, R. W. (1984). Psychology in its world context. *American Psychologist, 39*, 1017–1025.

Saccuzzo, D. P., & Kaplan, R. M. (1984). *Clinical psychology*. Boston: Allyn & Bacon.

Sales, B. D. (Ed.). (1983). *The professional psychologist's handbook*. New York: Plenum Press.

Sanford, F. H. (1951). Annual report of the executive secretary. *American Psychologist, 6*, 664–670.

Sexton, V. S., & Misiak, H. (1984). American psychologists and psychology abroad. *American Psychologist, 39*, 1026–1031.

Shakow, D. (Ed.). (1947). *Recommended graduate training program in clinical psychology*. Washington, DC: American Psychological Association.

Stapp, J., Fulcher, R., & Wicherski, M. (1984). The employment of 1981 and 1982 doctoral recipients in psychology. *American Psychologist, 39*, 1408–1423.

Strother, C. R. (Ed.). (1956). *Psychology and mental health*. Washington, DC: American Psychological Association.

Watson, N., Caddy, G. R., Johnson, J. H., & Rimm, D. C. (1981). Standards in the education of professional psychologists: The resolutions of the Conference of Virginia Beach. *American Psychologist, 36*, 514–519.

Webb, W. B. (1962). The organization of psychologists, their training and their employment. In W. B. Webb (Ed.), *The profession of psychology* (pp. 34–49). New York: Holt, Rinehart & Winston.

Werner, C. M. (1985). Comment: There is hope for graduate education. *American Psychologist, 40*, 855–857.

Chapter 2
Credentialing in Psychology

Hogan (1979) has reviewed the many definitions of a profession and found that most definitions stress the fact that an organized entity exists to represent and advance the development of the group. Following the agreement that professions are organized groups of individuals, the most important characteristic seems to be the fact that they promote standardized training in knowledge and skill areas to stated criteria; furthermore, that objective is also promoted and monitored by the formal establishment. It has been argued that the training leads to ". . . a way of thinking based on a scientific background and body of knowledge shared in common with other psychologists, augmented by special skills and knowledge based on education and training in the specialty area" (Bardon, 1981, p. 209). Finally, it has been noted that virtually all professions have codes of ethics that emphasize public service. While such altruistic considerations of the professional are considered critical to their definitions, Hogan states that some writers also have included the business motivations of the profession.

In marketplace terms, Beales (1980) points out that professionals are unique in that they generally fill two roles, "the consumer's agent and a principal in the transaction" (p. 125). Given that the professional not only diagnoses, that is, sells information, but also recommends treatment that he or she can deliver, the dual role represents a conflict of interest. The problems confronting the consumer include the risk of misdiagnosis, excessive diagnosis leading to unnecessary or inappropriate treatment, and low quality treatment. While other service personnel also hold this dual role (e.g., auto mechanics), the need for regulation rises as the need to protect the consumer increases, such as when the ability to assess the quality of the service is difficult. Thus, regulation addresses this problem by dealing with the quality of production inputs, the quality of the professional.

Credentialing is the mechanism, then, by which a profession regulates itself or is regulated. It can take place at several levels and implies that a relationship exists between the credential and the competency of the practitioners within the profession. In fact, some authors have conceptualized the construct for competence to vary as a function of the particular credential that is held (Koocher, 1979). This discussion centers on a description of the various types of credentials that exist in psychology. The value of the credential is the validation purpose it serves for the public, that in fact the bearer of the credential has fulfilled requirements and training to participate in the profession.

PSYCHOLOGY CREDENTIALS

Graduate Degree

The most basic credential is often overlooked in credentialing discussions: The graduate degree stands for what might be argued as the most important element of any profession. Graduate programs are academic in nature, and one should be able to assume that those programs advertising their intent to train professionals can be expected to maintain high standards for graduation. The degree, then, serving as one of the psychology credentials, has potentially the most credibility for insuring the entry-to-the-field competence of the novice professional. Longitudinal samples of the graduate's behavior under increasingly demanding conditions, which involve direct and indirect evaluations, support this conclusion. However, this premise is based on the assumption that the professional degree is not strictly academic, but contains sequenced, supervised professional practice (i.e., practicum and internship). Certainly, we can expect that a professional degree serves to confirm that the entry-level knowledge and skills expected of the professional psychologists have been mastered to some minimum criteria as determined by the experienced, even expert professionals doing the training.

Doctoral level training in psychology is often designated by award of the doctor of philosophy (PhD) or the doctor of psychology (PsyD) degree. PhD programs have typically embraced a *scientist-professional* (subtle differences in the meaning of this hyphenated concept are embodied in terms such as scholar-professional, scientist-practitioner or practitioner-scientist) model of training for a number of years, as adopted at the Boulder Conference (Raimy, 1950). More recently (Korman, 1974), the Vail Conference endorsed a recommendation that the highest professional degree be the PsyD. The Vail Conference participants reasoned that where "primary emphasis in training is on the direct delivery of professional services and evaluation and improvement of those services, the PsyD degree is appropriate." Thus, the PhD was conceptualized as appropriate when the primary training emphasis is on the development of new knowledge in psychology. The arguments for each degree will be reviewed in the Issues section of this chapter.

In addition to departments of psychology in universities, professional programs in psychology exist in a variety of organizational settings, such as freestanding schools of professional psychology, autonomous professional schools in academic settings, medical schools, and colleges of education, all of whom may award one or both of these degrees.

Licensure

Perhaps the most commonly identified credential, licensure, remains the least understood because of confusing terminology and the mixed purposes and functions for which it was envisioned. There are at least three types, or levels, of licensure acts. Technically, a *licensing* act grants not only the use of professional title to those individuals meeting established criteria, but also restricts the practice in the profession as defined therein. Thus, the often used synonomous term, a *practice* act. It is the most restrictive of the three types of self-regulation. *Certification*, on the other hand, usually is established primarily to restrict the use of title (or derivatives of the title, such as "psychological" in the case of psychology) and is not concerned with the restriction and/or protection of professional practice except where the person wishes to use the title *psychologist*. These acts are in fact referred to as "title" acts or permissive laws. While both of these forms of licensure laws are mandatory (in the sense that the practitioner is required to hold the credential in order to practice), a more voluntary type of licensure called *registration* is receiving some attention today. It requires no criteria such as passing an exam or meeting minimum educational or other prerequisites before permission is granted to practice. A registration law proposal has been made for psychotherapists in which the practitioner would file relevant information with the state (e.g., education, experience, intended field of practice, methods, goal of treatment, fees, etc.), and a board of registration would be responsible for disciplinary enforcement (Hogan, 1979). In this model, practitioners would be required to provide the client with sufficient information (full disclosure) of their services and the practice subject to direct evaluation by the client.

Licensure represents the mechanism by which state governments protect the public health, morals, safety, and general welfare of their citizens (Council of State Governments, 1952). The state identifies a regulatory agency to carry out this function by establishing a separate board for the occupation or profession. In fact, licensing laws are estimated to affect 20% to 30% of the work force, with the number of licensed occupations or professions involved numbering 500 (Hogan, 1979). Generally, the occupational or professional groups seek this type of legislation with the purpose of protecting the public from harm from incompetent, unethical, or unscrupulous practitioners. This goal is accomplished by establishing entry requirements and mechanisms for regulating professional conduct.

The first psychology licensure law was passed in 1945, but it was not until 1977 that all 50 states had such a statute. At that time it was estimated that there were 28,000 licensed psychologists. The American Psychological Association (1967) adopted a Model for State Legislation to assist states in planning new legislation or considering amendments and it remains the current policy of the organization. A model licensing law that updates the 1967 APA model is in draft form (APA, 1986). It is available from a subcommittee of the APA's Committee on Professional Practice, and may be presented to that organization's Council of Representatives for adoption in 1987.

Obviously, the conditions existing in each state, such as manpower needs and issues of a state's sovereignty, have led to less uniformity in compliance with licensure laws than some would like. Because compliance with federal standards is required before insurance reimbursement is realized, there has been some standardization.

Licensing laws are generally administered by an independent board staffed by the profession for its own regulation; in other instances the board operates within another state agency such as a department of licensing and regulation or department of health. Usually the board is composed of licensed psychologists and, recently, public members. Most laws place the responsibility for selecting board members with the governor. Because some type of formal or informal input from the profession is also involved, the state psychological associations exert a certain degree of influence. Generally, then, the charge to the board is to insure that the statute is carried out in protection of the public rather than as advocacy for the profession or licensed professional.

Psychology boards are members of the American Association of State Psychology Boards (AASPB) whose purposes involve promoting sound administration and facilitating communication among member boards. The AASPB has also begun recommending policy to its member boards. However, the primary task of the organization is the semiannual preparation of two, essentially non-overlapping, forms of the *Examination for Professional Practice in Psychology* (EPPP) for administration in April and October. A multiple-choice exam of approximately 200 items in length, the EPPP is standardized for use by licensing boards, and measures knowledge of basic psychology relevant to professional practice, ethics, and professional affairs. (All states use at least one complementary assessment procedure). A separate AASPB brochure, *Information for Candi-*

dates, is available from the AASPB or the state licensing board, and explains how to prepare for the exam. The content of the examination, beginning with the 1987 administrations, will be based on the results from three projects which were undertaken to ensure the content validity of the EPPP. The first project assembled a "Blue Ribbon Panel of psychologists who defined the scope of professional practice in psychology in terms of performance domains, roles and the knowledge required to perform the roles" (Myers & Rosen, p. 8). A job analysis of professional psychologists work completed by 1,585 licensed psychologists resulted in an "inventory consisting of 59 responsibilities and 61 procedures, techniques, and resources" (Myers & Rosen, p. 12). A 25-member panel of psychologists combined the data from the job dimensions and the domains of practice into five dimensions. The content outline for the exam is briefly summarized as follows:

Dimension I: Problem Definition/Diagnosis
   Responsibility 1: Conduct interviews/meetings, observe other
                    information from client/patient and relevant
                    others.
   Responsibility 2: Select, administer and score the instruments
                    and techniques and interpret the results.
   Responsibility 3: Organize and evaluate collected information
                    and plan for additional information needed;
                    then formulate a working hypothesis.
Dimension II: Design, Implementation and Assessment of Intervention
   Responsibility 4: Design, conduct and evaluate interventions and
                    programs to promote effective functioning.
Dimension III: Research and Measurement
   Responsibility 5: Design and implement research and report
                    conclusions and recommendations.
Dimension IV: Professional/Ethical/Legal Issues
   Responsibility 6: Take steps to ensure adherence to professional,
                    governmental and judicial guidelines and regulations for professional and scientific activities.
Dimension V: Applications to Social Systems
   Responsibility 7: Develop, conduct, evaluate and modify
                    interventions, strategies and programs designed
                    to promote effective functioning within the social
                    system.
   Responsibility 8: Evaluate physical, technological and social
                    environments of the system.
   Responsibility 9: Evaluate the human resource needs of the
                    environments of the system.

0708381

It is important to recognize that since its inception in 1961, the AASPB has been independent of the APA, and therefore represents the group of psychologists legally charged with regulation of the profession. Consequently, issues will be addressed from that perspective as well as purpose.

Six elements seem to recur in professional licensing laws or acts (Rubin, 1980). First, the state psychology licensing board, as described in previous paragraphs, serves by appointment of the governor. Because licensing boards are generally self-sustaining bodies (receiving no funds from the state), their expenses and those of the staff are compensated through applications and annual license fees. Second, the act defines minimum education, experience, and fitness qualifications for licensure. Usually regional accreditations of the university from which the graduate has received his or her degree are required. Documentation of the major field of study as psychology is also required through review of transcripts. Third, during the initial stages of state licensure, "grandparenting" provisions also have been included. Fourth, a code of ethics is stated, either by referencing to the APA Ethical Principles (1981a) or restating those concepts. Fifth, these acts provide the disciplinary action to be taken in accordance with the ethical code and in other instances, such as committing an illegal act. Due-process mechanisms, normally from the state's administrative code or other reference, are employed in such instances. Finally, provision is made for prohibition of professional practice by unlicensed individuals.

In 1981, the number of licensed psychologists nationwide was estimated at 38,000. (Dörken & Webb, 1981). The addresses of state licensing boards can be found in each June issue of the *American Psychologist*, while APA's Board of Professional Affairs summarizes the state licensure or certification laws regulating psychological practice on a periodic basis. Among the information included in this summary are the following items: educational and supervisory requirements, renewal policy, ABPP recognition, and continuing education renewal expectations. The American Association of State Psychology Boards also publishes the most comprehensive description of licensing information in the U.S. and Canada (AASPB, 1986). They include information such as the type of statutes which exist, levels of licensing, rules and regulations, requirements for licensing (e.g., academic degree, exams, cut-off scores, etc.) and description of the board.

SPECIALTY PROFESSIONAL CREDENTIALS

Specialty professional credentials, which are nationally recognized, go beyond the degree and licensure demands for practice and directly assess the competency of the experienced psychology professional. The academic degree and licensure could, in one sense, be described as entry credentials that validate the beginning professional's training and competency. Only where continuing education requirements exist for the renewal of a license can it be said that professional growth is a criterion for continued possession of that credential. By contrast, the specialty credentialing bodies generally require licensure and several years of experience before applications are accepted. The criteria of these groups usually involve direct evidence of the applicant's professional behavior as part of the examination period.

The question has often been raised concerning the benefits and value of specialty professional credentials. Certainly, there is some prestige value associated with these credentials, given the rigor of the examination process and the judgment of senior colleagues regarding one's professional work. However, it might also be argued that the process of working toward and preparing for this credentialing serves as a sound professional development activity. To a certain extent, some of these credentials may aid in the licensure re-application process needed when one moves from one state to another, and may increase the number of referrals of clients who are moving to new areas.

It is not unreasonable to expect trainers in professional psychology programs, and in particular, the directors of such programs, to represent the best attributes as professional role models. In fact, the APA accreditation criteria suggest that the director be recognized in some way by professional associations for their contributions (e.g., Fellow in an APA Division) or possess the ABPP diploma. Finally, Congress has provided the Veterans Administration (VA) with the authority to pay a bonus of up to $10,000 for those clinical or counseling psychologists who hold such credentials, although it has not been implemented. A similar recognition is now being considered by the Department of Defense. One state, Missouri, through its Department of Mental Health, provides automatic pay raises for psychologists who pass rigorous national examinations. Finally, the potential exists for school psychologists to advocate for such recognition through state departments of public instruction within the career development plans being adopted across the country.

Five examples of specialty credentials in psychology will be presented next. The objective of the credential and qualifications for application and examination procedures are included in the discussion. Addresses for each of the boards can be found at the end of this chapter.

Diplomate of the American Board of Professional Psychology

Established in 1947, the American Board of Examiners in Professional Psychology was incorporated and later renamed the American Board of

Professional Psychology (ABPP). The purpose of the organization, originally initiated by the APA but now an independent entity, is to promote
professional psychology. Candidates for examination for the Diplomate
of the ABPP credential "must demonstrate outstanding competence in
psychological evaluation and intervention skills, depth and currency of
scientific and professional knowledge in their practice area as well as
knowledge of and commitment to the profession of psychology and to the
Ethical Principles of the American Psychological Association" (ABPP, 1983).

The ABPP diploma is currently awarded in the following specialty
areas: clinical, counseling, industrial-organizational, forensic, neuropsychology, and school. This list of specialty areas reflects two recent
changes in the structure of ABPP. The American Board of Clinical Neuropsychology (ABCN) established a joint arrangement with ABPP in 1984.
Under the arrangement, ABPP will serve as the umbrella organization
where fiscal and administrative matters are concerned. On the other
hand, ABCN will contractually be responsible for renewing the credentials and conducting relevant examinations. In 1985, the American Board
of Forensic Psychology (ABFP) affiliated with ABPP for a 2-year trial
period. As with the ABCN arrangment, the ABFP will have a representative on the ABPP Central Board and each of its six regional boards.
During this trial period, ABFP will retain its separate identity and corporate status. A number of ABCN and ABFP members held the ABPP
diplomate as well. Approximately 16% of eligible APA members currently hold the ABPP credential.

Psychologists who have a doctoral degree in psychology as defined by
the education and credentialing criteria (to be discussed later) and 4
years of postdoctoral experience in a psychological practice area recognized by the ABPP may apply for the ABPP credential. The application
must be in the candidate's area of specialty unless formal postdoctoral
training has taken place. A doctoral internship or field experience based
on 1,800 hours of training is also required. The application process consists of review to determine if the applicant meets the following criteria:
(a) adequacy and extent of basic training; (b) amount, breadth, and
quality of professional experience; (c) special competence; and (d) reputation among professional colleagues. A preliminary review in which
would-be applicants submit only their educational and internship credentials is possible.

Following acceptance of the application, the ABPP candidate is asked
to submit a written work sample representative of his/her professional
practice, including assessment of individual(s), group(s) or situation(s),
and professional efforts to effect or influence change. The last step of the
process involves the ABPP examination, which is conducted by a committee of diplomate examiners in one of the six ABPP regional boards of
the country. Those regions are designated as Northeastern, Mideastern,

Southeastern, Midwestern, Intermountain, and Western. Each of the specialties has representatives on these boards. The boards identify examiners and review the recommendations of the examining committee. The regional concept facilitates this phase of the application by making arrangements for the exam to take place within a convenient area of the country for the applicant. It is interesting to note that chairs from the regional boards meet as a committee to review and assure uniformity of examining procedures within the respective specialty examinations. The examination, which covers 4 hours and uses the work sample as a springboard for discussion, is to cover the interrelated areas of (a) effectiveness of the candidate's efforts toward constructive intervention based on realistic assessment of the presented problems; (b) awareness of the relevance of research and theory; and (c) sensitivity to the ethical implications of professional practice. The examination involves an observation of the candidate in a typical professional activity.

The ABPP is now in the process of establishing a series of Specialty Advisory Committees, one advisory committee for each of the six specialties currently represented on the ABPP board, to advise the board on the following matters, as well as other issues that may ultimately develop. Their immediate purpose will be (a) to "monitor" the examination process of candidates within each specialty in which ABPP awards the diploma to assure that the body of knowledge and the in vivo experience on which the candidates are evaluated is representative of that specialty; (b) to advise the board on maintaining up-to-date assessment procedures of board candidates; and (c) to assist with the designing of more efficient evaluation procedures.

In addition to the application and examination fees, annual membership dues are required for those holding the ABPP diploma. The charging of these dues began in 1983, when the ABPP became a membership organization. Members receive the *Directory of ABPP Diplomates*, vote for the nominees for the "Distinguished Contributions to Psychology" award, and receive other privileges. The ABPP publishes a newsletter semiannually, *The Diplomate*.

Guidelines for revocation of the ABPP diploma exist for failure "to maintain a reputation among professional colleagues for standards of personal integrity which are irreproachable as a representative of the profession of psychology in the community or failure to maintain affiliation with the American Psychological Association or, where applicable, the Canadian Psychological Association" (ABPP, 1985, p. 8).

American Board of Family Psychology (ABFamP)

The American Board of Family Psychology, Inc. (ABFamP) was established to provide a service to the profession, other professionals, and the public by recognizing and diplomating qualified psychologists with advanced competence in the clinical practice of marital, sex, and family therapy. It was founded by members of the Division of Family Psychology (Division 43) of the APA (formerly the Academy of Family Psychology and the Academy of Psychologists in Marital, Sex, and Family Therapy, established in 1958) as a result of deliberations at their annual meeting held in conjunction with the 1980 meeting of the American Psychological Association. The ABFamP, although autonomous, continues its affiliation with Division 43 and is incorporated as a nonprofit corporation. It maintains and publishes a Register of Diplomates as a service to the public.

The ABFamP diplomate credential is designed for psychologists with current professional work involving practice of a special proficiency. To qualify for candidacy, each applicant must have a doctorate in psychology, including a 1,500-hour internship; hold licensure or certification in psychology; be a member of the APA or CPA (Canadian Psychological Association); have completed at least three graduate courses in one of the two aforementioned proficiencies (marital/sex therapy or marital/family therapy) along with two graduate clinical practice courses in the proficiency; and have 5 years of full-time, postdoctoral experience. Upon receipt of validation of such training and experience and application materials, an oral examination based on one or more work samples in the specialty area is conducted by a committee of three diplomates of this board. An interesting feature of this credential is that "certification" as a diplomate is granted only for a period of 5 years. Diplomates are required, at the end of the 5-year period, to present evidence of a minimum of 60 hours of continuing education in order to qualify for renewal of their credential. Specific information regarding the requirements and application for membership can be obtained by writing the Academy of Family Psychology.

American Board of Psychological Hypnosis (ABPH)

The purpose of the ABPH is "to certify psychologists in the sub-specialty of clinical or experimental hypnosis" (ABPH, 1983). While the ABPH credential is not necessary for practice or research in this area, it serves to identify a high level of competence in the field. Application and examination procedures are similar to the ABPP model. Applicants must have a doctoral degree in psychology, and either be a member or demonstrate eligibility for APA membership. They also must have 5 years of acceptable experience, including 2 years of supervised experience. For the clinical section they must be licensed or certified, and possess (or show eligibility for) the ABPP diploma in clinical or counseling psychology. Applications must be supported by three letters of reference.

If the application is accepted, a work sample is submitted. For clinicians, this typically consists of a brief case history and a tape recording or transcript of one or more therapy hours in which hypnosis plays a significant role. Researchers submit reprints or copies of one or more scholarly papers. Board examinations are held three times per year and are conducted by three psychologists who are either ABPH diplomates, Fellows of the APA, or otherwise well-qualified as decided by the chief examiner. The examination lasts approximately 2 hours and deals with theoretical and conceptual issues pertaining to hypnosis, the nature of the candidate's relevant clinical practice, knowledge of extant significant literature, ethics, and professional matters. Researchers should be aware of the issues and problems of research design and methodology in hypnosis research.

Further information and application materials can be obtained by writing the Secretary-Treasurer of the ABPH. The address of the current officer is available from the secretary of APA'S Division of Psychological Hypnosis (Division 30), which can be obtained by referring to the most current June issue of the *American Psychologist*.

American Board of Forensic Psychology (ABFP)

This board grew out of a specialty certification study committee of the American Psychology-Law Society. Established in 1978, its purposes are to provide a service to the public by identifying qualified practitioners of forensic psychology and promoting forensic psychology as a specialty within professional psychology. The board consists of nine diplomates, five who are officers and four who are members at large. Candidates must be members of good standing in the APA, CPA, or the American Psychology-Law Society and have earned a doctoral degree in psychology; exceptions can be made to the latter criterion. They must be licensed psychologists who have accumulated at least 1,000 hours of experience over a minimum of a 5-year period in forensic psychology. As of January 1987, at least 200 hours of supervision must also be documented in the forensic specialization.

As part of the application procedure, a work sample must be submitted once the application is accepted. If the work sample is deemed acceptable, a 3-hour oral examination is then scheduled with a three-member examining committee comprised of Diplomates in Forensic Psychology.

Candidates should expect the examination to cover forensic content as well as their own area of specialty. It may also include hypothetical situations from which the candidate will be asked to draw psychologically sound conclusions, and to justify the conclusions on both legal and ethical grounds. (ABFP, 1983)

The Board publishes a *Register of Diplomates in Forensic Psychology* containing appropriate information concerning diplomates. In addition to the fees attached to the diplomate certification process, a fee is charged for renewal certificates. The ABFP became an affiliate of the ABPP in 1985 (see ABPP discussion).

Certification of the Association of Behavioral Analysis (ABA)

Since 1980, the ABA (see chapter 5) has offered certification as a Behavior Analyst. Eligibility includes work on a minimal degree in one's area of professional training in the human services and membership in the ABA (full, student, or affiliate). Certification is intended to be a formal indicator of competence as a practicing behavior analyst. It requires professional master's-level practitioners to document their professional competence in disciplines where licensing/certification is limited to doctoral-level practitioners. Working to qualify for ABA certification is also intended to serve as a professional growth experience.

The examination consists of two stages. The first stage is multiple-choice with some essays, including analysis of "behavioral vignettes." Its purpose is "to assess the applicant's verbal competency with respect to basic behavioral principles and to establish the applicant's eligibility for his/her practicing or specialty competency in behavior analysis" (ABA, 1985, p. ix). The second stage involves a more extensive assessment and monitoring of performance in an area of specialization (e.g., behavioral clinical, behavioral analysis in education). The exam may be retaken as often as necessary to achieve proficient performance.

OTHER RELEVANT CREDENTIALS

National Register of Health Service Providers in Psychology (Register)

The Register publishes a list of psychologists who voluntarily apply and meet the criteria as health service providers in psychology; it does not evaluate quality or competence of listed individuals. A Health Service Provider in Psychology is defined by the Register as a psychologist, certified/licensed at the independent practice level in his/her state, who is duly trained and experienced in the delivery of direct, preventive, assessment and therapeutic intervention services to individuals whose growth, adjustment, or functioning is actually impaired or is demonstrably at high risk of impairment. (Council of National Register, 1985, p. xxii)

The criteria for listing also includes the holding of a doctoral degree and at least 2 years of supervised experience in health services in psychology, of which at least 1 year is in an organized health service training program, and 1 year is postdoctoral. Specific guidelines for defining supervised experience of internships are spelled out and include a minimum of 1,500 hours completed within 24 months.

As of 1983, approximately 13,500 registrants were listed in the publication of this nonprofit organization, which is also run separately from the APA. The information for each psychologist includes name, highest degree earned, preferred mailing address and telephone number, the state(s) in which licensed or certified, and diplomate status. Optional characteristics that may be listed for registrants who so choose are their theoretical orientation, the health service offered, specialized services offered, ages served, and language fluency. An alphabetical listing as well as a state listing of registrants is provided.

The register will make this list available to consumers of health services, health service organizations, health and welfare organizations, governmental agencies such as the National Institute of Mental Health, and the general public. A number of public and private insurers have informally recognized this registry for purposes of insurance reimbursement.

In addition to the application fees, there is an annual renewal fee. Guidelines exist for removal of a psychologist from listing when there is significant violation of professional ethics or standards of practice.

Certification—State Department of Public Instruction

Not to be confused with the type of psychology licensure discussed earlier and issued by a psychology board, this educational credential is issued by the state's education agency. This credential is created by legislative action similar to a licensure statute and pertains to the qualifications of the educational personnel working in the public schools, that is, teachers, administrators, and specialized personnel such as guidance counselors and social workers.

Initially, certification eligibility was determined by *course requirements*— submission of transcripts resulted in a documentation of successful completion of prescribed courses. A more recent procedure involves *program approval*. Program approval models require that training programs stand a similar evaluation to that involved in accreditation (see next section of this chapter). If approved, graduates of the program are certified, pending satisfaction of any other requirements. Some states now require that applicants take the National Teachers Examination or a similar state examination. Certification can be permanent or provisional, pending completion of a certain number of years of successful teaching experience. Certification can also be time-related with a renewal procedure contingent on completion of continuing education requirements.

Psychologists who are interested in becoming full-time employees of a school system will be most interested in this type of credential. Certification for school psychologists requires this type of credential; however, certification for school psychologists requires separate criteria from those specified for other professionals. Again, as with the variability among psychology licensure laws, this certification follows no standard plan. There may be several levels of school psychology certification: i.e. master's degree, specialists (60-hour master's or its equivalent), and doctorate. On the other hand, only one certification level may exist. As with licensure laws, there is no reciprocity among states with respect to this credential.

INSTITUTIONAL CREDENTIALING

One important individual credential sometimes overlooked is graduation from an *accredited* institution. The graduate degree, mentioned earlier, represents an individually oriented credential, which derives credibility indirectly, then, from the quality review of the institution. These reviews are conducted by accrediting agencies and/or associations. However, the U.S. Commissioner of Education determines which agencies and associations are reliable authorities to evaluate the quality of training offered by educational institutions with programs.

An accrediting body is concerned with either evaluation of educational entities as a whole, or educational units or programs within institutions. Examples of the former include regional and national accrediting commissions, National Institutional Accrediting Bodies (e.g., American Association of Bible Colleges; National Association of Trade and Technical Schools) and Regional Institutional Accrediting Bodies (e.g., Accrediting Commission for Senior Colleges and Universities/Western Association of Schools and Colleges; Commission on Colleges/Southern Association of Colleges and Schools). Specialized accrediting bodies include commissions on accreditation established by national professional organizations such as the American Psychological Association (accredits doctoral programs in clinical, counseling, and school psychology), National Council for Accreditation of Teacher Education (baccalaureate and degree programs), American Bar Association (law professional schools), Council on Social Work Education (baccalaureate and master's degree programs). In some instances, this latter group also evaluates freestanding professional or occupational schools. These commissions or national accrediting agencies have no legal control over educational institutions or programs. "They promulgate standards of quality or criteria of institutional excellence and approve or admit to membership those institutions that meet the standards or criteria" (DHEW, 1978). Most of the institutions attain eligibility for federal funds through accreditation by one of these recognized bodies. Accreditation is a voluntary process.

The Council on Postsecondary Accreditation (COPA) is a nongovernmental organization that "foster(s) and facilitate(s) the role of accrediting agencies in promoting and insuring the quality and diversity of American *postsecondary* education (DHEW, 1978). The COPA performs three primary functions: They recognize the accrediting members as well as coordinate and periodically review the work of those groups to insure they serve the broader interests of society as well as their membership. A similar council exists for secondary education.

APA Accreditation—Programs and Internships

The American Psychological Association, through the Office of Accreditation, accredits doctoral level programs in clinical, counseling, and school psychology, or appropriate combinations thereof, as well as predoctoral internship programs. The APA is recognized by COPA and by the U.S. Commissioner of Education to conduct this accreditation. A voluntary program, the accreditation is conducted in order "to promote excellence in programs designed to educate and train professional psychologists and to provide professional and objective evaluation of these programs as a service to the public, prospective students, and the profession" (APA, 1986, Appendix A, p. 1). There are three categories of accreditation. *Full* accreditation is granted to programs that meet the criteria in a satisfactory manner. *Provisional* accreditation is granted to programs making initial application that do not meet all criteria, but for which "there is a reasonable expectation that they will be met within a foreseeable period of time from the date of the initial site visit" (APA, 1986, Appendix A, p. 1). A program that has been awarded full accreditation may be placed on *probation* when the committee has evidence that it is not currently in satisfactory compliance with the criteria. Fully accredited programs are reviewed every 5 years, provisionally accredited programs every 3 years, and probationary programs each year. Programs with accreditation are listed each year in the December issue of the *American Psychologist*.

Following acceptance of the application materials, programs are site-visited by a team of psychologists. Visiting team members are selected through a nomination procedure by the Education and Training Board of the APA. Visits are generally conducted over a 2-day period and include interviews with program faculty, department faculty, students, and administrators. A site-visit team submits a report regarding the criteria covering the institutional setting; the manner in which cultural and individual differences are reflected in all aspects of the program; the training model and curricula; the qualifications of the faculty; characteristics of the students; the adequacy of the facilities; and systematic, intensive practicum and internship training. It is important to note that education in general psychology (including instruction in scientific and professional ethics and standards, research design and methodology, statistics, psychological measurement, and history and systems) is expected for every doctoral program. Each student must also demonstrate competence in the following substantive areas: biological bases of behavior; cognitive affective bases of behavior; social bases of behavior; and individual behavior. Course requirements in the specialty areas are also required. These criteria in large measure reflect the interorganizational conference on Education and Credentialing in Psychology (Wellner, 1978), which considered the relationship between education and credentialing in the field. The core curriculum, in particular, was developed at that conference.

Separate criteria also have been established for the accreditation of independent internship centers. These criteria include the administrative, procedural, selection, programmatic, and organizational aspects of this phase of training.

In May 1985, by authority of the APA Board of Directors, the Education and Training Board appointed a task force to review the scope and criteria for accreditation of education and training for professional psychology. That task force submitted its first report in April of 1985 (Brickman, 1985). Following a reaction period, in which comments from various constituencies within psychology are solicited, a second report followed by a second review stage is planned before final recommendations are made.

NCATE/NASP Accreditation

The National Association of School Psychologists (NASP), through its affiliation with the National Council for the Accreditation of Teacher Education (NCATE), has participated in the accreditation of master's and doctoral level school psychology programs located in schools of education. As a result of the overlap with APA accreditation of doctoral programs in psychology, an APA/NASP Task Force was established in 1979 to identify similarities and differences in the accreditation standards and process followed by the APA and NCATE. From this effort, a Joint Accreditation Pilot Project between the APA and NCATE/NASP accreditation was implemented which resulted in a recommended plan for future accreditation visits that could be held jointly. However, at this time, the NCATE has moved to focus their accreditation efforts at the unit level (e.g., schools of education) rather than the program level.

DESIGNATION

For a number of years, there have been calls for development of a formal mechanism that would identify/designate a training program as a "psychology" program. State psychology licensing boards, in particular, find themselves in a peculiar position of having to judge whether or not a program is in psychology when transcripts carry a different program title (e.g., human development), but applicants for licensure, and sometimes faculty, argue its validity on the grounds that the program is "psychological in nature." Similarly, students applying to graduate school may have similar questions regarding the nature of a program, as do other consumer groups and federal or state agencies. While various accreditation mechanisms exist, there currently is no nationally agreed-to criteria by which all programs wanting such recognition could be reviewed. Without a designation process, the field faces the prospect of a definition evolving from case law, policies of other independent organizations, and federal and state statutes and regulations. Also, students are not always assured that programs meet the educational requirements. Finally, users of psychological services (clients, legislators, school district personnel directors, etc.) cannot assume that the person claiming to be a psychologist will have the educational background to provide safe, effective, and appropriate service.

As a result, the APA has been engaged in an exploration of a plan for the designation of graduate programs in psychology. In 1985, the Council of Graduate Departments of Psychology opposed such an effort on several grounds. Philosophically, it was argued that the time was not ripe for standardization given the rapid changes in the field. Practically, academic freedom seemed to be at risk with such a movement, and the process was seen as a threat to accreditation. Also, programs feared that if they were not designated, whatever the reason, they might face lawsuits of various types. After much discussion, the APA Council of Representatives voted at their August 1985 meeting to suspend their discussions of designation (and the recommendations being made by a task force) until the task force on the structure of APA (see chapter 6) made its final report. In the meantime, the AASPB and the Register have decided to collaborate on a psychology program designation plan.

For the moment, then, three sources of identifying psychology programs exist. First, there is the APA accreditation process discussed in chapter 2 on credentialing. Next, the APA does publish the *Graduate Study in Psychology and Associated Fields* for those interested in graduate study in psychology. This publication is organized into four sections:

I. Departments and Schools of Psychology *and* APA-Accredited Programs Offering the Doctoral Degree;
II. Other Departments Offering the Doctoral Degree;
III. Graduate Departments of Psychology Offering Less than the Doctoral Degree;
IV. Other Graduate Departments Offering Less than the Doctoral Degree.

APA-accredited programs, it should be noted, are listed in Section I even if their departments are not labeled as psychology departments. Within each section, institutions are listed alphabetically by state. In addition, a "List of Programs by Degree Offered" is also provided and provides valuable locator assistance to the reader.

The information presented by the "Graduate Study" book is provided voluntarily by institutions and includes data on requirements, facilities, and financial assistance. For schools that did not respond, only the institution's name, department, address, telephone number, and chairperson's name are provided. Otherwise readers can expect to find the following information on the department:

1. University name, department, address, and telephone number;
2. APA accreditation status;
3. Year that information was provided, chairperson, faculty size;
4. Programs and degrees offered;
5. Application information;
6. Student information;
7. Degree requirements;
8. Admission requirements;
9. Tuition for full-time study;
10. Housing and daycare;
11. Financial assistance;
12. Special group considerations, training opportunities; and
13. Additional comments (departments are given an opportunity to indicate their orientation, objectives or emphases, internship requirements, special facilities or resources).

The last section of this book addresses questions related to graduate school application, such as selecting the program, and describes APA accreditation.

Finally, the Council for the National Register of Health Service Providers in Psychology (discussed in chapter 1) have published annually since 1981 a listing of doctoral programs in psychology; the publication is entitled *Designated Doctoral Programs in Psychology*, and is available by writing to the *National Register*. The list of programs is designed to facilitate the *National Register's* review of individual applications for listing in the *National Register*; the list does not include all the programs that meet their stated guidelines. The guidelines used for defining (designating) a doctoral degree in psychology are listed in Table 2.1. These guidelines were originally developed at the Education and Credentialing Psychology Meeting in 1977. This latter group included invited psychologists, representing invited organizations and divisions as well as related APA boards and committees. The *National Register* Designation editions list programs by state and include the APA accreditation status of a program if appropriate. The *National Register* supports development of a comprehensive designation system to serve the public and prospective students, and as noted earlier, will collaborate with the AASPB to develop a more comprehensive system.

SOME ISSUES

Specialty Emergence and Recognition

Professionals have been both blessed with the benefits of the knowledge explosion our society is experiencing and overwhelmed at the same time. In order to keep up with the ever-increasing information base, we are witnessing what some have described as an alarming shrinkage in our expertise range. The basic sciences present one startling example of this phenomenon in that one may no longer be an expert on the cell, but rather an expert on one aspect of the cell, such as cell motility. Applied professions have also experienced this trend toward specialization. For example, medicine, law, and dentistry have moved toward formal methods of recognizing specialities within their professions. To further illustrate this point, consider the surgery specialty of medicine, which has become further specialized so that plastic surgery, neurosurgery, and thoracic surgery, among others, have emerged.

Schnaps and Sales (1983) summarized the benefits of specialization as not only a mechanism for keeping up with the knowledge base (competence), but as furthering quality care, increasing access to quality services for the consumer, maximizing the quality of services through exter-

Table 2.1. National Register Guidelines for Defining Doctoral Degree in Psychology

---

The following criteria will be used to identify doctoral programs as psychology programs:

1. Programs that are accredited by the American Psychological Association are recognized as meeting the definition of a professional psychology program. The criteria for accreditation serve as a model for professional psychology training.

OR
All of the following criteria, 2 through 10:

2. Training in professional psychology is doctoral training offered in a regionally accredited institution of higher education.
3. The program, wherever it may be administratively housed, must be clearly identified and labeled as a psychology program. Such a program must specify in pertinent institutional catalogues and brochures its intent to educate and train professional psychologists.
4. The psychology program must stand as a recognizable, coherent organizational entity within the institution.
5. There must be a clear authority and primary responsibility for the core and specialty areas whether or not the program cuts across administrative lines.
6. The program must be an integrated, organized sequence of study.
7. There must be an identifiable psychology faculty and a psychologist responsible for the program.
8. The program must have an identifiable body of students who are matriculated in that program for a degree.
9. The program must include supervised practicum, internship, field or laboratory training appropriate to the practice of psychology.
10. The curriculum shall encompass a minimum of three academic years of full time graduate study. In addition to instruction in scientific and professional ethics and standards, research design and methodology, statistics and psychometrics, the core program shall require each student to demonstrate competence in each of the following substantive content areas:
    (a) Biological bases of behavior: Physiological psychology, comparative psychology, neuropsychology, sensation and perception, and psychopharmacology.
    (b) Cognitive-affective bases of behavior: Learning, thinking, motivation, emotion.
    (c) Social bases of behavior: Social psychology, group processes, organizational and systems theory.
    (d) Individual differences: Personality theory, human development, abnormal psychology.

In addition, all professional education programs in psychology will include course requirements in specialty areas.

From the Council for the National Register of Health Service Providers in Psychology (1986). *Designated doctoral programs in psychology*. Washington, DC: Author. Copyright 1986 by the Council for the National Register of Health Service Providers in Psychology. Reprinted by permission.

nal control, such as full fee reimbursement for certified professionals, reducing fees, and enhancing the satisfaction of the professional. The problems they see include the inverse of the results claimed above, along with a diminishing of the generalist's competence and the loss of a systems perspective on the part of specialists.

Nobel laureate Sir Peter Brian Medawar has also raised the concern that increasing specialization will limit science by making a broad synthesis of information impossible. Scientists "can no longer get their bearings in the great sea of knowledge" because "scientific frontiers have become so advanced that they are beyond the comprehension of any one man" (Best, 1984). However, Medawar did go on to state that this situation may not be an insurmountable problem given the development of the computer.

The APA is now exploring the desirability and feasibility of recognizing specialties. Currently, four specialties (clinical, counseling, industrial-organizational, and school psychology) have tacit recognition, as indicated by the existence of *Guidelines for Providers of Psychological Services* in these areas (APA, 1981b). Present plans include the use of specialty definitions criteria in a simulation to determine the feasibility of establishing a formal recognition system. Within this process, a distinction is made between a specialty (whose parameters include a body of knowledge, client populations served by the specialty, techniques and technologies employed by the psychologist, and the settings for the services) and a proficiency (which includes the knowledge and skills forming the bases for services in one of the four specialty parameters as a minimum requirement for definition).

Psychology specialties are currently recognized by the ABPP, the National Register of Health Services in Psychology, some state psychology licensing boards, and individual professional credentialing boards providing their own self-recognition. One related question, then, involves the adequacy of regulation, given the proliferation of the specialty recognition mechanisms that do exist—is there a need to organize these efforts to bring about a systematic development of the field? Another question relates to the issue of whether generic training as an applied psychologist must take place before specialist recognition, at which time a "journeyperson's" credential (versus the advanced-expertise notion embodied by the ABPP diploma) is necessary. It is interesting to note that APA accreditation criteria as well as the specialty guidelines include a generic psychology training core.

Competency-Based Credentials

While degrees and diplomate credentials, which have been discussed earlier, require observation of actual professional practice as well as examination on the practice sample by "experts" in that professional area, licensing and certification credentials usually do not contain such eligibility criteria. Consequently, concern has been voiced that the prime purpose of these credentialing requirements, protection of the consumer, in effect is not met by what is essentially a "paper" review. While these regulating laws often contain provisions for pre- and/or post-supervisory experiences (with prescribed, periodic supervisee evaluations submitted to the board by the supervisor), they still may not involve direct observation and review of the supervisee. A recent trend has involved the exploration of "assessment center" type examinations in which simulated rather than actual cases are used to evaluate the candidate's professional skills and ethical sensitivities. Similarly, videotaped vignettes could be employed with microcomputer interactive diagnosis and/or management case examinations.

In psychology, the use of such procedures as part of the initial or renewal credential procedures is in the exploration stage. It does need to be noted that in spite of its logical and common-sense appeal, the technology required to develop these cases may not be as readily available as it may initially seem. Furthermore, in some instances the prohibitive cost involved in such individualized examination procedures continues to be a realistic factor impeding rapid progress.

Entry Level in the Profession

Usually conceptualized as the level at which independent practice may begin, the entry level in the psychological profession, as defined by the APA, involves the attainment of the doctorate degree. A perennial issue has been the status of master's or specialist's degree-trained (60 semester hours) individuals in the profession. It is argued that they often engage in roles that are similar to or exactly the same as the PhD-trained psychologists' roles, particularly in public agencies and institutions. Also, after building years of experience with certain populations, these master's or specialist's degree professionals in fact may be more competent than the new PhD recipient. The question of independent practice in the private sector highlights questions relevant to this issue, such as the minimum training and supervised practice (if any) to be required for functioning independently.

Training Models: PhD or PsyD?

For over 30 years, psychology professional education has followed the Boulder Conference (Raimy, 1950) concept of the scientist-practitioner. It argued that the practicing psychologist would embody the attributes of the scientists in that he/she would contribute to the knowledge base as a researcher. At the same time, in exercising their specialty the careful evaluation and application of prior knowledge would be reflected in their practice. The integration of these two underpinnings formed the rationale for the award of the PhD in particular.

The emergence of the practitioner approach to training (Korman, 1974) as a viable alternative has resulted in the increasing acceptance of the PsyD degree. The practitioner model subscribes to most of the same values found in the scientist-practitioner model (Korman, 1974), but endorses this model as an additional form of professional training signifying a basic service orientation. Thus, in place of the PhD dissertation, the PsyD project allows for greater flexibility in defining the appropriateness of the project so that it is relevant to the professional role for which the candidate is preparing to enter. Advocates of this model (Peterson, 1976b) argued that it is difficult to train professional psychologists thoroughly except through explicitly defined professional programs. While professional schools might find it difficult to promise that graduates of their programs would contribute to the knowledge base upon which the practice is based, a liberally defined scholarly inquiry would be embraced. Similarly, some aspects of the scientific method are seen as applicable to professional practice, but not always possible or even warranted.

SUGGESTED READINGS

Licensing

Wiens and Menne (1981) have written about common misperceptions of the licensing process in a straightforward, easily understood manner. They deal with such propositions as, for example, licensing keeps those not licensed from delivering psychological services, licensing controls the number of people in a particular field, and licensing does not help consumers or society in general. Gross (1978), meanwhile, presents the counterpoint of these arguments in discussing what he labels the "myth of professional licensing." He concludes in this review of historical, economic, and sociological research that the promise of public protection actually institutionalizes a lack of accountability to the public. In a similar vein, Danish and Smyer (1981) raise the concern that licensing proposals, along with accreditation and third-party activity, may lead to serious unintended consequences.

Credentialing

Hogan's (1979) four-volume treatment of the regulation of psychotherapy presents a comprehensive view the serious student of this subject will want to review. Volume II contains the most general information regarding regulation. Koocher (1979), on the other hand, uses the concepts of face validity, content validity, and criterion-related validity to review levels of credentials in terms of the construct of professional competence.

Training

The need for the doctor of psychology degree is argued by Peterson (1976b) in an article where he defines the concept of professional psychology; discusses the similarities and differences of scholarly, scientific, and professional pursuits; and the advantages to the consumer and profession of adopting a degree that is employed restrictively by psychologists. Barlow, Hayes, and Nelson (1984) examine in detail the development of the scientist-practitioner training model. They note the basis of the model in the goal of training students in both research and practice, the rationale that research must be a vital part of the applied psychology field, that the profession can find people capable of doing both, and that involvement with the clinical practice brings one in contact with the important research issues and will provide much needed financial support for later efforts. They then go on to explore the factors that have inhibited the realization of this training objective while themselves presenting research strategies for integrating science and practice. Korman's (1974) article summarizes all of the recommendations of the Vail Conference, such as a "career-lattice" concept of training, the desirable characteristics of professional training, continued professional training, training of minority groups and women, as well as service delivery systems and the social context. Meanwhile, Perry (1979) argues for the continuance of the Boulder Conference model of training, because alternate models are unnecessary or undesirable; he also states that quality of training is the real issue.

Meltzoff's (1984) paper presents arguments for a clinical orientation versus a research orientation in training graduate students. The author, however, has a clear, strong orientation toward the scientist-practitioner model. The reader is afforded an opportunity to review some of the major differences in philosophy of the two orientations as well as some of the practical issues in the field. Issues such as cost relevancy and need are discussed.

Stern (1984) writes a thought-provoking article on the training of graduate students, in which he expresses concern with advocates of only one professional training model. The article examines some of the assumptions associated with professional training in psychology and finds a number of points of confusion that need to be addressed.

Marwit's (1983) article is one of many exploring the PhD versus PsyD debate. He surveyed graduate students in PhD and PsyD programs and asked them questions about the Vail Conference resolution, their career aspirations, and their preference for a PsyD or PhD program.

Defining a Professional

The Flexner (1915) article is often cited for its six-part definition of any profession. Peterson (1976a) examines professional psychology, with special emphasis on clinical applications, in terms of what he considers the most important dimension of a profession: "a demonstrably useful, educationally communicable technology, based in a complex, reasonably well established intellectual discipline" (pp. 573–574). A comprehensive treatment of the "professionalism" movement is provided by Moore (1970). In this book, the author examines, in detail, not only the emergence of the notion of professionalism, but also considers the professional's role with peers, clients, and the general public. In a scholarly manner, Moore sheds light on the attractiveness and the limits of this occupational development.

The list in Box 2.1 gives addresses of a number of credentialing organizations for the profession.

Box 2.1. Addresses of Credentialing Organizations

American Association of State Psychology Boards
Executive Officer: Randolph P. Reeves
                     100 Corporate Square
                     P.O. Box 4389
                     Montgomery, AL 36103

American Board of Family Psychology
6501 Sanger, Suite 15
P.O. Box 7977
Waco, TX 76714
(817) 776-6081

American Board of Forensic Psychology
Record Secretary: Swen Helge, PhD, PC
                    1701 River Run, Ste. 310
                    Fort Worth, TX 76107
                    (817) 334-0611

American Board of Professional Psychology
Suite 313, 2100 E. Broadway
Columbia, MD 65201
(314) 875-1267

(continued)

Box 2.1. Continued

American Board of Psychological Hypnosis
Secretary, Division 30
William C. Coe
Department of Psychology
California State University
Fresno, CA 93740
(209) 294-2691

American Psychological Association
1200 Seventeenth Street, N.W.
Washington, DC 20036
(202) 955-7600

Association for Behavioral Analysis
Department of Psychology
Western Michigan University
Kalamazoo, MI 49008
(616) 383-1977

Council for the National Register of Health
    Service Providers in Psychology
1200 Seventeenth Street, N.W.
Washington, DC 20036
(202) 833-2377

Council on Postsecondary Accreditation (COPA)
1 Dupont Circle, N.W., Suite 305
Washington, DC 20036
(202) 452-1433

REFERENCES

American Association of State Psychology Boards. (1986). *Handbook of licensing and certification requirements for psychologists in North America*. Washington, DC: Author.

American Board of Forensic Psychology. (1983, December). *Summary brochure*. Author.

American Board of Professional Psychology. (1983). From the editor. *The Diplomate, 3,* 4.

American Board of Professional Psychology. (1985). *Policies and procedures for the creation of Diplomates in Professional Psychology*. Columbia, MO: Author.

American Board of Psychological Hypnosis. (November, 1983). *A guide to the American Board of Psychological Hypnosis*. Indianapolis, IN: Author.

American Psychological Association. (1981a). Ethical principles of psychologists. *American Psychologist, 36,* 633–638.

American Psychological Association. (1981b). Specialty guidelines for the delivery of services. *American Psychologist, 36,* 639.

American Psychological Association. (1986). *Accreditation handbook*. Washington, DC: Author.

American Psychological Association. (1986). *Proposed revision of APA 1967 model guidelines for state licensure*. Washington, DC: Author.

American Psychological Association, Committee on Legislation. (1967). A model for state legislation affecting the practice of psychology. *American Psychologist, 22*, 1095–1103.

Association for Behavior Analysis. (1985). *Eleventh annual convention program*. Kalamazoo, MI: Author.

Bardon, J. I. (1981). A personalized account of the development and status of school psychology. *Journal of School Psychology, 19*, 199–210.

Barlow, D. H., Hayes, S. C., & Nelson, R. O. (1984). *The scientist practitioner*. New York: Pergamon Press.

Beales, III, J. H. (1980). The economics of regulating the professions. In R. D. Blair & S. Rubin (Eds.), *Regulating the professions* (pp. 125–142). Lexington, MA: Lexington Books.

Best, K. (1984, March 28). Nobel laureate: Basic questions elude scientists. *Durham Morning Herald*, p. 1, section B.

Brickman, L. B. (Ed.). (1985). *Issues and concerns: Graduate education in psychology*. Washington, DC: American Psychological Association.

Council for the National Register of Health Service Providers in Psychology. (1985). *National register of health service providers in psychology*. Washington, DC: Author.

Council for the National Register of Health Service Providers in Psychology. (1986). *Designated doctoral programs in psychology*. Washington, DC: Author.

Council of State Governments. (1952). *Occupational licensing legislation in the states: A study of state licensing legislation licensing the practice of professions and other occupations*. Chicago: Author.

Danish, S. J., & Smyer, M. A. (1981). Unintended consequences of requiring a license to help. *American Psychologist, 36*, 13–21.

Department of Health, Education & Welfare, Office of Education, Bureau of Higher and Continuing Education, Division of Eligibility and Agency Evaluation. (1978). *Nationally recognized accrediting agencies and associations*. Washington, DC: Author.

Dörken, H., & Webb, J. T. (1981). Licensed psychologists on the increase, 1974–1979. *American Psychologist, 36*, 1419–1426.

Flexner, A. B. (1910). *Medical education in the United States and Canada*. New York: Carnegie Foundation for the Advancement of Teaching.

Flexner, A. B. (1915). Is social work a profession? In *Proceedings of the National Conference of Charities and Corrections*. Baltimore, MD: Social Work.

Gross, S. J. (1978). The myth of professional licensing. *American Psychologist, 33*, 1009–1016.

Hogan, D. B. (1979). *The regulation of psychotherapists, Volumes I–IV*. Cambridge, MA: Ballinger Publishing Co.

Koocher, G. P. (1979). Credentialing in psychology: Close encounters with competence? *American Psychologist, 34*, 696–702.

Korman, M. (1974). National conference on levels and patterns of professionals training in psychology. *American Psychologist, 29*, 441–449.

Marwit, S. J. (1983). Doctoral candidates' attitudes towards models of professional training. *Professional Psychology: Research and Practice, 14*, 105–111.

Meltzoff, J. (1984). Research training for clinical psychologists: Point–counterpoint. *Professional Psychology: Research and Practice, 15*, 203–209.

Moore, W. E. (1970). *The professions: Roles and rules*. New York: Russell Sage Foundation.

Myers, R. A., & Rosen, G. A. (1986, August). *Research digest: The examination for professional practice in psychology*. Montgomery, AL: American Association of State Psychology Boards.

Perry, N. W. (1979). Why clinical psychology does not need alternative training models. *American Psychologist, 34*, 603–611.

Peterson, D. R. (1976a). Is psychology a profession? *American Psychologist, 31,* 572–581.

Peterson, D. R. (1976b). Need for the Doctor of Psychology degree in professional psychology. *American Psychologist, 31,* 792–798.

Raimy, V. C. (Ed.). (1950). *Training in clinical psychology.* Englewood Cliffs, NJ: Prentice-Hall.

Rubin, S. (1980). The legal web of profession regulation. In R. D. Blair & S. Rubin (Eds.), *Regulating the professions* (pp. 20–60). Lexington, MA: Lexington Books.

Schnaps, L. S., & Sales, B. D. (1983, August). Specialization in psychology: Lessons from other professions. In B. Sales, P. Bricklin, & J. Hall (Eds.), *Manual for the identification and continued recognition of proficiencies and new specialties in psychology: Second draft.* Washington, DC: American Psychological Association.

Stern, S. (1984). Professional training and professional competence: A critique of current thinking. *Professional Psychology: Research and Practice, 15,* 230–243.

Wellner, A. M. (Ed.). (1978). *Education and credentialing in psychology: A proposal for a National Commission.* Washington, DC: American Psychological Association.

Wiens, A. N., & Menne, J. E. (1981). On disposing of "straw people." *American Psychologist, 36,* 390–395.

Chapter 3
Ethics and Standards

Psychology as a profession has a moral dimension relative to professional practice. It is embodied within the ethical code developed by the American Psychological Association (APA, 1981a) and codes developed by virtually every national-level professional group providing treatment services to the public. Additionally, licensing and regulatory boards have adopted rules for professional conduct based upon the APA Ethical Principles.

Individual professionals may support their professional code for practical reasons such as a desire for respect and a good reputation within the professional community or the possible loss of license by the licensing boards. However, most professionals support their professional code because they believe it is good and justifiable. It must be kept in mind that mere acceptance of a code by professionals does not demonstrate that its principles are morally sound. One needs only to look to the past relative to the treatment of the mentally disabled to realize that ethical behavior is related to what is currently acceptable within the broader context of society, and existing standards will change as technologies advance and society changes.

It is indeed quite possible that an immoral code could be adopted much in the same manner that laws that discriminate against minorities have existed. If, then, an ethical issue is also a moral one, the specific questions relative to professional conduct and motivation are not nearly as important as the underlying moral principles of the professional code. Therefore, it well serves all psychologists to pause, read carefully, and reconsider the Preamble to the APA Ethical Principles.

PREAMBLE

Psychologists respect the dignity and worth of the individual and strive for the preservation and protection of fundamental human rights. They are committed to increasing knowledge of human behavior and of people's understanding of themselves and others and to the utilization of such knowledge for the promotion of human welfare. While pursuing these objectives, they make every effort to protect the welfare of those who seek their services and of the research participants that may be the object of study. They use their skills only for purposes consistent with these values and do not knowingly permit their misuse by others. While demanding for themselves freedom of inquiry and communication, psychologists accept the responsibility this freedom requires: competence, objectivity in the application of skills, and concern for the best interests of clients, colleagues, students, research participants, and society. In the pursuit of these ideals, psychologists subscribe to principles in the following areas: 1. Responsibility, 2. Competence, 3. Moral and Legal Standards, 4. Public Statements, 5. Confidentiality, 6. Welfare of the Consumer, 7. Professional Relationships, 8. Assessment Techniques, 9. Research With Human Participants, and 10. Care and Use of Animals.

Acceptance of membership in the American Psychological Association commits the member to adherence to these principles.

Psychologists cooperate with duly constituted committees of the American Psychological Association, in particular, the Committee on Scientific and Professional Ethics and Conduct, by responding to inquiries promptly and completely. Members also respond promptly and completely to inquiries from duly constituted state association ethics committees and professional standards review committees. (APA, 1981a, p. 633)

This general statement of the code indicates a concern on the part of psychology with each individual's sense of self-worth and dignity. For example, the importance of both understanding people and helping them understand themselves, the promotion of the general welfare of citizens and research subjects, the need to be aware of abuses of power and influence held by psychologists, and a more general acceptance of responsibility are evident. The 10 general principles offer general guidelines for making moral and practical decisions about research, teaching, consulting, and clerical work.

What is not accomplished by the APA Ethical Principles, nor is it the purpose of the statement, is the exploration of the philosophical rationale and issues underlying the principles. It is incumbent upon the individual psychologist to interpret problematic concepts like duty, rights, responsibility, and individual worth; and to be able to apply these values to the ethical guidelines and professional practice. This responsibility can be, at times, quite difficult for the practicing psychologist inasmuch as one's morality, the ambiguity of the guidelines, the unclear nature of the problem at hand, and the immediacy of the situation cause conflicts more frequently than the general public might suspect.

The Preamble admirably points out that while the APA Ethical Principles focus on rules of professional conduct, and hence moral issues, they do not provide all the answers relative to professional conduct. As with all rules and codes, they are never completely comprehensive to all situations, and the exceptions raise moral problems for the practitioner. Often, psychologists are faced with decisions wherein there exists a conflict of obligations in terms of professional duties or even between professional standards and human obligations. In the moral reasoning process, psychologists must examine their personal values, as these values may influence their choice of action. The main point is that despite the attempts of the profession to develop standards to promote the direct well-being of clients, moral issues are abundant.

PRINCIPLES

The development of ethical principles has been a continuous process since 1938, when the American Psychological Association formed a special committee to consider the adoption of an ethical code. Generally speaking, ethics of the profession reflected the level of sophistication of the profession, and indeed as the profession has grown, so has the complexity of the ethical principles.

The 1938 committee investigated and resolved ethical complaints; most of its work was informal in nature. In 1940, the Committee on Scientific and Professional Ethics (CSPEC) was created as a standing committee to consider ethical complaints. However, the development of a formal code of ethics did not begin until 1947 with an incident collection process; APA members in 1948 were asked to submit incident reports detailing ethical problems. Based upon over 1,000 reports, six categories were derived: (a) public responsibility, (b) client relationships, (c) teaching, (d) research, (e) writing and publishing, and (f) professional relationships.

These reports were used to prepare a number of drafts of an ethical code and designated for reactions and debate to psychology departments and at state, regional, and national professional meetings. This process has been reviewed extensively by Golann (1970) and reports by the committee on ethical standards for psychology in 1951 issues of the *American Psychologist* (APA, 1951a and 1951b). According to Golann (1970), the first formal code was adopted in 1953, with a revised version featuring 18 general principles published in 1959. The 1959 version featured a 3-year trial period. In 1977, after 9 years of work and numerous revisions, another version evolved. The latest revision, entitled "Ethical Principles of Psychologists," was adopted January 24, 1981, by the APA Council of Representatives and published in the June 1981 issue of the *American Psychologist* (1981a). This revision contained both substantive and grammatical changes in each of the nine ethical principles, plus a new 10th principle entitled "Care and Use of Animals."

Essentially, the process involved in adopting new standards within the APA involves drafting of revisions of present standards based upon complaints and prevailing issues within the profession by CSPEC. The proposed changes are then given to the membership for reactions and comment. After several revisions are drafted, the final proposal must be presented to the APA Council of Representatives for approval.

Additionally, within the complexity of the APA, there are numerous other committees, panels, and task forces that generate issues and policy statements that influence the work of CSPEC in developing and monitoring standards and practices. Thus, through the APA office, members of one committee will generate policy statements and solicit comments and reactions from other committees. As a result, there are numerous influences operating within the APA that directly or indirectly influence the thinking relative to ethical codes and standards.

It is very important to understand that the ethical principles and standards of psychology will continue to be reviewed. A number of areas remain unclear and continual clarification and additions will need to be made that reflect the ethical thinking and standards of the profession.

In addition to the ethical principles, eight policy statements have been developed by CSPEC regarding the care and use of animals, guidelines for conducting growth groups, guidelines for telephone directory listing, and standards for providers of psychological services. These are referenced in the APA Ethical Principles, and while they are not part of the principles, the professional psychologist should be familiar with these documents, especially those related to their professional areas of practice. The "Standards for Providers of Psychological Services" are discussed following the Enforcement section of this chapter; by contrast, the guidelines related to academic and research psychologists are omitted, along with statements relative to telephone listing. Telephone listing provisions are out of date considering the changes that have occurred due to legal decisions, which will be discussed in the Issues section of this chapter. The "Ethical Principles in the Conduct of Research with Human Participants" (APA, 1982) can be reviewed as needed.

Up to this point, the focus has been upon the ethical code of the American Psychological Association, with mention of similar codes of other professional organizations. Members of the American Psychological Association, as well as other states and national organizations, are voluntarily expected to adhere to these standards by virtue of their professional membership. By the same token, psychologists not belonging to APA, or to state psychological associations that have adopted the APA Ethical Principles, are not necessarily bound by the same standards.

ETHICAL COMPLAINTS: PROCEDURES

The APA and state associations have jurisdiction only over their members, and provide enforcement through organizational ethics committees. However, all 50 states and the District of Columbia have statutory licensure or certification laws. Based upon each law, rules of professional conduct are promulgated and for the most part are identical to the APA Ethical Principles. As a result, the practicing psychologist, choosing not to voluntarily join a professional organization, will end up being accountable to the APA Standards or a similar code.

Koocher (1983) points out that the most important control for ethical violation lies in a prevention plan. Most violations can be avoided if four basic strategies are followed. He believes that first, the psychologist must be informed; it is important to be familiar with laws, rules, principles, standards, practices, and issues in the delivery of psychological services. The second strategy is to be sensible. The attributes of common sense, a cooperative spirit, and openness and honesty will all enhance professional relationships. Third, the psychologist must think preventively. It is important to think ahead about possible problems and take preventive measures, such as written agreements with clients and colleagues. The final strategy is to ask for advice. Colleagues, ethics committees of state organizations, and licensing board members are good sources for discovering issues, alternatives, and guidelines for avoiding problems. Consultation is the best method for avoiding problems.

As previously implied, within the profession of psychology, the enforcement of ethical standards historically has been the jurisdiction of professional associations. When ethical violations occurred, they came to the attention of another psychologist. The second psychologist, as a first step, was urged to make an informal contact with his/her colleague to discuss the ethical concern on a confidential basis. The intention, or ideal resolution, would be that both parties would react with a sense of professionalism which would resolve the situation. When angry, defensive reactions or unethical behaviors continued to exist, the next step would be to contact state and/or national ethics committees. However, as indicated, these bodies only have jurisdiction over their members, with the severest penalty being expulsion from membership. For this reason, the APA and most state associations will not accept resignations by members under investigation for an ethical complaint. Resignation from the organization would remove the psychologist from the association's jurisdiction. In essence, the profession was responsible for policing itself.

As mentioned earlier, CSPEC is the APA's official committee for handling complaints of members' unethical misconduct. This committee has the power to investigate or adjudicate allegations of unethical behaviors that may be harmful to the public. This charge is provided for in the APA bylaws, the Rules of Council, the Ethical Principles of Psychologists (APA, 1981a), and CSPEC's own Rules and Procedures (Hare-Mustin & Hall, 1981). As stated previously, the most any professional association can do as a sanction for the violation of ethical principles is to expel an offending member. Although that event seldom occurs, in light of the size of the APA's membership, lesser sanctions such as censure or stipulated resignation are more common. Methods for responding to complaints have been elaborated upon more fully by Hare-Mustin and Hall (1981) with illustrated case examples.

When filing a complaint against a psychologist, one may choose to work through CSPEC if the psychologist is a member of the APA, or with the respective state licensing board if legal violations are involved. The CSPEC procedure is to write a confidential letter to the administrative officer for ethics, including the following information: name of the member psychologist being complained against, the special misbehavior, and the reason why this behavior was considered to be unethical. Documenting evidence is helpful. Attempts are then made to resolve the matter.

The administrative officer shares the information with the chair of CSPEC, to determine if the behavior is considered to be unethical and falls within the jurisdiction of the committee. Unlike licensing boards, CSPEC will ask for authorization to use the complainant's name in contacting the psychologist. The philosophy dictating the inclusion of such information is that the psychologist has the right to know the name of the accuser; the case will not proceed forward until such permission is given. An exception to this rule involves situations of probable cause for action—*sua sponte* or without a specific complaint—usually when there is available public documentation, such as a court record or newspaper clipping, to warrant CSPEC to proceed on its own initiative.

CSPEC will typically take one of the following actions. It may choose to take an educative position with the psychologist and close the case. On the other hand, information can be sought from other sources such as APA members, boards, or committees; divisions of the association; state ethics committees; state licensing boards; or the American Board of Professional Psychology (ABPP). Finally, CSPEC may appoint a fact-finding committee under the following conditions: (a) the charges are serious, and if sustained could lead to censure, probation, stipulated resignation, or expulsion; (b) the committee is unable to get necessary information by correspondence or other written materials; and (c) an on-site investigation is highly likely to produce such information (Hare-Mustin & Hall, 1981).

Dispositions can be informal and involve a cease and desist order, or may involve one of the following: censure statement; requirement for supervision; rehabilitation; training or psychotherapy; probation or education; or referral to a state association for review. When the complainee rejects CSPEC's informal attempts to resolve the matter, the case is forwarded to the APA Board of Directors, who may administer the sanction of expulsion or a lesser penalty after specified due process is assured. Again, the reader wishing further elaboration is referred to Hare-Mustin and Hall (1981) for case examples, and Hall and Hare-Mustin (1983) regarding the types of ethical complaints received by CSPEC. They also elaborate on a task force, which developed a draft for sanctions based upon three levels of inappropriate or unethical behaviors, ranging from inappropriate but not unethical behavior to clearly unethical behavior. Sanctions may range from educative and advisory, to educative warnings with inappropriate behavior. Reprimands, censure, stipulated resignations, and expulsion provide the range of sanctions with regard to unethical behavior. Reports of such action are reported directly to APA members on an annual basis, usually at the time of dues renewal. Mills (1984), as well as Sanders and Keith-Spiegel (1980), also elaborate on the APA adjudication procedures.

LEGAL ENFORCEMENT

Since the advent of licensing laws and the creation of state licensing boards with the explicit charge to protect the public, enforcement within the last 5 years has increasingly become a major function of state regulatory boards. As indicated in chapter 1, competence through the credentialing process is difficult to guarantee and has been a controversial issue over the last 15 years within the profession. However, the role of regulatory boards relative to credentialing notwithstanding, the public deserves protection against incompetent and unethical behavior on the part of licensed psychologists.

During the 1970s and early 1980s, credentialing issues have occupied most of regulatory boards' time and resources. As the credentialing issues become increasingly resolved through modification in state laws and rules, litigation, and the national examination process, board activities have become increasingly investigative and enforcement-oriented. It may be safe to say, at this point in time, that state boards have supplanted professional organizations relative to enforcement and will continue to do so in the future. As a result, it is important for the professional psychologist to understand fully the state licensing board's role in the process of enforcement of regulations and standards.

The state regulatory board generally has jurisdiction over those individuals who hold a license or who, as a result of being registered with the board, are enabled to hold the title of *psychologist* and to practice psychology. It is important to note again that some states have "title" laws that regulate the title of *psychologist*, while other states have "practice" laws that specify what is considered to be the practice of psychology. For example, Ohio lists procedures in its rules (Ohio Administrative Code, 1981) that, in the judgment of the board, require professional expertise in psychology. These include, but are not limited to:

A. Sensitivity training
B. Confrontation groups
C. Hypnotic techniques for psychotherapeutic purposes (diagnosis and treatment)
D. Individual intelligence testing
E. Psychological diagnosis and personality evaluation
F. Individual and group psychological psychotherapy
G. Psychological psychotherapy such as, but not limited to, implosive therapy, aversive therapy, and desensitization
H. Couples and family psychological psychotherapy
I. Psychological psychotherapy for sexual dysfunction.

Discussion of this example relative to its strengths and limitations is beyond the scope of this chapter; however, it does serve as a good illustration of a "practice" law. The advantage of having practice provisions enables the boards to prosecute, usually through civil or criminal court, those individuals who practice psychology without a license either through the misuse of the title or involvement in illegal practice (e.g., psychological testing). It should be noted that most laws do provide an "exempt status" for specialties, such as a school psychologist certified by a state department of education and employed by a board of education, or for disciplines such as the pastoral counselor or social worker; these exemptions vary from state to state. Some states also have jurisdiction over individuals who are registered with the board under the supervision of the licensed professional psychologist, such as interns, psychological assistants, or examiners.

Violations relative to licensed individuals are usually prosecuted by the state attorney general and unlicensed individuals by local district attorneys. While it cannot be fully documented, initially boards were concerned with pursuing the unlicensed person. As the public and practitioners alike have become more knowledgeable, these situations have lessened considerably and boards have become more concerned with regulating the profession.

It is very important to reiterate that boards have no authority to enforce standards of practice unless these are specified in statute or in Rules and Regulations. The peer-imposed standards (e.g., APA Ethical Principles,

Standards for Providers of Psychological Services) are often embodied in the state law or regulations, usually by paraphrasing them, and occasionally by reference. In the latter situation, the disadvantage is that standards might change and become more ambiguous and more difficult to enforce, or even that such changes might not be in the best interest of the consumer.

State licensing boards essentially respond to complaints from consumers or professional psychologists. Occasionally, the board will respond to noted irregularities with site review visits or formal investigations. In other instances, boards will become involved when court findings have been found against a psychologist, such as with welfare or third-party payment fraud. Cases may also be referred to boards by state ethics committees or third-party payers who review case procedures. While the procedure is not systemized, it appears that consumers, professional psychologists, and others are becoming increasingly aware of the role of the licensing boards regarding enforcement and are reporting violations.

A significant deterrent to reporting violations is the complainant's fear of legal action against her/himself—particularly from a colleague. Most boards will not reveal the name of complainants unless they will be involved in the actual hearing process; some states (e.g., California) have laws protecting persons who report suspected violations without malice. In some instances, boards who have an investigating process prefer to have complaints made directly to the board and are not concerned about having the psychologist first contact the offender.

Board action is determined to be relevant when there are:

1. Violations of statute.
   (a) Unlicensed practice of psychology as defined in the state statute.
   (b) Violations related to the practice of psychology by licensed individuals (e.g., moral turpitude, fraud).
   (c) Laws such as felonies, unrelated to the practice of psychology. Note: Some states, such as California, require the felony to bear a substantial relationship to the licensed practice in order for the board to take action.
2. Violations of rules and regulations.
   (a) Rules of professional conduct.
   (b) Gross negligence.
   (c) Incompetence.
3. Violations of other licensing boards and action taken by other boards.
4. Disciplinary actions or denial of license by the psychology board of another state.

Psychologists need to read and be very familiar with the law and rules of the state in which they practice psychology. Violations and subse-

PAAP-E

quent penalties can be prevented through knowledge and consultation, along with understanding the potential seriousness for violations.

Investigations

With suspected violations, the licensing board will initiate a formal investigation. The investigation is either done by board members themselves, or a designated state department of investigation which assigns a state investigator to the case who, in turn, works closely with the board. The primary advantage of board members investigating a case is their intimate knowledge of the profession and the subsequent manner in which violations can be hidden. An added function is the commitment board members have to the maintenance of the integrity of the profession. This orientation may be contrary to public opinion, which often assumes that regulating boards operate to protect the profession from the public, and will take little action.

State investigators have considerable expertise in investigating procedures, thereby eliminating the need to train new board members as investigators. However, they also serve on numerous boards and are less knowledgeable about the profession, and sometimes have less commitment to extend investigations when impasses are reached; the time commitment for any investigation can be quite extensive, a factor board members must consider when taking on a case.

Some states have explicit due rights procedures spelled out in detail, while others are vague. In some instances, states may employ undercover investigators. Investigators and hearings are also expensive. States do vary as to fiscal support and other resources for investigations and hearings, with some required to pay for such expenses solely from renewal and application fees, while others are supported from general revenue funds.

At any rate, clear guidelines for investigators are usually established. When a formal hearing results from an investigation, the investigator does not participate as a member of the panel if he or she is a board member. Likewise, board members who work with state investigators are not involved. Previous bias can be avoided in this way. Finally, whatever the resolution of the case, the originator of the complaint is given information about the disposition.

HEARINGS

If a complaint is found to have validity, formal charges may be filed with the board, along with notification to the accused psychologist of an opportunity for a formal hearing. Because of time and expense, formal consent agreements sometimes can be reached through negotiation relative to guilt and punishment. In other instances, when consent cannot be reached, or either party does not want to reach an agreement, the case proceeds to a formal hearing.

Although procedures vary among states, the most common model is for hearings to be held by the board itself, usually with a hearing officer presiding who is familiar with legal procedures. Some boards have the authority to appoint a hearing officer with the case reviewed by the board. The drawback with the use of outside hearing officers is that unless they are familiar with psychological practice, real issues relative to ethical practice and harm to the client may not be fully appreciated by the presiding officer.

During the hearing, the state's case is presented by the deputy attorney general of the state. The defendant is also represented by legal counsel. In some states, witnesses may be subjected to subpoena and are sworn in so that cross-examination is permissible. The formal hearing is quite similar to trial proceedings, only with more flexibility and leniency. The American Association of State Psychology Boards (AASPB), working with the Texas Board, has developed a videotape of a model hearing, which makes both educational and interesting viewing and can be secured upon request from AASPB or state licensing boards (Texas Board of Examiners, 1985).

Butler and Williams (1985) analyzed hearings of the Ohio Board of Psychology from 1972 to 1983, and concluded that when a complaint reached the hearing stage there was, in most instances, enough evidence to warrant a conviction. In most states, after weighing the evidence the board has the authority to reprimand, suspend, or revoke the license. Both suspension and revocation can be stayed, with a period of probation and specified term of probation. If the terms of the probation are violated, the original punishment is activated. Combinations of these actions can be given (e.g., suspension of 1 year, stayed with 30 days actual suspension plus conditions of probation). The advantage of staying is that the board has both a surveillance and rehabilitation mechanism. The Psychology Examining Committee of California has issued a set of disciplinary guidelines to aid boards in reaching decisions. The guidelines were reproduced in the *AASPB Newsletter* (Psychology Examining Committee of California, 1979). Most boards further believe that publicity of actions taken may be useful, both as a deterrent and as evidence that the board is doing its job.

PROFESSIONAL STANDARDS

While the APA Ethical Principles (APA, 1981) provide the foundation for professional practice, other standards have been developed that will directly affect the practice of psychology in the future. The standards and guidelines of practice serve to provide a linkage between the ethical code and the requirements set by state statute relative to the practice of psychology.

State laws regulate the practice of psychology, and in many respects represent the consumers' and other interested parties' attempts to regulate professional conduct from outside the profession. The various standards of practice are attempts to regulate practice from within the profession itself. However, standards developed by the APA generally tend to be more restrictive and emphasize a higher level of practice than state legislative requirements, especially regarding entry level requirements and competence for practice. Jacobs (1983) points out that the reason for this emphasis lies within the political process itself, whereby legislative actions result from a more heterogeneous mix of interested parties, in contrast to professional organizations, which represent a fairly consistent professional viewpoint.

State laws basically emphasize minimum levels of entry and competency in order to provide services to the public, while professional standards are designed to upgrade the profession in order to demonstrate to the public that the profession itself seeks to maintain both high entry level qualifications and standards for competence. State laws are primarily designed to protect the public, while professional standards have both public and professional objectives.

Despite the differences, state statutes have been influenced by professional organizations. Indeed, Hogan (1979) has charged that laws have served the profession rather than the public, unnecessarily restricting the latter's access to qualified providers. Furthermore, Gross (1978) had previously emphasized that while licensing gives a profession autonomy and public recognition, it also legitimizes the power of the profession to gain a monopoly over practice. In many respects, legislative actions have lent to higher and tighter standards, a longer period of training, and an extended period of supervised practice.

The paradoxical relationship between standards and laws has not prevented additional criticism of licensing boards in terms of monitoring and prosecution of violations. In part, this type of criticism during the late 1970s and early 1980s led to the passing of "sunset laws," whereby in several states licensing laws were provisionally repealed. It is important to note that psychology has fared well under such legislative "sunset" reviews. The development of standards and guidelines by the APA and other groups does serve to enhance public accountability, as the profession is forced to review its practices and procedures.

Professional standards are designed to provide not only guidelines to the individual professional, but to offer mental health and agency directors, schools, and corporate officers with a blueprint for organizing and staffing psychological service units. "Standards of practice have come to fill an essential need not fully met by the profession's or society's previous methods to insure safety, quality, orthodoxy, effectiveness, accessibility, economy, and accountability to potential users of psychological services" (Jacobs, 1983, p. 45).

Guidelines for Providers of Psychological Services

The "Specialty Guidelines for the Delivery of Services" (1981b) are the latest extension of the national Standards for Providers of Psychological Services, originally adopted by the APA on September 4, 1974 (APA, 1974). The intent of these standards/guidelines is to improve the quality, effectiveness, and accessibility of psychological services to all who require them.

The original 1974 standards were revised in January 1977 and provided generic standards for the delivery of services (APA, 1977). As stated previously, while admission to the practice of psychology is regulated by state law, the APA has consistently supported generic licensing. However, professional psychology has evolved into four recognized specialties—clinical, counseling, school, and industrial/organizational (I–O) psychology—which are supported by university training programs. It was felt by many within the APA that after the 1977 standards were adopted, the knowledge base in each of these areas was developed to the point that a uniform set of specialty guidelines were possible and desirable. The present guidelines, which were adopted in June 1980, and revised and published in the June 1981 issue of the *American Psychologist*, were intended to educate the public and the profession regarding the types of services available from the specialties within the profession (APA, 1981). For an excellent historical review of the development of these guidelines, the reader is referred to Jacobs (1983), in which he details the ongoing process within the APA for the 20 years preceding the adoption of the present standards.

The content of each specialty's set of guidelines reflects a consensus of university faculty and public and private practitioners, regarding the knowledge base, services provided, problems addressed, and clients served by that specialty. The specialty guidelines are further intended to specify, after the grandfathering period, the qualifications by which psychologists can hold themselves out to the public as *specialists* in a given area. These guidelines were intended to be applicable to only those psychologists who wish specialty designation, and do not apply to other psychologists.

Each specialty guideline adheres closely to the format and wording of the generic Standards (APA, 1977), and the Standards still remain the basic policy statement. While the APA is still committed to generic licensure, they also recommend the specialty guidelines' use as "an authoritative reference for use in credentialing specialty providers by such groups as divisions of the APA and state associations, and boards and agencies that find such criteria useful for quality assurance" (APA, 1981c, p. 640).

The APA Committee on Professional Standards (COPS) was established in January 1980, and is charged with keeping the APA Standards and Specialty Guidelines responsive to the needs of the public and the profession. It is also charged with "continually reviewing, modifying and extending them progressively as the profession and science of psychology develops new knowledge, improved methods, and additional modes of psychological services" (APA, 1981c, p. 640). Revisions can be expected in the next several years. In fact, as of winter 1986, COPS has begun work on a revision of the APA's generic Standards document. It is anticipated that the Specialty Guidelines will then undergo a similar review.

Each set of guidelines begins with a Definition section, which defines Providers of (Specialty) Psychological Service. Professional (specialty) psychologists are defined as those who have doctoral degrees from APA-accredited programs or fit specific criteria. Interestingly, the criteria are quite similar to the Designation Project for Programs in Psychology adopted by the American Association of State Psychology Boards (AASPB) and the National Register in August 1985. The future impact of the Designation Program on these definitions is probable. Exceptions to training definitions are for I–O psychologists, because of a lack of a consensus statement regarding educational and training requirements, and school psychology, because of ongoing dialogue between the APA and the National Association of School Psychologists relative to doctoral/nondoctoral training and joint accreditation of training programs. Also defined in this section are specialty psychological services, a service unit, and users of the specialty psychological services.

In terms of psychological services, there are a common set of generic services for clinical, counseling, and school guidelines. These are assessment and evaluation, intervention, consultation, program development, evaluation, and supervision. The I–O guidelines specify selection and placement of employees, organizational development, training and development of employees, personnel research, improving employee motivation, and design and optimization of work environments.

It should also be noted that the I–O guidelines do not provide separate sections dealing with the psychological service unit and users of psychological services, leaving open the organizational framework for the delivery of services.

Following the Definitions section, there are four areas of guidelines: *Providers, Programs, Accountability,* and *Environment.* The Providers area details eight specific guidelines covering adequacy of services, supervision, administrative responsibility, development and practice relative to professional competence, training, and encouragement to develop innovations. The Programs section includes guidelines on psychological service units, policies, and procedures. Guideline 3, Accountability, involves client welfare, autonomous practice, and evaluation and accountability of services. The fourth guideline, Environment, places psychology within a larger context of society. The content of the I–O guidelines, in comparison to the other specialties, have some basic differences, especially concerning the generic standards. The training tends to be more flexible and omits the composition and organization of the service unit, as well as several other differences.

The APA's generic Standards and Specialty Guidelines appear to be important documents relative to the future practice of psychology. The APA may well decide that these will eventually serve as guidelines not only to its membership but for the general public as well. More likely, the Standards and Guidelines will also serve as standards relative to local, state, or national peer-review efforts. While peer-review procedures do not have direct enforcement power, they still wield considerable influence. This impact is especially true in state-level review systems. The review system should provide the general public with strong evidence that the profession fully intends to protect the consumer and maintain competent and high quality services.

STANDARDS FOR PSYCHOLOGICAL TESTS

The *1984 Joint Technical Standards for Educational and Psychological Testing* is a joint document of the APA, the American Educational Research Association, and the National Council on Measurement in Education (APA, 1984). This document provides a comprehensive set of standards regarding test use, and special issues related to linguistic/cultural differences, testing the handicapped, testing the aged, and computerized adaptive testing.

The *1984 Joint Technical Standards* is the latest revision, with the first sets of "testing standards" developed in 1954 (APA, 1954), and a second revision in 1966 (APA, 1966). These two sets of standards presented the proper content of manuals provided by the test publisher. A later revision in 1974 added the requirements for test users (APA, 1974).

The standards are for both publishers and users of tests. While the standards apply to those who publish tests and test developers who are developing an instrument that has widespread use, users of tests are expected to utilize psychological tests only in accordance with the standards. Users are expected to evaluate the evidence of validity of the instrument, recognize and limit practice to professional qualifications, maintain test security, as well as meet the standards for interpretation of test results. In making interpretations, the user should be cognizant of potential test bias or client characteristics such as ethnic or cultural minority situations, which might reduce the validity of the test results. Along with reporting test data, the psychologist should also report, and provide evidence for, any relevant cautions of bias or other suspected problems. Additionally, each technique needs to be valid for the intended purpose of the assessment. This expectation implies a thorough knowledge about the technical test data, including normative procedures, and reliability and validity findings, in order to ascertain appropriate use of the instrument. An excellent resource for further reading is the special issue of the *American Psychologist* (1981d) which carefully delineates and discusses the current controversies in psychological assessment.

NASP Professional Conduct Manual

The National Association of School Psychologists (NASP) has also developed both *Principles for Professional Ethics* (1984a) and *Standards for the Provision of School Psychological Services* (1984c), which are both published in the *Professional Conduct Manual* (1984b). The manual also includes Procedural Guidelines for the Adjudication of Ethical Complaints. These documents serve as an example of how a specialty within psychology has evolved its own set of documents relative to professional practice.

The NASP code of ethics is specific to the practice of school psychology, dealing with areas of professional competency; relationships with students, parents, community, and related professionals; and professional practices in school and private settings. It is a comprehensive document and a valuable asset for school psychologists who wish more specific guidelines than that provided in the APA code.

The Procedural Guidelines for the Adjudication of Ethical Complaints makes the NASP Ethics and Professional Conduct Committee responsible for the investigation, hearings, and recommendations resulting from its deliberations. However, expulsion from membership requires a confirmation by a two-thirds vote of the NASP Executive Board, with a majority ratification by the Delegate Assembly.

The *Standards for the Provision of School Psychological Services* (1984b) represents NASP's position on the delivery of comprehensive school psychological services. Similar to APA Standards and Guidelines, they are intended to educate the public and profession regarding appropriate professional practice. They also are designed to provide direction to students and trainers in school psychology and administrators of school psychological services. The NASP Standards were developed from numerous NASP documents, such as *Standards for the Provision of School Psychological Services* (NASP, 1978) and *Standards for Training and Field Placement Programs in School Psychology* (1984d), as well as ideas from the APA Specialty Guidelines, and ideas and suggestions from the general membership. As a result, the standards are considerably more extensive than the APA Specialty Guidelines with standards for administrative agencies (federal and state), employing agencies, and the delivery of comprehensive school psychological services. The latter section includes topics dealing with the organization of services; autonomous functioning; independent practice; continuing professional development; and accountability. The document is designed to provide future direction for amendments to state statutes and rules, and it is hoped that local school psychology units will incorporate these standards into practice.

SOME ISSUES

Competence

While methods for adequately analyzing competence are not clear and precise, the issue regarding the professional responsibility to achieve and maintain competence is absolute. Psychology is an amalgamation of orientations, approaches, and techniques. For example, the outcome of therapy often depends upon a blend of the type of problem, client, method, and therapist; the measure of successful outcome is often difficult to determine. Given the psychologist's training and other factors, a psychologist can be competent in one setting and incompetent in another. Despite these difficulties, psychologists are expected to practice within the bounds of activities and settings they are qualified to conduct.

From the standpoint of the individual psychologist, "competence" involves the ability to honestly assess one's own professional strengths and limitations, and often a willingness to refer or not to treat a client whose problem is beyond the competence of the psychologist. This decision can be a difficult problem for the professional. At present, the psychologist is issued a general license and conceivably engages in any type of evaluative or therapeutic practice. Often consumers are uninformed about the differences in training, and often assume that a psychologist, for example, who is well trained in individual psychotherapy might also have the appropriate training and skills in marital or family therapy. It is unfortunate but true that some psychologists make the same erroneous assumption—that their license allows them to practice in any applied area of psychology, regardless of training or supervised experience.

Because of the lack of clear identification by the public and self-limiting behaviors on the part of the individual psychologists, licensing boards must deal with problematic relationships between competency and training in several ways. In attempting to determine relevant training, boards begin by specifying degree requirements: that is, master's or doctoral degree in psychology or equivalent program. While the PhD is essentially the entry-level requirement, content and standards of programs vary considerably, so that this does not provide a sufficient sole determiner of competence. While it is contended that the doctoral degree was designed to develop high standards to protect consumers, others have argued that the real issue is third-party reimbursement. The addition of a general examination tends to test knowledge, although it has begun more recently to focus on general practice issues. An additional criterion is that of supervised experience, whereby a licensed professional endorses the psychologist's clinical abilities and clinical judgment. Some boards, such as California's, structure oral examinations based upon clinical case vignettes to further assess competency.

Many malpractice suits involve competency issues, where both therapeutic ability and judgment are called into question. At this point, the psychologist most often defends himself or herself, and licensing alone does not provide an adequate defense. The psychologist must be able to demonstrate adequate academic preparation, including didactic and practica, as well as clinical supervision relative to this particular situation. A defense relative to the reasonable judgments made in a case begins with basic competence.

The major focus relative to competence has been discussed mainly in terms of psychotherapy; however, competence is also an issue in testing, consultation, teaching, and research. Basic coursework and supervised training in specific tests and techniques, for example, Rorschach or WAIS-R, as well as report writing, also involves a basic sensitivity about labeling. Consulting in agencies, schools, and industries requires different academic preparation and training for each area. Teaching requires keeping abreast of new knowledge as well as ethical considerations of the course content. Research involves working with one's level and competence regarding designs as well as subject welfare, including the obtaining of valid consent from subjects.

Confidentiality

Confidentiality is designed to protect the privacy and welfare of clients. At the same time, *privilege* and *confidentiality* are frequently confused concepts, creating issues for the psychologist whereby knowledge and sensitivity are needed. Privilege (communication) is a legal term, granted by state laws to clients, which defines the type of relationships that prevent information learned as part of such relationships from being disclosed in legal proceedings, or to third parties without the expressed consent of the client. While the psychologist (or other professional) is explicitly named in the statute, the privilege exists for the client. If the client waives the privilege, the psychologist may be compelled to release the information or testify. Privilege is also rarely absolute, and in some situations, such as child abuse, the psychologist may be legally required to make a report to the authorities. Because state laws do vary, psychologists are urged to make themselves aware of the nature and status of privileged communication in their own state.

Confidentiality, in contrast to privilege, refers to a professional standard of conduct and as such, is an ethical principle without a legal basis. Therefore, in ordinary situations, a professional is obligated through a professional code of ethics not to discuss information about a client with anyone. Regarding the disclosure of information, two types of problems can occur: (a) the psychologist, through carelessness, reveals confidential information; and (b) the psychologist makes a decision to reveal information. In the first instance, information can be revealed by professors teaching classes and not sufficiently disguising case examples from their practice, maintaining open filing systems while allowing nonprofessionals to have access to information, and in consultation with other staff. These situations can easily occur, and create problems if not monitored carefully by the psychologist.

The second problem, regarding the conscious decision to release information, creates the greatest controversy, especially in terms of situations that would justify this decision. The focus of this controversy involves the "clear danger to the person or to others" clause in the APA Ethical Principles (1981). In some instances, psychologists must make a difficult decision when the client will move from talking about harmful situations to actually taking action. While physical harm to self or others may present more obvious choices, insidious forms of harm, such as financial ruin, create the necessity for a difficult decision.

The classic Tarasoff case (*Tarasoff v. Regents of University of California*, 1976) is discussed in chapter 4 and raises the issue of whether or not the psychologist has a duty to protect all potential victims. The extent of this responsibility has generated numerous concerns which have yet to be fully answered.

Psychologists need to be aware that changes have been made in the laws regarding the release of information allowing freer client-to-records access. Institutional records (e.g., clinical, school, agency) generally have client access, while private practitioners and working notes are not covered by specific legislation. Generally, records do not belong to the client, but rather to the practitioner. Caution, however, is advised for the psychologist relative to working notes, because of the sensitive nature of the psychologist's impressions and the possibility of such speculation being subpoenaed in a court action. Regular reviews and summaries are recommended.

Psychologists need to have written permission from the client prior to releasing any records or information and fully alert the client of any possible hazards involved. All information should consider both the need-to-know basis of the recipient and the use of the information and impact upon the client.

Dual Relationships

Dual relationships in psychotherapy arise when a connection exists outside the therapeutic alliance with the client as a lover, friend, family member, student, or business partner. Dual relationships distort the objectivity in therapy and compromise the therapeutic relationship.

Holyroyd and Brodsky (1977), in a survey of 657 licensed psychologists, reported that 5.5% of the male therapists and 0.6% of the female therapists had sexual intercourse with their clients. Sexually intimate behavior is considered to be a serious ethical violation which carries severe penalties with licensing boards. Prolonged suspension or revocation of the license are common penalties. Moreover, the legal costs in terms of defense before boards and civil suits by clients are to the point of becoming astronomical. Legal fees in sexual malpractice suits are usually not covered by liability insurance carriers. The financial and professional devastation itself notwithstanding, psychologists are advised to avoid dual relationship situations because abusing the trust, influence, and power involved in their professional relationship can result in harm to their clients.

Keith-Spiegel and Koocher (1985) list a number of precautions psychologists can take to protect themselves against unwarranted claims of sexual misconduct:

1. Before attempting any form of non-erotic touching or verbal compliment that could be considered flirtatious or suggestive, thoroughly know your client's psychological functioning. Some clients may remain unsuited to these types of displays for the duration of therapy.
2. If uneasy feelings about attraction dynamics are perceived as emanating from a client, consult a trusted, sensitive, and preferably experienced colleague about the proper course of action with this particular client.
3. If a client is open and direct about erotic feelings or a desire for a sexual relationship, deal with these impulses in a way that protects the client's self-esteem. Taylor and Wagner (1976) suggest that the therapist express a feeling of flattery followed by a firm declaration that such behavior

cannot ever occur between them, because it is both a serious ethical violation and potentially harmful. Then the therapeutic issues surrounding the attraction can be handled.

4. The truly fearful therapist might consider some practical safeguards, including the following:

    a. Conduct therapy in a group practice setting where other people are around.

    b. Furnish the office tastefully, but in a businesslike manner. Avoid decor and furniture that suggest a too-cozy ambience.

    c. Avoid offering therapy sessions in other than a traditional, professional setting. (p. 260)

While psychologists who deal with clients in a professional manner need not be overly concerned about unwarranted accusations, the psychologist's feelings of sexual attraction should not be ignored. Often it is unwise to discuss these feelings in the therapy session, but rather in consultation with a colleague, especially when the desire exists to act upon these feelings. In such instances, termination and referral is advisable. For further reading about this issue and dual relationships from a variety of perspectives, chapter 10 in Keith-Spiegel and Koocher (1985) is highly recommended.

Advertisements

Historically, until the mid-1970s, psychologists operated under the guidelines for telephone directory listings published in the *American Psychologist* (APA, 1969). Announcements or listings were limited to name, highest relevant degree, narrow area of specialization, address, and phone number. Announcement to colleagues regarding the establishment of the practice was also acceptable. In response to Federal Trade Commission rulings based upon the Supreme Court ruling (*Goldfarb v. Virginia State Bar*, 1975), relative to ethical codes in the legal profession that heretofore had prohibited advertising, price competition, and overall competitive practices, the APA Ethics Committee made some substantial shifts in its position. The Ethical Principles now allow advertising by psychologists, within limits.

At this point in time, advertisements are considered appropriate if modesty, caution, and accurate representation of qualifications and credentials are exhibited. Simple factual statements are still considered the most appropriate format to use. However, exaggerated claims, direct solicitation of clients, testimonials, and evaluative comments range from illegal violation of some licensing laws, to ethical violations of the APA Ethical Principles, to just "tacky" misrepresentations.

Currently, the most controversial examples involve Yellow Pages listings. Disagreement exists relative to the style of advertising, ranging in most directories from simple name, address, and phone number to complex display ads that display a long list of specialties.

Licensing boards are constantly reviewing the telephone listings relative to appropriateness of the listing and to prevent nonpsychologists, including supervisees, from listing under "psychologist." Subtle misrepresentation is a real issue, and within the absence of firm guidelines because of the Federal Trade Commission rulings, difficult to prevent. Psychologists have been known to list services clearly beyond their areas of competency in order to attract clients. Other psychologists may list degrees (e.g., PhD), when the degree was awarded in another field or from an unaccredited institution. The latter situation is usually a direct violation of state licensing laws, and will result in charges being filed against the psychologist.

Media Relationships

The entire field of mass media increasingly has become an area of concern for the psychology profession. On the one hand, as the profession matures, the media looks toward psychology for answers which, in turn, if handled correctly can enhance the profession in the eyes of the public. On the other hand, some forms of mass media are geared to sensationalism, hype, and superficiality. This is sometimes related to poor journalism, while at other times it occurs just by virtue of the media's format, time allowance, and topic in a particular situation. Often psychologists are hard pressed to avoid becoming involved in media situations where sensationalism, exaggeration or superficiality, as defined in the APA Ethical Principles, are present.

Psychologists find themselves interviewed by newspaper journalists, making guest appearances on radio and television, or promoting books on psychological procedures. A particularly heated issue has been the "advice-giving" situations, whereby the separation from psychotherapy has been difficult to determine. Prior to 1981, the APA prohibited psychologists from offering psychological services or products for the purpose of diagnosing, treating, or giving personal advice to individuals through the mass media. In 1981, the code of ethics was modified so that while individual diagnostic and therapeutic services still belonged in a private professional context, personal advice given through public lectures, newspaper and magazine articles, and broadcast media were allowed as long as the psychologist uses current relevant data and exercises a high level of professional judgment.

This change in position, while not totally satisfactory, is an attempt to begin to deal with a realistic emerging problem in a positive manner. The difficulties in deciding what constitutes "personal advice" from diagnosis and therapeutic interpretation is extremely unclear. In addition, the issue of what constitutes current relevant data and sound professional judgment is, at best, arguable.

This issue ultimately rests upon the competence and expertise of the giver of advice in relationship to the welfare of the public. The impact of psychology upon the public is the primary concern, but how the profession will proceed in handling this situation is still unclear.

From another aspect, however, it is clearly inappropriate for psychologists to endorse products or to be compensated for the endorsement. Koocher (1983) gives two reasons for this conclusion: (a) if the product is psychological in nature, it will stand on its own scientific merit; and (b) if the product is not psychological in nature, the psychologist is using his or her professional stature to endorse a product that is misleading the public. In a sense, the psychologist would be using undue influence to manipulate the public for personal financial gain.

In summary, psychologists need to exercise considerable caution when dealing with the media. Ultimately, the psychologist is responsible for how his or her name is used, and the statements or advice given. It needs to be continually recognized that often the goals of the media may be in conflict with those of the individual psychologist and the profession.

Supervision

An area of increasing concern of licensing boards has been in the area of supervision. For clarity, supervision can take the form of training in order to prepare the supervisee for licensure, or work supervision when the supervisee becomes, in essence, an extender of the psychologist. In the first situation, training standards as well as licensing laws provide guidelines and rules for training. In the second instance, state licensing laws provide the parameters for supervision.

With the increase of availability of third-party reimbursement, supervision has become a viable method for private practitioners and agencies to increase revenues. As a result, agencies may pressure psychologists to utilize "sign off" procedures on case reports and insurance forms for a large number of cases and supervisees. At the same time, private practitioners may actively seek supervisees to the point where adequate work or training supervision is also not provided.

In terms of most licensing laws, supervisees do not have any professional status. They are extensions of the psychologist who is legally responsible for all of the psychological work of the supervisee. This legal responsibility extends to any malpractice or negligence action of the supervisee. Sloppy or inadequate supervision practices place the psychologist in a vulnerable position, in terms of both litigation and with the licensing board. Licensing boards are increasingly revising their rules relative to supervision and providing stricter enforcement in this area.

The lack of quality supervision also affects the supervisee, especially in terms of training supervision, where the trainee is dependent upon the quality of supervision to provide the foundation for future professional practice. In order to be licensed, 1 or 2 years of supervised experience are necessary, and unfortunately, some students may end up in situations that provide far less than good supervision and experience. In summary, psychologists who undertake supervision need to be familiar with state laws. They have a professional and legal obligation to provide quality supervision. They also need to make clear to clients, as well as supervisees, the nature and expectations relative to the supervisory relationship.

SUGGESTED READINGS

Ethics in Psychology: Professional Standards and Cases by Keith-Spiegel and Koocher (1985) is a good personal reference text that covers all areas of psychological practice, with interesting case examples. This book is the most recent and comprehensive text in the field of ethical behavior in psychological practice, with the case examples drawn from APA files.

In 1980, the APA Board of Professional Affairs charged its Committee on Professional Standards (COPS) to develop a casebook for providers of psychological services. The focus of the cases would be quality assurance problems that come to the attention of that committee, or the Committee on Academic Freedom and Conditions of Employment, or the Committee on Scientific and Professional Ethics and Conduct. Since 1981, three to four cases have been presented in each June archival issue of the *American Psychologist*. The cases deal with implementation of the APA Specialty Guidelines and are in the specialty areas of clinical, counseling, industrial/organizational, and school psychology.

For those psychologists specializing in group, marital, and/or family therapy, the ethical issues are often quite different, not necessarily in principle, but rather in some practice situations. The *APA Guidelines for Group Therapists* (1973) is a necessity for those therapists working with multiple clients in a group setting. A number of basic issues, including confidentiality, are covered. Several authors have written good articles and chapters about some of the legal issues regarding marital and family work. Hines and Hare-Mustin (1978) discuss the ethical issues in family therapy, and Margolin (1982) offers a comprehensive set of the legal and ethical issues in marital and family therapy. The psychologist in practice is often required to work with couples and families. These practice modalities present some unique ethical and legal ramifications, especially concerning confidentiality, and the reader is urged to review these articles inasmuch as the *APA Ethical Standards* does not cover such situations.

At a broader level, Haas and Fennimore (1983) have compiled a bibliography of 171 publications between 1970 and 1981 related to ethical and legal issues in professional psychology. They are grouped under the following eight topics: issues, malpractice, patients' rights, licensure, therapist sexuality, sexism and bias, ethics in teaching, and training.

Finally, guidelines dealing with complex ethical issues are not easy to develop. While the rights of individuals and groups need protection, the value systems inherent in religion, economics, philosophies of thought, ethical codes, and the law can lead to very different conclusions. Tymchuk (1981) presents a two-part ethical decisionmaking model that can help the professional examine a situation systematically and identify the factors influencing a decision.

REFERENCES

American Psychological Association. (1969). Guidelines for telephone directory listing. *American Psychologist, 24*, 70–71.

American Psychological Association. (1973). *APA guidelines for group therapists.* Washington, DC: Author.

American Psychological Association. (1974). *Standards for providers of psychological services.* Washington, DC: Author.

American Psychological Association. (1977). Standards for providers of psychological services. *American Psychologist, 32*, 495–505.

American Psychological Association. (1981a). Ethical principles of psychologists (rev. ed.). *American Psychologist, 36*, 639–681.

American Psychological Association. (1981b). Specialty guidelines for the delivery of services (APA Committee on Professional Standards). *American Psychologist, 36*, 639–681.

American Psychological Association. (1981c). Specialty guidelines for the delivery of services by clinical psychologists. *American Psychologist, 36*, 640–651.

American Psychological Association. (1981d). Testing: Concepts, policy, practice and research. *American Psychologist, 36*, 997–1189.

American Psychological Association. (1982). *Ethical principles in the conduct of research with human participants.* Washington, DC: Author.

American Psychological Association. (1984). *Joint standards for educational and psychological testing.* Washington, DC: Author.

American Psychological Association, Committee on Ethical Standards of Psychology. (1951a). Ethical standards for psychology. *American Psychologist, 6*, 427–452.

American Psychological Association, Committee on Ethical Standards of Psychology. (1951b). Ethical standards for psychology. *American Psychologist, 6*, 626–661.

American Psychological Association, Educational Research Association and National Council on Measurement in Education. (1954). Technical recommendations for psychological tests and diagnostic techniques. *Psychological Bulletin, 51*, 201–238.

American Psychological Association, Educational Research Association and National

Council on Measurement in Education. (1966). *Standards for educational and psychological tests and manuals*. Washington, DC: Author.

American Psychological Association, Educational Research Association and National Council on Measurement in Education. (1974). *Standards for educational and psychological tests and manuals*. Washington, DC: Author.

Butler, R. W., & Williams, D. A. (1985). Description of Ohio State Board of Psychology hearings in ethical violations: From 1972 to the present. *Professional Psychology: Research and Practice, 16*, 502–511.

Golann, S. E. (1970). Ethical standards for psychology. Development and revision, 1938–1968. *Annals of the New York Academy of Sciences, 169*, 398–405.

Goldfarb v. Virginia State Bar, 421 U.S. 773 (1975).

Gross, S. J. (1980). The myth of professional licensing. *American Psychologist, 33*, 1009–1016.

Haas, L. J., & Fennimore, D. (1983). Ethical and legal issues in professional psychology: Selected works, 1970–1981. *Professional Psychology: Research and Practice, 14*, 540–548.

Hall, J., & Hare-Mustin, R. (1983). Sanctions and the diversity of ethical complaints against psychologists. *American Psychologist, 38*, 714–729.

Hare-Mustin, R., & Hall, J. (1981). Procedures for responding to ethical complaints against psychologists. *American Psychologist, 36*, 1494–1505.

Hines, P. M., & Hare-Mustin, R. T. (1978). Ethical concerns in family therapy. *Professional Psychology, 9*, 165–171.

Hogan, D. B. (1979). *The regulation of psychotherapists*. Cambridge, MA: Ballinger.

Holyroyd, J. C., & Brodsky, H. M. (1977). Psychologists' attitudes and practices regarding erotic and non–erotic physical contact with patients. *American Psychologist, 32*, 843–849.

Jacobs, D. F. (1983). The development and application of standards of practice for professional psychologists. In B. D. Sales (Ed.), *The professional psychologist's handbook* (pp. 19–75). New York: Plenum Press.

Keith-Spiegel, P., & Koocher, G. P. (1985). *Ethics in psychology: Professional standards and cases*. Hillside, NJ: Erlbaum.

Koocher, G. P. (1983). Ethical and professional standards in psychology. In B. D. Sales (Ed.), *The professional psychologist's handbook* (pp. 77–109). New York: Plenum Press.

Margolin, G. (1982). Ethical and legal considerations in marital and family therapy. *American Psychologist, 37*, 788–801.

Mills, D. H. (1984). Ethics education and adjudication within psychology. *American Psychologist, 39*, 669–675.

National Association of School Psychologists. (1978, May). *Standards for the provision of school psychological services*. Washington, DC: Author.

National Association of School Psychologists. (1984a). *Principles for ethical practice*. Kent, OH: Author.

National Association of School Psychologists. (1984b). *Professional conduct manual*. Kent, OH: Author.

National Association of School Psychologists. (1984c). *Standards for the provision of school psychological services*. Kent, OH: Author.

National Association of School Psychologists. (1984d). *Standards for training and field placement programs in school psychology*. Kent, OH: Author.

Ohio Admin. Code §§ 4732-5-02 (1981).

Ohio Rev. Code Ann. § 4732 (Baldwin 1972).

Psychology Examining Committee of California. (1979, March). Disciplinary guidelines. *AASPB Newsletter, 15*, 38–43.

Sanders, J. R., & Keith-Spiegel, P. (1980). Formal and internal adjudication of ethics complaints against psychologists. *American Psychologist, 35*, 1096–1105.

Tarasoff v. Regents of the University of California, 551 P 2d 334, 131 Cal. Rptr. 14 (1976).

Taylor, B. J., & Wagner, N. N. (1976). Sex between therapists and clients: A review and analysis. *Professional Psychology, 7,* 593–601.

Texas Board of Examiners. (1985). *Mock disciplinary hearing* (Videotape). Montgomery, AL: American Association of State Psychology Boards.

Tymchuk, A. J. (1981). Ethical decision making and psychological treatment. *Journal of Psychiatric Treatment and Evaluation, 3,* 507–513.

Chapter 4
Legal Impact in Practice

The practice of psychology has become increasingly regulated. In fact, it appears that over the last 15 years federal legislation, state legislation, and court decisions have coalesced to actually control the practice of psychology. As a result, the professional organizations have been relegated to a less influential role than ever before in some areas of practice. This chapter explores the increasing impact the legal system has upon the practice of professional psychology. In many ways, the legal system has essentially determined how applied psychology will be financed relative to health care and third-party payments, and ultimately the shape and scope of how psychologists will function.

Whether this legal influence is beneficial to the profession is arguable. There was a time, as recently as the 1960s, when applied psychology functioned relatively independently of the legal system, and was guided essentially by professional standards developed by the APA. With the advent of state licensure laws, freedom of choice laws at the state level relative to third-party reimbursement, and federal legislation of a variety of health plans, psychology fully entered the arena of the provision of health care services. Additionally, legislation related to the delivery of mental health and developmental disabilities services, as well as regulations governing access to records, have had a further impact upon the profession. In all instances of federal regulation, the Department of Health and Human Services has published a series of complex and controversial regulations implementing these statutes. Adding to legislative regulation are court decisions relative to testing and evaluation, malpractice, and other areas that will continue to shape the functioning of the profession.

In this chapter, state laws will be discussed first, as they have had the most direct impact upon general practice, followed by a review of federal legislation, mostly related to federal programs and agencies. Mental health and developmental disabilities legislation and relevant court decisions will then be discussed. Finally, inasmuch as psychologists most likely will at one time or another be involved in court hearings, the basics of being an expert witness are presented.

THE LEGAL SYSTEM

The legal system is governed by both statutes and court decisions. Legislation is enacted in developing laws. However, because laws are often written in broad terms, the courts must often apply and interpret the statutes. When a court renders a decision that creates a new legal principle, that court and lower courts in the same jurisdiction are bound to apply the precedent to future cases with similar facts.

Statutory laws, like court decisions, exist in each of the 50 states as well as on the federal level. The statutes are binding only in the jurisdiction in which they are passed. Outside of the state, they do not have direct influence on any court. General compilations of statutes are called "codes," which are published by state agencies (e.g., state psychology boards) or contracted out to private publishers for publication. Federal statutes can be found in the *United States Code*, which is the official government publication. However, there are two unofficial popular publications—West Publishing Company's *United States Code Annotated* and Lawyers Cooperative Publishing Company's *United States Code Service*—that are updated annually.

Another area of law comes from administrative agencies that have been delegated broad rule-making authority by Congress or state legislatures. These agencies (e.g., psychology boards) need to have specialized knowledge and time beyond the limits of legislation to develop and promulgate rules on all areas of government control. State governments usually have a manual or "redbook" giving information about these various state agencies. However, the most expedient method of obtaining information may be to contact the state agency directly for a set of rules. At the federal level, since 1735 the federal government has published the *Federal Register*, which is a daily gazette on documents of the administrative and executive branches. The regulations collected for the *Federal Register* are arranged by subject and published in the *Code of Federal Regulations*.

Often the courts must apply, interpret, and fill in the gaps of the various statutes. The cumulative body of court decisions within a jurisdiction is called common (judgment) law. When a court lays down a decision which becomes a new principle of law, the court and lower courts in the same jurisdiction are bound to apply that precedent to future cases. In terms of other courts, however, depending upon the reasoning, these decisions are only persuasive and not binding. Consequently, because of the volume and complexity of the legal decision-making process, it is virtually impossible for the practicing psychologist to be current with the precedent-setting cases relative to the profession. Professional organizations (state and national) regularly provide legal updates and are an invaluable resource to the practitioner.

Psychologists should be aware of the basic structure of the American judicial system. Cases can be decided in the trial, intermediate, appellate, or highest court levels within the state or federal systems. Typically, at the federal level, the court nomenclature in descending order is:

1. U.S. Supreme Court.
2. U.S. Court of Appeals.
3. Federal District Courts.
4. Specialized Courts (e.g., Court of Claims).

At the state level, the various court levels are:

1. State Supreme Court.
2. Appellate Court, Superior Court.
3. County Courts.
4. District Courts.
5. Court of Common Pleas.
6. Specialty Courts (e.g., Family Court).

Initial case testimony is given in trial courts. The losing party may appeal to the appellate court, which does not receive new testimony, but rather, decides if the law was applied properly at the lower level. A subsequent appeal is made to the Supreme Court, which has the right to decide if the case should be heard before considering the appeal itself.

STATE STATUTES

The professional practice of psychology is most directly affected by state laws. State licensure, in particular, has been the basis for the maturing of the profession. The insurance industry, influenced by the direct recognition of psychology as a health provider through freedom of choice laws, also falls under state jurisdiction. The regulation of health insurance through state laws and insurance plans has directly influenced the practice trends in psychology.

Licensing Laws

The first state to enact legislation in the form of a psychology law was Connecticut in 1945, followed by Virginia in 1946 and Kentucky in 1948. Approximately half of the states and six of the Canadian provinces had adopted such statutes by 1970. Missouri was the last state in 1977 to include such provisions. As of this date, all Canadian provinces, with the exception of Newfoundland and Prince Edward Island, provide for the regulation of psychological services (Stigall, 1983).

The relationship of these laws relative to credentialing has been fully discussed in chapter 2 and, with regard to disciplinary actions, in chapter 3. While most laws provide both direct recognition of psychologists and procedures to obtain a license, approximately 42 states and the Canadian provinces of British Columbia and Quebec further provide a definition of the actual practice of psychology. These laws specify services or functions that can be legally performed by a psychologist. The range of scope and practice includes diagnosis and treatment, psychological psychotherapy, biofeedback, hypnotherapy, and behavioral modification as examples. However, many of these definitions are rather unclear and vary considerably from state to state.

In essence, the development of licensing laws has paralleled the growth of applied psychology. Licensure laws have allowed psychologists to be recognized as independent providers of services. Without state statute authority, psychology would not have been able to effectively enter the health care industry, aided by legislation at the state level regarding insurance benefits to clients for psychological services.

Freedom of Choice

Dörken (1983) reported that by June 1982, 36 states and the District of Columbia had passed "freedom of choice" legislation embracing 87% of the population. Freedom of choice legislation essentially creates a choice for the consumer relative to mental health services. Directly changing state insurance laws, freedom of choice legislation requires insurance companies to recognize licensed psychologists as mental health providers and provide coverage at the same level as psychiatrists in the treatment of mental and emotional disorders. As a result, the consumer has a broader range of options when seeking services.

Without the various state freedom of choice laws, insurance companies' recognition of psychologists is strictly voluntary. Some major carriers have voluntarily recognized psychologists, especially for psychological testing at a physician's referral, while others such as Blue Shield (e.g., the extended litigation in the Virginia "Blues" case—Resnick, 1985) have been reluctant. Although psychologists' fees are comparatively lower than those of psychiatrists, when the number of providers is expanded, the costs for insurance companies are considerably increased.

Insurance laws apply to the state in which they are written. Basically, if an insurance carrier has a beneficiary in the freedom of choice state, it must reimburse psychological practice in that state. Conversely, if the beneficiary lives in a state without such legislation, the carrier will most likely not provide the reimbursement. Thus, for major insurance companies, reimbursement policies differ considerably from state to state. To further complicate the issues, in some instances, reimbursement will depend upon the state in which the master contract was written. If the contract was written in a state requiring reimbursement for psychological services, then for the most part, the company will retain the reimbursement policy regardless of the state of residence held by the provider. Often in these instances, and in states without specific provisions for licensed psychologists, the companies will utilize the *National Register for Health Care Providers in Psychology* (see chapter 2) to determine the qualifications of the provider (Council, 1985).

States that do have specific provisions for licensed psychologists, in terms of specific language and reference to licensed psychologists, include New Jersey, New York, California, Maryland, Massachusetts, and Ohio. In other instances, the legislation provides for mandatory coverage, mandatory when the insurance group requests that psychology be recognized for reimbursement. In other situations, psychology reimbursement has been a negotiated issue. With insurance laws varying so much between states, beginning practitioners should study carefully the legislation in the state in which they plan to practice. State psychological associations are usually most helpful in this regard.

Not only need the prospective practitioner be aware of the reimbursement procedures in a particular state, but also, the minimum standards required in that state for recognition as a health care provider should be reviewed. In some states, licensing itself is sufficient, while in others, as indicated previously, National Health Care Provider registration is a necessity. In the future, issues relative to training, degree, and nature, as well as the setting of supervised experience, may play a larger and more specific role in the determination of eligibility as a reimbursable health care provider.

With most of the freedom of choice legislation having been passed since 1970, psychology will still have to continue its efforts in this area. With counselors and social workers working extremely hard to get licensing recognition, and then subsequently seeking access to reimbursement, insurance companies will continue to fight the expansion of the providers' pool.

Already, there have been developments that negate state insurance laws. For example, large companies underwrite their own policies in collaboration with the major insurer and thus, become a "self-insured" program. An example has been the General Motors Corporation working with Blue Cross/Blue Shield to develop contracts in which psychological services were not included. Through being qualified as a "self-insured" body, GM did not have to adhere to state insurance laws. The basis for such arrangements is found in the Employee Retirement Income Security Act (ERISA, Public Law 93-406) which takes precedence over state laws regarding employee benefit plans. However, the issue of the ERISA exemption status has been in litigation for some time, so long-term implications are unclear.

On June 3, 1985, the U.S. Supreme Court reached a decision in *Metropolitan Life Insurance Company v. Massachusetts* which upheld the freedom of choice laws. The case stems from a situation in Massachusetts involving the Travelers Insurance Company, where the court was asked to decide the issue of whether the ERISA does actually preempt state insurance laws. The court's decision was limited and applied only to self-insured companies; such companies are almost always exempt from state regulation due to other federal court decisions related to ERISA. In essence, the court decided unanimously that states have broad powers to regulate health insurance offered by insurance companies. Specifically, states can mandate coverage by insurance companies for mental health, alcoholism, childbirth, and related benefits.

In regard to mandated benefits applied to third-party insurance carriers, the benefits are now on firm constitutional grounds. On a practical basis, if a state has a mental health mandate law that requires carriers to provide a minimum of "mental health" coverage and a freedom of choice law, then for residents of this state, reimbursement is required for psychologists under both statutes, provided that the insured person's employer's home office is in this same state. If, however, the employer's home office is in another state, then only the freedom of choice law would apply. However, the *Metropolitan Life v. Massachusetts* Supreme Court decision applies only to situations not specifically covered by state law, including, in most states, health maintenance organizations, preferred provider organizations, and "self-insured" programs such as the GM Plan. Thus, while the decision was vital and helpful, the increase in self-insured programs is still a critical matter.

In order to deal with the self-insured situation, on November 27, 1985, the Cleveland (Ohio) Academy of Consulting Psychologists and three Cleveland area psychologists filed suit against General Motors because their employees would be only reimbursed for mental health services rendered by a physician. At issue is whether self-insured programs should be exempt from state insurance laws. The plaintiffs' argument is based upon a 1985 *Michigan United Food and Commercial v. Baerwaldt* decision in the Sixth Circuit Court of Appeals which ruled that a company cannot claim to be self-insured when its purchase of insurance is to protect itself against catastrophic losses. As in most cases of litigation, the outcome may not be determined for several years.

Workmen's Compensation

The area of workmen's compensation and rehabilitation services involves disability evaluations and therapeutic services to job-injured or otherwise disabled workers. Nationally, the need for these services is quite extensive; however, psychology has not as yet become involved in this service area to any great extent. In 1971, Montana, and later, California (1978), were the only two states with recognized psychological services under workmen's compensation laws. In Ohio (1974), psychologists became recognized in the state compensation fund. Federally, clinical psychologists were given recognition in 1975 with the passing of Public Law 93-416, which amended the Federal Employee Compensation Act for work injuries to federal employees.

Dörken (1979) provided a review of workmen's compensation programs by state. Workmen's compensation plans are casualty/liability insurance which cover all injury-related medical care. Dörken reported that this area is a major insurance market with over $1 billion paid in medical and rehabilitation expenses in 1970; premiums in California alone in 1976 exceeded $1.5 billion. It is quite probable that psychological aspects of industrial disability will become increasingly important. Psychological services of an evaluative nature, rehabilitative therapy, and even case reviews by psychologists can become a viable market for psychologists. Psychologists interested in this market should assertively review opportunities within their respective states.

Psychologists have been recognized since 1975 as providers for rehabilitation services for the severely disabled, through the Rehabilitation Act of 1973—Public Law 93-112. Individual states receive a fixed dollar/formula amount to provide rehabilitation services when a disabled individual can become employable. Most states employ rehabilitation counselors and psychologists in either a direct service or consultative role. When contracting for psychological services, the rate of reimbursement is usually lower than the prevailing rate for similar services in the private sector.

FEDERAL LAW RELATIVE TO REIMBURSEMENT

Medicare

Medicare is that part of the Title XVIII of the Social Security Act that provides health insurance funds for all citizens 65 years of age and older. The plan is financed from Social Security revenues for Part A, Mandatory Coverage, and includes a voluntary Part B, Supplemental Coverage, which is available for purchase. Part A does not cover all services and has deductibles. The state can cover these costs under Part B if they so choose. Individuals may also purchase private insurance to provide complete coverage.

Psychologists are limited to evaluative services when functioning as an independent practitioner. Intervention services can also be provided when under the direction and supervision of a physician within the physician's facilities and when billed by the physician. As a physician extender, there is no dollar or visit limit on services. When private supplementary insurance is purchased, some insurance plans do provide for psychological services in states with freedom of choice laws; however, reimbursement is usually considerably limited.

Various attempts have been made to have psychologists recognized as independent providers according to the terms of legislative amendments. To date, none of these attempts has been successful.

Medicaid

Medicaid, part of Title XIX of the Social Security Act, provides funds to states for health care to families with dependent children, the blind, aged, or disabled whose incomes are insufficient to meet the costs of health services. In order to assist families and individuals attain or retain self-care capabilities, Medicaid further provides rehabilitation and other services.

States independently determine eligibility for services within fairly broad federal guidelines. The states also determine the types of assistance, reimbursement schedules, and provider eligibility. Thus, each state essentially has its own assistance programs with the freedom to determine the extent to which psychological services will be recognized. Therefore, when a state chooses to include psychological services in its plan, it has great latitude in determining the extent of services and the controls that are imposed.

As of 1982 (Resnick, 1983), 25 plans have some form of reimbursement for psychological services. Testing and therapy were given direct reimbursement for independent services in 13 states: California, Kansas, Maine, Massachusetts, Minnesota, Montana, New Hampshire, New Jersey, New Mexico, New York (except New York City), Ohio, Utah, and West Virginia. Physician referral for testing and therapy was required in Connecticut, Georgia, Hawaii, Indiana, Oregon, and Vermont. Illinois and Michigan recognized only testing and referral, while medical supervision was required in Arkansas and Nebraska. Tennessee also required a medical referral and physician billing. Wisconsin psychologists are recognized through state contracts. Dörken and Webb (1981) also indicated that testing is given recognition for reimbursement, however, at levels lower than customary rates.

Due to the striking differences between plans and the intermediating role of physicians, Medicaid and Medicare account for only a very small portion of claims submitted by psychologists (Dörken & Webb, 1980). Psychologists are required to be eligible as recognized professionals under the state plan and then apply to have a number assigned to them in order to bill for services. In some states, recognition and services change frequently, lending confusion to practitioners. As a result of the bureaucratic problems and low rates for reimbursement, psychological services to the poor are limited to public agencies, with independent practitioners having little involvement with this strata of society.

CHAMPUS

The U.S. Department of Defense instituted through congressional action the Civilian Health and Medical Program of the Uniformed Services (CHAMPUS) in 1956. The plan, which was broadened in 1966, provides civilian health care resources for active-duty and retired members of the armed services and their dependents, when services are limited in the military treatment facilities and direct care system. This program has experienced tremendous growth over the last decade, as the Department of Defense and Congress have recognized the health care needs of military families and have tied the development of national defense readiness to the health status and economic well-being of Uniformed Service beneficiaries (DeLeon & VandenBos, 1980).

This program is modeled after private insurance programs and has insurance orientation in providing health care reimbursement for civilian medical services. With over 8.6 million lives covered, this is the single largest health care plan in the country. Under administrative directive since 1974, and Public Law 94-212 in 1976, clinical psychologists have been recognized as independent health care providers. (In this instance, as in most dealing with federal laws, the term *clinical psychologist* is used generically to mean applied or specialty psychologist.) While the title itself is not defined, licensed psychologists with 1 or 2 years of supervision who have passed a national exam, as well as "grandparented" psychologists, are recognized providers. Thus, reimbursement is available for psychologists who meet certain qualifications. First, reimbursement is limited to qualified providers and to services according to the law that are "medically or psychologically necessary." Second, psychologists listed in the *National Register of Health Service Providers in Psychology* are recognized automatically, while others must apply and have a credential review by the fiscal intermediary, which is usually an insurance company such as Aetna or Blue Shield (Dörken, 1983).

An additional unique feature of this program has been the peer review plan initiated in 1977 with the American Psychological Association and the American Psychiatric Association. The actual processing of claims did not begin until the latter part of 1979. Essentially, dialogue between the professional organizations and Department of Defense was necessary in order to develop peer review criteria and procedures regarding psychological and psychiatric outpatient services; treatment criteria, review protocols, and reviewer manuals needed to be developed. Administrative liaisons with each association and approximately 350 psychiatric and 400 psychological peer reviews had to be identified and prepared, as well as report forms and protocols designed (Claiborn, Biskin, & Friedman, 1982).

Rodriguez (1983) provides an excellent review of the issues that need resolution with such peer review programs. Considerable concern was expressed by both professions regarding the uses and possible misuses of clinical information that would be submitted for peer review. Bent (1982) has described the need for additional control of confidential information as third-party payers in general have increasingly asked for more information in their efforts to assure quality and cost control of health care. Despite the focus of concern, Rodriguez reports that records are maintained with strict care and respect for privacy. To date, there have been no known breaches of confidentiality; however, the issue of confidentiality and privileged communication resting with client and professional, excluding third-party payers, is still not fully resolved to everyone's satisfaction. Further concern has also been expressed about the validity of information from providers, the standards and types of services imposed relative to health care, quality and theoretical orientation of the reviews, and financial costs for the entire system.

Reimbursement for services will be contingent upon quality review procedures to the extent that fees represent the usual, customary, and reasonable (UCR) rate for the profession within the practice area, as well as representing the provider's own UCR rate. The UCR rate is determined by the 75% level of the fees charged for services. The reimbursement level and individual UCR rates are adjusted annually.

The end result of this plan will require psychologists to demonstrate the benefit from services in order to have such services maintained in a treatment plan. Psychologists will also have to meet the standards of the profession. The system is designed to promote cost effectiveness, accountability, and limit services to those demonstrated as effective.

Another aspect of this program of practical interest is the element of benefit coordination provision with other insurance plans to prevent duplication of payments. When using Medicare or other insurance, the other insurance must be used first before CHAMPUS benefits can be utilized. CHAMPUS will cover psychological services not covered under other plans. The practitioner will still have to bill the other plan prior to submitting for CHAMPUS reimbursement.

Federal Employee Health Benefit Act

Federal employees are covered for health insurance under the Federal Employee Health Benefit Act. In 1975 (Public Law 93-363), clinical psychologists were recognized as independent providers. The plan itself is authorized through independent insurance companies, with Blue Cross/Blue Shield being the largest and Aetna the second largest. In all, there are about 20 plans, each differing according to benefits involving psychological services. In all, these plans cover over 10 million individuals.

Clinical psychologists are recognized by Blue Cross/Blue Shield as having a license, doctoral degree in psychology, and 2 years of clinical experience in a recognized health setting. Listing in the National Register is also acceptable for direct recognition.

While reimbursement is generally consistent with private plans, group prepayment plans such as Health Maintenance Organizations (HMO) and Independent Practices Associations (IPA) are not required to recognize psychological services. Because of a general exclusion clause in Public Law 93-363, recognition of psychologists is not mandatory in group practice prepayment plans. For other traditional plans, reimbursement procedures are generally the same as when submitting any insurance claim.

LEGAL REGULATION OF PRACTICE

In a more direct manner, the legal system, especially the courts, has had an impact upon the practice of psychology. Congress and federal administrative agencies, particularly, have passed legislation related to handicapped children, with the Handicapped Children's Early Education Assistance Act of 1968. The Rehabilitation Acts of 1973, the Education for the Handicapped Amendments of 1974 (Public Law 93-380), the Family Education Rights and Privacy Act (the Buckley Amendment), and the Education for All Handicapped Children Act of 1975 (Public Law 94-142), are examples of legislation that has affected the practice of psychology for the last decade.

Federal and state courts have also been active, especially concerning decisions regarding the placement of minority children in special education classes, and with handicapped persons in general. The courts have also been involved with cases relative to licensing and malpractice by psychologists. Additionally, mental health laws have involved patient rights, as well as directly influencing the work of forensic psychologists. The last decade has seen increased legal regulation of the profession.

Psychological Assessment

Psychologists, especially school psychologists, have been most directly affected by the Education for All Handicapped Children Act of 1975. This act provides educational and "related" services for handicapped children. States that fail to meet this requirement are subject to the termination of federal funding. Psychologists are directly involved with the identification and, to some extent, therapy of these children; practicing psychologists should be familiar with the provision of this act, as well as relevant state regulations. States may have a system for the identification of all handicapped children in the state from birth to the age of 21. Schools must provide adequate identification procedures which often include psychological assessment. The following are considered to be handicapping conditions: mental retardation, impaired hearing, deafness, speech impairment, visual handicap, serious emotional disturbance, orthopedic impairment, other health impairment, or special learning disabilities. Children who have learning problems that primarily are the result of environmental, cultural, or economic disadvantage are excluded.

Psychologists outside the school should be aware that once a child is identified as having a suspected handicap, schools are required to perform a multidisciplinary team evaluation upon the child; this often includes evaluation by a school psychologist. Extensive requirements also exist for involving parents in every step of their child's placement process, beginning with full and informal consent for the evaluation. Three-year evaluations are required for children placed into a special program, although they can be scheduled sooner at the request of the parents. Often, these evaluations are performed by the school psychologist, although independent evaluations by outside psychologists may be performed. When the latter's recommendation differs from the school's team, this discrepancy must be considered by the multidisciplinary team.

Every child placed into a special education program must have an individual educational program (IEP) developed by special placement teams. Psychologists involved with the evaluation should also be involved in developing the IEP. In addition, there are provisions for psychological counseling for children and parents. This intervention may be done by school psychologists, or contracted privately by parents, and at public expense if recommended by the IEP team.

A series of court decisions have been rendered regarding nondiscriminatory assessment of the handicapped. The most important decision by far has been the *Larry P. v. Riles*, 1979. The courts essentially maintained that the practice of placing children solely on the basis of an intelligence test resulted in a disproportionate and harmful impact on black children, in violation of the equal protection clause. The court issued a preliminary injunction, and, in 1979, a permanent injunction against the administration of individual intelligence tests to place black children in educable mentally retarded classes. However, in 1980, in *PASE v. Hannon*, the Illinois district court determined that the WISC-R and Stanford-Binet tests, when used in conjunction with other criteria as defined in Public Law 94-142, do not discriminate against black children in the Chicago public schools. A more complete analysis of these complex cases and others is provided by Bersoff (1982).

Psychological Records

The Family Education Rights and Privacy Act (Buckley Amendment) changed the tradition of limiting access of psychological reports. The 1976 regulations were incorporated into Public Law 94-142, which gave the right of parents of handicapped children to inspect and review all educational records. Parents of the handicapped can also review all records pertaining to identification, evaluation, and placement in special education programs.

It is generally agreed upon that psychological reports are open to inspection by parents; however, whether the right of parental review extends to test questions and protocols is questionable. As of this date, there are not any cases that answer this question. Excluded from the definition of educational records are those documents retained as personal records or notes by the psychologist. Therefore, the determining factor has been whether the test protocols have been made available to others. If not, then the protocols remain as personal notes and are not available for parental inspection. However, the situation reverses itself if the protocols are kept in a place where others have access to them, or if they have been revealed to others in a case conference. Therefore, when test reports are shared in making placement decisions, they are considered to be part of the child's educational records. This issue is of concern to the private practitioner functioning in an independent evaluation role, whose concerns may be different from those of the psychologist employed by the school system.

Informed Consent

A general legal principle involves not only consent for evaluation or therapeutic services, but also the understanding that the client must be fully informed about this evaluation and any treatment that is required. This requirement includes not only the client, but also the parents or guardian in the case of children or adolescents. The court must be the provider in the care of mentally incompetent persons.

Children are basically considered as not being capable of full under-standing concerning psychological evaluation and treatment, and the courts have determined that the parents need to give consent prior to any formal psychological services for their children. When there is evi-dence as to direct physical and psychological abuse of the child, the psychologist might decide to initiate involvement without parental con-sent, although such action is very risky. The same procedure exists for adolescents; however, states increasingly have given them greater free-dom to independently seek outside assistance regarding certain kinds of medical problems such as venereal disease and other sex-related prob-lems. In general, the courts have still consistently shown a preference for parental control where assistance to minors is concerned.

SOME ISSUES

Hospital Privileges and Practice

DeLeon, Pallak, and Hefferman (1982) reported that approximately 10% of the APA membership were estimated to be employed in hospital settings. Access to hospitals for psychologists has been an ongoing struggle with the medical profession. For psychologists interested in health care delivery along with treatment of mental and emotional disor-ders, hospital privileges provide an important link with the medical community. This contact is especially important relative to referral re-sources as well as client access. Additionally, insurance reimbursement is greater for inpatient than outpatient services.

For the last 15 years, psychologists have worked with the Joint Com-mission on Accreditation of Hospitals (JCAH). Zaro, Batchelor, Gins-berg, and Pallak (1982) describe psychologists' ongoing struggle over the previous 10 years, through formal and informal means, to receive formal membership in JCAH, as having very limited results. At the same time, since approximately 1978, psychologists also have actively sought com-parable legislation at the state level. In 1978, California was successful in obtaining staff membership and/or clinical privileges for licensed psy-chologists. Then, with the passage of State Bill 259, California became the first state to recognize the independent and autonomous practice of psychology in hospital settings. In 1982, the District of Columbia City Council enacted legislation that extended to psychologists, as well as other licensed health care professionals, the right to admit patients to psychiatric hospitals and to provide therapy to clients admitted to hospitals. While still able to deny privileges to individual psychologists, the bill prohibited District of Columbia hospitals from denying access and privileges to psychologists, podiatrists, nurse midwives, nurse practitioners, and nurse anesthetists as a class.

State laws, as such, do not pose a problem for psychologists seeking medical staff recognition. Buklad and Ginsberg (1982) reported that many states have laws or regulations affecting hospital medical staffs. These state codes comprise four categories:

1. States with laws that do not address the specific issue of the terms of medical staff membership (5 states);
2. States with hospital laws defining "medical" staff in terms broad enough to include psychologists (9 states);
3. States with hospital laws requiring some physical supervision, but not limiting staff membership to physicians and dentists (8 states);
4. States with hospital codes or regulations that could permit the JCAH to dictate about matters of staff and governance organizations (28 states), therefore, considerable effort had been placed with both JCAH by APA, as well as state legislative action on the part of state psychological associations.

In 1979, the Ohio Attorney General filed suit in federal court against JCAH, the Ohio Medical Association, and the Ohio Psychiatric Association for alleged violations of federal and state antitrust laws. This action was the result of psychologists being denied full access to practice in JCAH accredited facilities on the grounds that it represented a restraint of trade; that is, psychologists were prevented from practicing to the fullest extent of their licenses. While this suit was waiting to be heard, JCAH developed a new set of standards in December of 1983. The new standards were a clear relaxation of hospital staff privilege standards for psychologists, which prompted the Ohio Attorney General's office to dismiss the antitrust suit which had started 4 years earlier.

The JCAH standards have become part of the *Accreditation Manual for Hospitals* (Joint Commission, 1983). They allowed that psychologists licensed to practice independently may be on the staff of hospitals, and that clinical privileges for psychologists will be dealt with on an individual basis. This action leaves the issue of hospital privileges up to individual hospital boards. A part of the clarification is that psychologists are more interested in working in a clinical or consulting capacity within the hospital rather than having admitting privileges per se. While psychologists have gained significantly from AMH medical staff chapter revisions, it is still up to the individual psychologist to actively pursue hospital medical staff membership.

Psychologists interested in hospital practice are referred to a primer prepared by the APA Committee on Professional Practice (COPP) that is specifically aimed at the hospital setting (APA, 1985). It covers such issues as staff privileges, organized staff membership, roles for psychologists in hospitals, and training for psychological work in hospitals.

Mental Health Legislation

The legal system, relative to laws pertaining to the mentally disabled, is based upon the medical model of mental disorder which, in part, assumes that disordered behavior is symptomatic of underlying illness. As such, these behaviors are not subject to personal control. Furthermore, the patient is not responsible for his or her behavior. The legal system, therefore, has established a set of laws treating the mentally disordered person differently than normal persons, based upon the scientific study of these disorders.

As a result, scientific research in medicine and psychology has had considerable impact upon the formulation of these laws. The legal system, in general, and lawyers, specifically, are not equipped to deal with the complexity of issues surrounding mental disorders; thus, they rely upon mental health professionals to reach conclusions that are primarily psychological, rather than legal, in nature. Traditionally, in addition to the scientific basis for special treatment of the mentally disabled, many experts believe that decisions about competence, freedom, and responsibility for the mentally disabled should be made primarily by professional psychologists. Therefore, the decision about issues and individual cases is determined by the legal system, but it has been argued that the major influence relative to treatment should be made by psychology experts.

This area of the legal system offers a diversity of fascinating cases, and represents a context wherein professional psychologists directly interface with the courtroom and lawyers. There are millions of such cases each year and, increasingly, psychologists are called upon to perform psychological evaluations and serve as expert witnesses.

The field of forensic psychology is a specialty area served by the American Board of Forensic Psychology associated with ABPP and with one of the American Psychological Association divisions (41) devoted to Psychology and the Law. However, most psychologists can expect to participate in some manner relative to being a mental health expert and provide expert testimony. Therefore, a brief overview of mental health laws will be presented, followed by a section discussing the role of an expert witness testifying in the courtroom situation.

Commitment

Civil commitment occurs when a person is admitted to a state hospital consistent with procedures defined in the state statutes. All states provide for voluntary or involuntary commitment, and psychologists interested in this area should consult the state statutes for procedures and regulations for specific information relative to their state.

All such laws do vary from state to state, but generally require that the admitted person have a mental disorder and behave in such a manner that he or she is deemed dangerous to self or others, or otherwise in need of care and treatment. For involuntary commitment, this "in need of care and treatment" provision is becoming quite rare and may possibly be ruled unconstitutional (e.g., *Lessard v. Schmidt*, 1976).

Therefore, most standards for commitment have focused upon the behavior of the individual, although what constitutes the standard for "dangerous" can be argued. Generally, the degree of danger must be specified, along with the degree of likelihood of dangerous behavior occurring, as a prerequisite to the court deciding in favor of involuntary commitment. Despite the professional difficulties related to making predictions, courts have upheld the constitutionality of "dangerous" commitment based on clinical prediction where no overt behavioral action had occurred (*Mathew v. Nelson*, 1978).

There are procedures in most state statutes for emergency and temporary commitment when imminent harm is demonstrated. In such instances, court hearings are bypassed and admissions can be made by a physician, police officer, or family member. Evaluation and treatment can be authorized for a specified period of time, ranging from 48 hours to 15 days in some states. This procedure is a tempting one to follow, as it bypasses cumbersome hearings. However, the civil rights of patients can also be easily violated so that care must be exercised in these situations. Because some state laws do not require imminent harm, involuntary commitments can far too easily occur. Additionally, once hospitalized, the patient is at a distinct disadvantage in arguing against a full commitment. Emerging commitments, in general, should be used only after careful consideration, and when necessary.

Morse (1983) argued that commitment is far too easily accomplished, even in full hearings. Due process procedures are violated with informal hearings that do not follow legally established standards and procedures. Morse believed that far too often, judges respond to these cases in a rough, paternalistic, and intuitive manner, relying mainly upon expert testimony given by the mental health professional. Moreover, there are few appeals to appellate courts that assure that state statutory standards are kept.

In contrast to adults, commitment of minors to mental hospitals is the statutory right of the parent or guardian. Such "voluntary" commitments are only subject to acceptance by the hospital. In essence, this provision gives parents absolute control over the custody or care of the child. The Supreme Court, in *J.R. v. Putnam* (1979), held that the child's due process rights were adequately safeguarded by the parents' concern and the independent evaluation of the medical expert performing the evaluation for admittance. In most jurisdictions, there are no due process procedures and formal hearings afforded children.

In such cases of "voluntary" hospitalization, release can be made at the request of the parent or a decision of the hospital. In cases where the professional expert believes, contrary to the parents, that further hospitalization is necessary, a petition must be made to the court that the state declare the child a ward of the court and assure guardianship.

The structure of the legal system places enormous responsibility upon the psychologist within the hospital setting, relative to the appropriateness of the admission. Involuntary hospitalization involves civil liberties issues and considerable social stigma for the child or youth. Hospitalization can be viewed as a method for some parents to scapegoat a behaviorally difficult child, and decisions to admit need to be made on the basis of the disorder and treatment efficacy. Moreover, the psychologist may be faced with administrative pressure to maintain the patient population. Psychiatric and mentally disabled children and youth are clear candidates for admission; however, the criteria for hospitalization of delinquent or difficult behaviorally disordered children or youth are far less clear.

Least Restrictive Environment

In the last decade, commitment for institutionalizations has dramatically decreased relative to length of stay. With the improvement of psychotropic medication treatment, community-based treatment has been proven to be as effective as institutionalization. At the same time, the community mental health movement has resulted in more outpatient services, rather than relying upon inpatient hospitalization (Musto, 1975; Rappaport, 1977). From a legal perspective, attempts have been made to ensure that hospitalization should be avoided or minimized, when appropriate, with the principle of "least restrictive alternative." This doctrine was amended by the United States Supreme Court in the 1960s through a number of cases and applies in relationship to psychology to civil commitment and placement of children in handicapped programs.

The least restrictive doctrine holds that when state regulations infringe on civil liberties that are guaranteed by the constitution in order to fulfill the state's purpose, they should only do so with the means least restrictive of those rights and interests. It is fair to assume that the state has a legitimate right to protect individuals or society through involuntary commitment of dangerous persons, or to place children in handicapped programs to provide quality education. However, such placements also impinge upon the freedom of the individual. The doctrine emphasizes that the state must investigate all available options and any alternatives not suitable to the individual. Hospitalization and placement should only be ordered when other alternatives are unavailable.

This doctrine was explored for the institutionalized retarded through a number of Supreme Court decisions (*Halderman v. Pennhurst*, 1979; *Halderman v. Pennhurst*, 1981). Briefly, this case, ultimately decided by the U.S. Supreme Court, began in 1977, when Terri Lee Halderman, a mental patient in the Pennsylvania Pennhurst State School and Hospital, filed a complaint involving the inhumane conditions, unrestricted use of constraints, dangerous over-medication, inadequate supervision, and lack of rehabilitative programs he encountered. In 1977, the Federal Court determined that the allegations were true. This case is complex and has a number of interesting issues; for more detail, the reader is urged to consult Morse (1983). However, the most important fact for purposes of this discussion is that the Supreme Court decision in 1982 held that the federal Developmentally Disabled Assistance and Bill of Rights Act did not grant the mentally retarded the right to habilitation in the least restrictive environment. The court decided the case strictly on the interpretation of the federal statutory language.

However, in another case arising against the Pennhurst institution (*Youngberg v. Romeo*, 1982), the U.S. Supreme Court decided in a patients' rights case that retarded persons are entitled to freedom from excessive restraint, appropriate training to ensure safety, and the ability to function free of bodily restraints. While the issue of institutionalization in a least restrictive environment for the mentally retarded has not been settled, the courts seem increasingly to be moving in that direction for all mental disorders.

The entire issue of hospitalization of mental patients is highly relevant to psychology. The National Institute of Mental Health reports that over 70% of mental health funds are spent on hospitalization. Kiesler (1981) reasoned that this allocation is due to inappropriate insurance mechanisms. The President's Commission on Mental Health (Platman, 1978) said, "The level and type of care given to the chronically mentally disabled is frequently based upon what services are fundable and not on what services are needed and appropriate" (p. 369). Despite the legal impact upon commitment procedures and the emergence of the community mental health movement, Kiesler (1982b), in an extensive study regarding hospitalization, found the following trends:

1. Mental hospitalization is increasing well in excess of the population rate. This includes inpatient episodes in hospitals with and without psychiatric units.
2. The site of hospitalization has changed dramatically—the state mental hospital and private mental hospital now accounts for only 25% of the total incidence of mental disorders.
3. Hospital stays at state and V.A. hospitals have decreased, but length of stays in general hospitals have remained stable.

Kiesler (1982a) suggested that the majority of patients treated for mental disorders could be treated more effectively and less expensively elsewhere. As Talbot (1981) indicated, the treatment modalities are available but specific programs do not exist. Psychologists involved in the area of diagnosis and treatment of the mentally disabled need to fully understand the legal, moral, and social issues relative to this population.

Expert Testimony

Psychologists are increasingly being called upon to testify as expert witnesses in administrative and judicial proceedings. Typically, these might include child abuse and custody hearings, competency hearings with the elderly, or in criminal defense and handicap issues with children in Public Law 94-142 hearings. Conceivably, most psychologists at one time or another will be called as an expert witness.

There are two types of witnesses, lay and expert, with considerable differences between each in terms of the actual testimony that is allowable. While lay witnesses have no specialized knowledge or skill in the subject matter in the area of testimony, expert witnesses, because of their experience and/or training, are called upon to give testimony in their field of expertise. Expert witnesses can give their opinion testimony and draw inferences from the facts concerned with the situation.

The legal definition of an expert witness, as set forth in Rule 702 of the Federal Rules of Evidence indicates:

> If scientific, technical, or other specialized knowledge will assist the findings of fact (the judge, hearing officer, or a jury) to understand the evidence or to determine a fact in evidence; a witness qualified as an expert by knowledge, skill, experience, or training, or educated may testify thereto in the form of an opinion or otherwise.

Thereafter, judges will tend to look at two issues relative to the admission of expert testimony: (a) whether the testimony is relevant to understanding the issue in a controversy; and (b) whether the expert possesses the necessary qualifications to deal with the subject matter.

Initially, in most hearings, the qualification of a witness will be established. Such documentation typically includes the educational background, skills, and experience of the witness. An expert need not be a nationally recognized authority; however, what must be demonstrated is that his or her level of education and experience meets the standards of the profession. Similarly, the opinions of the witness need only to be consistent with those reasonably held by others in the field.

A common dilemma when giving testimony for psychologists relates to privileged communications. Psychologists need to understand that, despite state statutes, privileged communication often is not required in some types of court hearings, especially when criminal action or child abuse is involved. In many instances, when a patient has received psychotherapy from the psychologist for a mental or emotional disorder, the court will respect the psychologist–client privilege. The privilege is waived where the patient is criminal or treated for legal purposes, or when a psychologist is involved in determining sanity in a criminal case. The difficulty arises in forensic situations where the psychologist must divulge information that is embarrassing and painful to the client. The psychologist in forensic work needs to understand that confidentiality is not consistent with the structure of the legal system. The specifics of privileged communication vary from state to state, and psychologists are advised to seek legal counsel regarding when testimony is required, versus when one has the right to refuse testimony.

Generally speaking, an expert witness is appropriate when the subject matter is beyond the knowledge level of the layperson. Psychologists, when qualified by training and experience, testify in a number of areas. However, psychologists need to be concerned with two general questions before agreeing to provide testimony: (a) Does our training and experience qualify us to be experts; and (b) Are the questions we are to address truly "scientific" or are they moral and social judgments presented under the guise of scientific conclusion? (Morse, 1983). A legal system adversarial in nature is designed to deal with conflict resolution in manners alien to a "scientific" or "client-centered" model. Thus, the psychologist is placed on one side or the other in a dispute, but with considerable pressure from each side to be placed in the role of an advocate. The psychologist may indeed have an opinion or even, at a more subtle level, a bias. It is appropriate at times, when representing a client, to become an advocate as long as the testimony remains within the bounds of scientific professionalism. In other words, opinions should always be based upon clinical and research evidence.

When testifying, the psychologist should thoroughly prepare the testimony beforehand, in order to alleviate nervousness. He or she should dress in a conservative style and use notes, if necessary, to remember facts and details. Typically, once her or his qualifications are established, the psychologist, in a narrative fashion, will offer testimony that lays the foundation for his or her conclusions. The testimony will review the evaluation procedures employed, including the nature and purposes of the tests or techniques involved; the psychologist will then be asked to form an opinion relative to the issue involved. As often as possible, it is helpful to relate the conclusion to the underlying facts in the assessment. Also, it is necessary to avoid the use of jargon or sweeping conclusions without sharing the reasoning process involved in reaching an opinion. When opinions are based upon an ambiguous scientific foundation, the psychologist should take even more care to demonstrate how the conclusions were reached. In general, the responses should be straightforward and related to the psychological data. If personal beliefs or sympathies are involved in the situation, such as in a custody case, admitting beliefs and sympathies honestly with an explanation is the best procedure. Cross-examination follows direct examination, and is designed to probe and expose weaknesses in the testimony. Opposing counsel may attempt to undermine the expert's qualifications, the quality of the assessment, and/or the basis of the opinion itself. Different attorneys practice various techniques of cross-examination, ranging from a "soft" manner to being hard and attacking. Trick questions in an innocuous style, complex questions involving several answers, misleading premises, provocative insinuations, and a bombardment of yes–no questions can be employed by the opposing attorney. However difficult or annoying this experience may be, the psychologist should not become argumentative or defensive. Careful preparation and/or well-laid-out testimony considerably reduces the attack in cross-examination. Testifying in court can be a fatiguing experience; if one takes the time to be well prepared, it can be a quite satisfying and educational experience.

Malpractice Liability and Insurance

Insurance rates for malpractice liability have risen dramatically in the last several years for psychologists, a trend that is part of a national crisis involving general liability coverage. There certainly has been a trend for malpractice suits in medicine and other professions to be pursued in cases involving injury, harm, or even dissatisfaction with the professional, regardless of fault. However, psychologists have also seen an increase in frequency of claims and size of settlements. Losses for insurance companies in 1963 totaled $13,000; in 1973, the total was $134,000. More recently, losses have averaged $2 million (Gable, 1983). As a result, insurance companies have increasingly failed to renew contracts covering psychologists and, at this point in time, the APA-endorsed insurance plan often provides the only option or the most affordable insurance available.

Despite an exclusion clause in most policies relative to the defense of psychologists in suits involving sexual relations with clients, such suits have still involved companies in increased cases and settlements.

Malpractice suits result from a number of situations in addition to sexual intimacy. These include negligence, issues of informal consent, disclosure of information, improper diagnosis, and suicide or homicide by clients. While other situations may occur, these areas have provided the greatest potential for liability.

Gable (1983) offers a number of general comments to help practitioners avoid legal entanglements due to professional negligence. He points out four "elements" of liability. These are:

1. That the practitioner owed a duty to the patient to conform to a professional standard of care and skill;
2. That there was a dereliction or breach of this duty by the practitioner;
3. That because of the dereliction of duty by the practitioner the patient suffered some injury or harm; and
4. That the practitioner's dereliction of duty was the direct or proximate cause of injury or harm suffered by the patient.

One form of negligence is the failure of the psychologist to conform to a professional standard of care and skill. While the quality of care and the technical skills employed are often resolved through litigation, in such instances the "local" standard has been a ruling guide. However, while the practitioner must hold only to an "average" standard, those who claim to be specialists in a given area must reflect a higher standard of practice, regardless of specialized training. When claiming to be a specialist, the professional needs to demonstrate current knowledge and skills through attendance at national conferences, workshops, or training courses.

The standards of care may be established through state licensing laws, as well as through national professional standards. Thus, a member of the APA also has to conform to ethical principles and standards of the APA that would help the court determine the standard of care involved in the litigated case. Thus, violations of ethical standards will, in most instances, increase the probability of liability.

Individual practice, however, need only be reasonable to the particular case. As long as the practice is usable to a "respectable minority" within the profession and not experimental in value, the risk of liability is clearly lessened. Nevertheless, the court still determines the standard that will apply in each case in the final analysis.

The court has also determined there must be *informed* consent to treatment. It is commonly accepted that clients must provide information to the client about the psychological treatment to be undertaken and any potential risks involved. In general, the psychologist needs to be honest and straightforward about the diagnosis given, the purpose of the treatment, methods to be employed, and prognosis. Additionally, the professional should have reviewed the possible negative outcomes that will accrue if treatment is not undertaken, along with the other alternatives for treatment being given to the client, in order to minimize the legal risks.

While misdiagnosis is more a medical problem involving physical disorders, psychologists, nonetheless, should exercise care in determining the mental diagnosis of clients. Slovenko (1973) points out that diagnostic error alone does not constitute liability, regardless of the harm. All of the diagnostic means available need to be utilized, and the lack of ordinary diligence and skill are the determining factors.

The most controversial situations have been when clients have committed suicide or homicide when under treatment; a typical situation has been when the client was released from the hospital where care and prevention were possible. In determining liability, Gable (1983) indicates that three factors are of importance: (a) the foreseeability of the patient's suicidal attempt; (b) the reasonableness of professional judgment in treatment; and (c) the dependability with which the client carried out the directions for treatment.

Psychologists may be held liable for foreseeable harmful acts of their clients, especially when the lack of reasonable care can be demonstrated. The usual standard applied is based on the question: did the hospital or practitioner follow the degree of care that a reasonably prudent person would have exercised under the same or similar circumstances? This standard can take into account the error variance in psychological diagnosis of client assessment. Psychologists, upon learning of a client's potentially dangerous behavioral inclinations, are urged to seek consultation and warn possible victims, since the courts may well in the future render decisions that favor the protection of potential victims.

The most well known case dealing with this whole matter has been *Tarasoff v. Regents of the University of California* (1976). The legal action was for the recovery of damages resulting from the murder of the plaintiff's daughter. Prosenjitt Podder was seen by a psychologist for treatment at a student mental health clinic. Podder, in the course of therapy, made repeated references about purchasing a gun and threatened to use it against his former girlfriend. The psychologist, recognizing the seriousness of the situation, by letter informed the campus police of the situation who, in turn, took Podder into custody. Being satisfied Podder was rational, the police released him. The evaluation of supervising psychiatrists apparently concluded that Podder was sane and commitment was not needed, and also directed that the psychologist's letter and notes be destroyed. Podder subsequently killed his former girlfriend.

The Supreme Court of California decided that when, in fact, a therapist does determine that a patient poses a serious danger of violence to others, he or she has a duty to exercise reasonable care to protect the foreseeable victim of the danger. While predicting violence is difficult, the court felt that the risk to potential victims outweighs the need of the client. Practitioners need to be aware that the duty is to "protect" the potential victim, which does not necessarily mean directly warning the person. The protection conceivably includes other reasonable methods, such as notifying the police, removing instruments/harm, continuous supervision by the family or community, modifying treatment, referral, or even commitment.

The Tarasoff decision has created considerable concern among professionals, because the duty to protect is not clearly defined. The decision to warn the victim is not covered in the APA Ethical Standards of Psychologists. The Tarasoff decision does not involve potential suicide victims, which the California Supreme Court in *Bullah v. Greenson* (1977) indicated in concluding that warning parents of a patient that she might commit suicide was not a logical extension of the Tarasoff decision.

Generally, malpractice liability has become a real issue for psychology as well as other professions. Risks relative to liability can be reduced by adhering to the Ethical Standards of Psychologists, as well as state statutes and rules relative to the practice of psychology. Discussions with clients relative to the nature of the professional relationships, confidentiality, and physical contact are enormously helpful. Written information and consent relative to practices that might be used and possible risks in treatment are a further necessity. Misunderstandings and prolonged treatment difficulties should result in consultation with colleagues. Referral to another practitioner in such instances, or the arrangement of alternative treatment, can also considerably lessen the possibility of litigation. Gable (1983) makes a strong point that good intentions are not sufficient to avoid malpractice liability. Following nationally recognized standards and customary and usual practice is the best method to reduce this risk.

SUGGESTED READINGS

Psychologists intent on doing their own legal research are referred to Knapp, Vandercreek, and Zirkel (1985). Along with an introduction to the legal system, this article concentrates on the legal resources and tools available to psychologists. This is an excellent starting point for psychologists wishing to review the law itself.

An area only briefly mentioned in this chapter relates to custody evaluations that may necessitate court appearances. Karras and Berry (1985) have reviewed this role and discuss the method and content of evaluations, and the need to serve as impartial evaluators. Ethical dilemmas associated with being an evaluator and the limits of conclusion are also discussed.

From another standpoint relative to courtroom testimony, Blau (1984) has written an article dealing with the specific issue of psychological testing to substantiate expert opinion in the courtroom. The appropriate use of tests for determining competence, personal injury issues, and children's status and needs are contrasted with more questionable use for insanity defense and dangerousness. Issues related to selection and application of tests, as well as supporting their use in a courtroom setting, are discussed. Another good source regarding this issue is Bersoff (1981).

Rosen (1977) explored the question of whether or not clients agree to sign release-of-information consent in order to increase their likelihood of receiving mental health services. The percentages signing varied noticeably with the clients' understanding of their options. In a different study, it was found that adolescents' disclosure was not related to conditions of assurance of confidentiality; rather, the physical conditions (quiet secluded surroundings) may be more influential in terms of the amount of disclosure (Kobocow, McGuire, & Blau, 1983).

In the Sales (1983) *The Professional Psychologist's Handbook*, there are two excellent chapters offering more extensive coverage into several areas covered in this chapter. Gable's exploration of malpractice liability covers this area from a very complete legal perspective. Morse also covers, in considerable depth, the principles of mental health law blended with the role of the psychologist.

In 1976, the Tarasoff decision resulted in a rethinking of the professional's responsibility to the public in regard to a potentially violent patient. The so-called "duty to warn" has raised a number of related, but complicated, issues. Some of these issues have been treated in subsequent court cases. Knapp and Vandercreek (1982) explore those decisions and present a number of helpful recommendations to psychologists faced with such circumstances.

Finally, Sarason (1982) has done a critical review of the Education for All Handicapped Children Act (Public Law 94-142), which includes a comprehensive treatment of the specific parts of the act.

REFERENCES

American Psychological Association (1985). *A hospital primer for psychologists*. Committee on Professional Practice of the Board of Professional Affairs. Washington, DC: Author.

Bent, R. J. (1982). Multidimensional model for control of private information. *Professional Psychology, 13*, 27–33.

Bersoff, D. N. (1981). Testing and the law. *American Psychologist, 36*, 1047–1059.

Bersoff, D. N. (1982). The legal regulations of school psychology. In C. R. Reynolds & T. Gutkin (Eds.), *The handbook of school psychology* (pp. 1043–1074). New York: John Wiley & Sons.

Blau, T. (1984). Psychological tests in the courtroom. *Professional Psychology: Research and Practice, 15*, 176–186.

Buklad, W., & Ginsberg, M. R. (1982). *State law and medical staff privileges for psychologists.* Washington, DC: American Psychological Association, State Association Program.

Claiborn, W. L., Biskin, B. H., & Friedman, L. S. (1982). CHAMPUS and quality assurance. *Professional Psychology, 13*, 40–49.

Council for National Register of Health Service Providers in Psychology. (1985). *National register of health service providers in psychology.* Washington, DC: Author.

DeLeon, P. H., Pallak, M. S., & Hefferman, J. A. (1982). Hospital health care delivery. *American Psychologist, 37*, 1340–1341.

DeLeon, P. H., & VandenBos, G. R. (1980). Psychotherapy reimbursement in federal programs. In G. R. VandenBos (Ed.), *Psychotherapy, practice, research, policy.* Beverly Hills, CA: Sage.

Department of Defense Appropriation Act of 1976. Pub. L. No. 94-212, 90 Stat. 153 (1976).

Dörken, H. (1979). Worker's compensation: Opening up a major market for psychological practice. *Professional Psychology, 10*, 834–840.

Dörken, H., & Webb, J. (1980). 1976 Third-party reimbursement experience: An interstate comparison by carrier. *American Psychologist, 35*, 355–363.

Dörken, H., & Webb, J. (1981). Licensed psychologists on the increase, 1974–79. *American Psychologist, 36*, 1419–1426.

Dörken, H. (1983). Health insurance and third party reimbursement. In B. Sales (Ed.), *The professional psychologist's handbook* (pp. 249–284). New York: Plenum.

Education for All Handicapped Children Act of 1975. Pub. L. 94-142 (20 U.S.C. §§ 1401–1461, 1975).

Education for the Handicapped Amendment of 1974. Pub. L. No. 93-380, § 611–621, 88 Stat. 484, 579–587 (1974).

Employee Retirement Income Security Act of 1974. Pub. L. No. 93-406, 88 Stat. 829 (1974).

Family Rights and Privacy Act of 1974. Pub. L. No. 93-380, 88 Stat. 571 (1974).

Federal Employee Compensation Act of 1974. Pub. L. No. 93-416, 88 Stat. 1143 (1974).

Federal Employee Health Benefit Act of 1976. Pub. L. No. 93-363, 88 Stat. 398 (1974).

Gable, R. K. (1983). Malpractice liability of psychologists. In B. Sales (Ed.), *The professional psychologist's handbook* (pp. 457–491). New York: Plenum.

Halderman v. Pennhurst State School and Hospital, 446 F. Supp. 1295 (E.D. pa. 1977), 451 F. Supp. 223 (E.D. pa. 1978), modified 612 F. 2'd. 84 (3d Cir. 1979).

Halderman v. Pennhurst, 451 U.S. 1 (1981).

J. R. v. Parham, 422 U.S. 584 (1979). (412 F. Supp. 112 [M.D. Ga. 1976]).

Joint Commission for Accreditation of Hospitals. (1983). *Creditation manual for hospitals.* Chicago, IL: Accreditation Council for Hospitals.

Karras, D., & Berry, K. (1985). Custody evaluations: A critical review. *Professional Psychology: Research and Practice, 16*, 76–85.

Kiesler, C. A. (1981). Mental health policy: Research site for social psychology. In L. Wheeler (Ed.), *Review of personality and social psychology* (Vol. 2, pp. 273–295). Beverly Hills, CA: Sage.

Kiesler, C. A. (1982a). Mental hospitals and alternative care: Noninstitutionalization as potential public policy for mental patients. *American Psychologist, 37*, 349–360.

Kiesler, C. A. (1982b). Public and professional myths about mental hospitalization. An empirical reassessment of policy-related beliefs. *American Psychologist, 37*, 1323–1337.

Knapp, S. J., & Vandercreek, L. (1982). Tarasoff: Five years later. *Professional Psychology: Research and Practice, 13*, 511–516.

Knapp, S. J., Vandercreek, L., & Zirkel, P. (1985). Legal research techniques: What the psychologist needs to know. *Professional Psychology: Research and Practice, 16*, 363.

Kobocow, B., McGuire, J. M., & Blau, B. I. (1983). The influence of confidentiality conditions on self-disclosure of early adolescents. *Professional Psychology: Research and Practice, 14*, 435–443.

Larry P. v. Riles, 343 T. Supp. 1306 (N.D. Cal. 1982) Aff'd 502 F 2d. 963 (9th Cir. 1974); 495 F. Supp. 926 (N.D. Cal. 1979).

Lessard v. Schmidt, 349 F. Supp. 1078 (E.D. Wis. 1972). Vacated and remanded on procedural grounds, 414 U.S. 473, new j'mt. entered, 379 F. Supp. 1376 (E.D. Wis. 1974). Vacated and remanded, 421 U.S. 957 (1975), prior j'mt. reinstated, 413 F. Supp. 1318 (E.D. Wis. 1976).

Mathew v. Nelson, 461 F. Supp. 707 (N.D. Ill, 1978).

Metropolitan Life Insurance Company v. Commonwealth of Massachusetts, 471 U.S. 724 (1985).

Michigan United Food and Commercial v. Baerwaldt, 767 F. 2d. 308 (1985).

Morse, S. J. (1983). Mental health law. In B. Sales (Ed.), *The professional psychologist's handbook* (pp. 339–442). New York: Plenum.

Musto, D. F. (1975). Whatever happened to "community mental health?" *The Public Interest, 39*, 53–79.

PASE v. Hannon. No. 74-C-3586 (N.D. Ill. 1980).

Platman, S. R. (Coordinator). (1978). *Report of the Task Panel on Deinstitutionalization, Rehabilitation, and Long-Term Care* (President's Commission on Mental Health, Vol. 2). Washington, DC: U.S. Government Printing Office.

Rappaport, J. (1977). *Community psychology.* New York: Holt, Rinehart & Winston.

Rehabilitation Act of 1973, 29 U.S.C. § 794, (1973).

Resnick, R. J. (1983). Medicaid, direct provider recognition. *Professional Psychology: Research and Practice, 14*, 368–373.

Resnick, R. J. (1985). The case against the Blues: The Virginia challenge. *American Psychologist, 40*, 975–983.

Rodriguez, A. R. (1983). Psychological and psychiatric peer review at CHAMPUS. *American Psychologist, 38*, 941–947.

Rosen, C. E. (1977). Why clients relinquish their rights to privacy under sign-away pressures. *Professional Psychology, 8*, 17–24.

Sales, B. D. (Ed.). (1983). *The professional psychologist's handbook.* New York: Plenum.

Sarason, S. B. (1982). *The culture of the school and the problem of change* (2nd ed.). Boston: Allyn & Bacon.

Slovenko, R. (1973). *Psychiatry and law.* Boston: Little, Brown.

Stigall, T. (1983). Licensing and certification. In B. Sales (Ed.), *The professional psychologist's handbook* (pp. 285–337). New York: Plenum.

Talbot, J. A. (1981). The national plan for the chronically mentally ill: A programmatic analysis. *Hospital and Community Psychiatry, 32*, 699–713.

Tarasoff v. Regents of the University of California, 551 P 2d, 334, Cal. Rptr. 14 (1976).

United States Code Annotated. St. Paul, MN: West Publishing Co.

United States Code. United States Government Printing Office, Washington, DC.

United States Code Service. Rochester, NY: Lawyers' Cooperative Publishing Co.

Youngberg v. Romero, 102 S. Ct. 2452 (1982).

Zaro, J. S., Batchelor, W. F., Ginsberg, M. R., & Pallak, M. S. (1982). Psychology and JCAH: Reflections on a decade of struggle. *American Psychologist, 37*, 1342–1349.

Chapter 5
Professional Development and Accountability

The position taken in this chapter is that the internship experience bridges the gap between the formal, initial training of professional psychologists and their immersion into the world of work. This transition stage, therefore, seemed an appropriate place to introduce the topic of professional development as a continuing responsibility of the practitioner. The next major topic of the chapter involves the continuing education responsibilities of the professional throughout his/her career. Several alternatives are discussed. Finally, professional accountability is introduced as a concept that should undergird the growth and development process as well. Therefore, it can be viewed both for its self-evaluative benefits as well as within the larger context of responsibility to clients.

INTERNSHIPS

Predoctoral Internships

Internships have typically been seen as the culminating degree requirement. For the most part, this training experience is planned in such a way that information and preliminary fieldwork can be integrated and applied under the guidance of a mentor. The internship usually takes place at a site separate from where the didactic work was completed, but under a coordinated arrangement with the training program so that it represents an application of that former training. It is distinguished from *practicum* experiences, which are also field experiences, but are typically tied to specific courses and therefore narrowly defined in terms of their educational objectives. While some practicums may not be tied to a course, the objectives remain relatively restricted in scope and are considered preparatory for the internship experience. These latter type "practicums" usually are scheduled for a full semester. Finally, the term *externship* has been used in the literature to refer to field assignments that are scheduled concurrently with coursework and the responsibilities of the extern are tied directly to the students' level of training (Reilly & Pryzwansky, 1973). An integrative field experience is planned throughout the training of the professional when the externship model of training is used.

Considered by the American Psychological Association (APA) (1986a) to be an essential component of doctoral training programs in professional psychology and crucial preparation for functioning as an independent professional, the internship is taken after completion of relevant didactic and practicum work. Thus, the internship is an experience that is geographically and administratively separate from the training program. It should precede the granting of the doctorate. The pre-degree requirement for the internship is seen by the APA as strengthening basic pedagogical requirements, as well as insuring that important functions remain the responsibility of the degree program, such as monitoring the quality of the experience and facilitating the practical concerns often raised with regard to the question of pre-degree versus post-degree arrangements. The internship in clinical psychology requires full-time experience for 1 calendar year or for 2 years of half-time experience. School and counseling psychology internships require a full-time experience for either the academic or calendar year or a half-time experience for 2 years. The practicum training is encouraged to be planned as early as is feasible in the doctoral program. A minimum of 400 hours is required for APA-accredited training programs, with at least 150 hours spent in direct service activities. A minimum of 75 hours of formal, scheduled supervision is also required. Activities such as attending case conferences and writing reports are recommended. The internship follows and constitutes an intensive as well as extensive experience. The intern's role clearly remains that of a trainee, however, and the total experience should reflect that objective; a minimum of 2 hours per week of formally scheduled supervision is required for APA-approved internship sites.

Other sources influence the way in which the internship is considered and emphasized. For example, the Council for National Register of Health Service Providers in Psychology (see chapter 2) includes among its listing criteria 2 years of supervised experience in an organized health service training. Because 1 year must be a postdoctoral experience, the internship can serve to fulfill part of the 2-year requirement. Twelve guidelines are used to identify internships in psychology (i.e., supervised experience in an "Organized Health Service Training Program") if it is not APA-accredited. These guidelines were also adopted by the

American Association of State Psychology Boards (see chapter 2) as guidelines for defining supervised experience in an organized psychology internship training program. The guidelines (Council, 1981) are as follows:

1. An organized training program, in contrast to supervised experience or on-the-job training, is designed to provide the intern with a planned, programmed sequence of training experiences. The primary focus and purpose is assuring breadth and quality of training.
2. The internship agency has a clearly designated staff psychologist who is responsible for the integrity and quality of the training program and who is actively licensed/certified by the state board of examiners in psychology.
3. The internship agency has two or more psychologists on the staff as supervisors, at least one of whom is actively licensed as a psychologist by the state board of examiners in psychology.
4. Internship supervision is provided by a staff member of the internship agency, or an affiliate of that agency, who carries clinical responsibility for the cases being supervised. At least half of the internship supervision is provided by one or more psychologists.
5. The internship provides training in a range of assessment and treatment activities conducted directly with patients seeking health services.
6. At least 24% of trainee's time is in direct patient contact (minimum 375 hours).
7. The internship includes a minimum of 2 hours per week (regardless of whether the internship is completed in 1 year or 2) of regularly scheduled, formal, face-to-face individual supervision with the specific intent of dealing with health services rendered directly by the intern. There are also at least 2 additional hours spent per week in learning activities such as case conferences involving a case in which the intern was actively involved; seminars dealing with clinical issues; co-therapy with a staff person including discussion; group supervision; additional individual supervision.
8. Training is post-clerkship, post-practicum, and post-externship level.
9. The internship agency has a minimum of two interns at the internship level of training during applicant's training period.
10. Trainee has title such as "intern," "resident," "fellow," or other designation of trainee status.
11. The internship agency has a written statement or brochure that describes the goals and content of the internship, states clear expectations for quantity and quality of trainee's work, and is made available to prospective interns.

12. The internship experience (minimum 1,500 hours) is completed within 24 months.

In addition, the American Board of Professional Psychology defines internships as consisting of 1,800 hours of field experience within a period of 2 years supervised by a psychologist (see chapter 2). Candidates in the different specialty areas should note any specific internship requirement criteria unique to their specialty. Finally, the APA Specialty Guidelines also make reference to the characteristics of internships (see chapter 3).

INTERNSHIP SITES

Several resources are now available for individuals planning an internship. In addition, the APA currently accredits internship sites and consortia for the clinical and counseling psychology specialties; therefore some attention will be directed toward describing that accreditation process in this section.

Association of Psychology Internship Centers (APIC)

Founded in 1968, the Association of Psychology Internship Centers (APIC) is a national organization representing psychology internship training interests. Its membership consists of institutions and agencies offering pre- and/or postdoctoral internships in professional psychology under the direction of a psychologist; the internship sites must be in accordance with eligibility standards and regulations set by APIC in their bylaws. There is a membership fee.

Originally founded as an informal group of psychologists involved in internship training who had needs to share information about mutual problems, APIC has grown into a formal organization. A major function of the organization is to publish annually the *Directory of Internship Programs in Professional Psychology Including Post-Doctoral Training Programs*. This directory lists the names of institutions offering internships in each state plus their addresses, telephone numbers, and APA accreditation status (i.e., full, provisional, probation, none), and a classification of the agency (e.g., state hospital, foundation, VA medical center, university counseling center, HMO, medical school, children's hospital, etc.). The names of the chief psychologist/psychology director and director of training for each institution are included, along with the internship starting date. Information on the characteristics of the site include the number of full-time and part-time psychologists, the number of funded interns, the total number of interns, the stipend amount, fringe benefits, and characteristics of the client population. Finally, information on program requirements and restrictions is provided and includes APA accreditation status, minimum number of prerequisite hours, and other special requirements. Applicants must write directly to the internship site for an application and more specific information. The directory may be purchased by writing APIC, P. O. Box 574, Knoxville, IA 50138. The cost is $40, and the new directory for each year should be available by September of the previous year.

It should be noted that APIC does not state that listing in the directory represents approval, evaluation, accreditation, or the like. APIC is bound by APA policies concerning intern applicants in that (a) intern applicants shall have completed practicum experience and be enrolled in a doctoral program in the relevant area of professional psychology for which they are seeking internship experience, and (b) the internship must be considered an essential component of the training for persons seeking to change to a professional specialty for which they were not originally prepared (see Change of Specialty section of this chapter).

APIC has adopted voluntary guidelines in order to create a fairer, less pressured climate for more compatible student internship matching.

APIC Policy Regarding Internship Offers and Acceptance

In past years, students, psychology program directors, and internship agencies have noted with dismay that extreme pressures are sometimes unfairly placed on students to accept early internship offers before there is time to consider other possibilities. In an effort to create a fairer, less pressured climate for more compatible student-internship matching, APIC has adopted the following voluntary guidelines:

1. APIC members are to include APIC guidelines in the material sent to applicants describing the internship.
2. Accepted applicants are to be notified no earlier than 8:00 a.m. Central Standard Time of the second Monday in February. Those applicants must respond no later than 12:00 noon Central Standard Time, the following day.
3. Alternate applicants accepted between 8:00 a.m. Monday and 12:00 noon Tuesday may be asked to respond by Tuesday noon CST, but not earlier.
4. Applicants accepted after Tuesday noon should be prepared to make a relatively quick decision, on the assumption that they have already considered any earlier offers.
5. Applicants whom agencies do not intend to consider for a position should be notified as soon as possible, preferably no later than the first Monday in February.

6. Applicants who are being thought of as alternates for the center's first choices may be notified of their alternate status, but not before 8:00 a.m. of the second Monday in February.
7. Once a center's positions are filled, all remaining applicants should be so notified.
8. Applicants who receive offers that do not comply with these standards are urged not to accept the offer, reminding the internship agency of APIC's guidelines and requesting the center's compliance. If the center does not respond favorably, applicants are urged to notify their director of training and APIC.
9. Directors of training programs are requested to insure that the above recommendations are followed by their students.
10. To help insure that training directors are aware of offers made to students, internship agencies are requested to send a copy of all letters confirming internship positions to the directors of training of those students who have accepted internship offers.
11. Students, agencies, and program directors are urged to report all violations of these guidelines to: Dr. Ronald B. Kurz, Department of Pediatric Psychology, Children's Hospital National Medical Center, 111 Michigan Avenue, N.W., Washington, DC 20010.
12. An offer to an applicant should state explicitly that it is contingent upon his/her not having made a prior commitment.

APIC also operates a clearinghouse, which assists internship candidates and internship training centers who fail to locate one another during the course of the annual notification period. Thus, it serves to supplement the regular procedures just described, but becomes operational only after the period of notification–acceptance of internship offers. Also, it is an information exchange *only* between directors of professional psychology graduate programs and directors of internship programs. Because access is limited, those pre- and postdoctoral applicants who have not accepted an internship position should contact the director of their graduate program. Directors then contact—by mail—the clearinghouse, which maintains a list of candidates and listings. Copies of that listing will then be sent to the program director. Directors (not applicants) may obtain this information by writing the APIC Clearinghouse, Texas Research Institute of Mental Sciences, 1300 Moursand, Houston, TX 77030.

The executive committee of APIC consists of six members, elected by the membership, who serve a 3-year term and may be reelected to one additional term. They meet annually at the APA Convention and usually at the time that the directors of psychology departments also hold their meetings.

Directory of Internship Programs in Clinical Child and Pediatric Psychology

This directory has gone through four editions since 1976. It lists internship programs by states under the headings "Predoctoral Internship," "Postdoctoral Internship," and "Postdoctoral Fellowship." The latter entry, Postdoctoral Fellowship, refers to "advanced (often specialized) training placed in the sequence of training post-doctorally and post internship" (Tuma, 1984, p. 1).

All internship and fellowship programs are designated as one of the following: "Pediatric Psychology," "Clinical Child Psychology," or "Combined Clinical Child and Pediatric Psychology." The listing and the information provided on the program was obtained by the directory author's survey of training facilities that were either known to have or were reported to have types of training programs.

The information provided includes the address of the facility as well as the chief and/or director of training's name and phone number, requirements for application, information regarding the internship (e.g., stipend, deadline for application) and the nature of training, the client load, and description of the basic setting and the personnel employed at the setting. The author notes that no attempt has been made to authenticate or evaluate the data that are listed; likewise it is pointed out that listing does not represent approval, evaluation, or accreditation.

Graduate Study in Behavior Therapy: Psychology Internship Program (1981)

The Association for Advancement of Behavior Therapy (AABT—see chapter 6 for address) has published information on training in behavior therapy; one such listing is the *Graduate Study in Behavior Therapy: Psychology Internship Program* directory. This listing provides information as follows: the name of the director and contact for each internship program, whether it is APA approved, the orientation of the program, and the seminars that are given. In addition, the department faculty members of each program are given with a notation of those faculty committed to behavioral therapy. The research area of the faculty is also provided. Finally, the emphasis on behavioral therapy is rated on a scale from 1 to 7 in the following areas: adult clinical; behavioral assessment; behavioral medicine; child clinical; community consultation; developmental disabilities; and teaching/classroom management. All information listed in the directory, including the ratings, are provided by the program.

APA Accreditation of Independent Internship Centers

APA accredits internship sites that are administratively independent of a single graduate department or school and draw interns from multiple sources. The internships are expected to provide the trainee with "opportunity to take substantial responsibility for carrying out major professional functions in the context of appropriate supervisory support, professional role modeling, and awareness of administrative structures" (APA, 1986, Appendix B, p. 18). A close working relationship is encouraged between the internship program and the graduate program in professional psychology, so that advisement and evaluation can be conducted in the most helpful manner. Criteria regarding the professional psychology staff of the internship site, selection of interns, and the program itself are also delineated.

A professional psychologist (see APA Standards, APA, 1977, for a definition) should be clearly designated to be responsible for the integrity and quality of the psychology internship training program. This individual should be an appropriate role model as demonstrated by recognition or distinction within professional associations (e.g., APA Fellow), possess the ABPP diploma, or otherwise reflect clear evidence of professional competence, participation, and leadership. All professional/psychology staff should be licensed/certified to practice in the state in which they work, and should have completed an internship in the appropriate specialty.

Internship selection is expected to be systematic, with the interns showing evidence of having completed practicum experience and enrolled in a relevant doctoral program. Applicants from programs awarding degrees in areas other than psychology are not considered eligible for the training. At least two interns should be in the setting, and their primary role should be that of trainee, with their client care services carefully supervised and part of an integrated training plan. At the same time they should be involved in evaluating both their own experiences and the supervision and instruction they receive. Evaluative sessions should be held and include the results of observations of interns' professional functioning. Two hours per week of formally scheduled individual supervision is considered minimum. Their activities should be organized and sequenced, with exposure to a variety of problems provided. In addition to opportunities for research they should learn ethical standards and apply them in their practice of psychology. Other specific program criteria are involved, along with guidelines covering consortia internship arrangements.

The application for initial APA internship accreditation includes a detailed documentation of staff and program. Following a site team visit, a report is submitted to the APA accreditation committee who then make a final decision. Four types of decisions can be made: (a) full accreditation, (b) provisional accreditation, (c) probation, for programs whose full accreditation is not renewed, (d) denial. Accredited programs must make detailed reports annually with site visits every 5 years thereafter. Currently, internships for clinical and counseling psychology have been accredited. Those internships that hold some level of APA accreditation are listed annually in the December issue of the *American Psychologist*; a supplementary list is published in the June issue.

CONTINUING EDUCATION

The professional's task of keeping abreast of current developments in his/her specialty, let alone his or her basic discipline and allied fields, is a formidable task in today's scientific world. The knowledge base is rapidly changing and expanding along with the increasing number of systems for accessing that information. The expense involved in maintaining a library, let alone a journal library, has risen to the point that it may not only be prohibitive but unwise from a space and practical standpoint. Therefore, while it has become axiomatic that professionals keep up to date in their field, other educational activities in addition to reading become increasingly important in that endeavor.

The concept of continuing education (CE) has been embraced by most professional organizations and is reflected in their major policy documents. While the APA does not have a CE requirement for membership, that idea is supported in many ways. For example, one criterion for assessing the faculty within training programs applying for accreditation is that they demonstrate professional dedication ". . . by obtaining licensure and/or by participating in continuing education (APA, 1986, Appendix B, p. 10)." Similarly, in the APA Ethical Principles of Psychologists (APA, 1981b, p. 634), Principle 2: Competence states the following: "They [all psychologists] maintain knowledge of current scientific and professional information related to the services they render." Furthermore, the APA Standards for Providers of Psychological Services (APA, 1977) repeats Ethical Principle 2 and in terms of providers interprets it more specifically (see Standard 1.5); that standard requires that these psychologists be prepared to show evidence periodically that they have kept up to date on ". . . current knowledge and practices through continuing education (APA, 1977, p. 498)." In several states the state psychology licensing board or state psychology associations do have CE requirements for relicensure or recertification; individual psychologists are advised to make note of any such requirements during the application for membership.

Formal APA CE Credit

The APA does promote the need for psychologists to refresh their knowledge and skills in various aspects of basic psychological education through the recognition of quality CE providers in psychology. Through the CE Sponsor Approval System, established in 1979, the APA approves institutions and organizations that provide CE activities; over 200 organizations participate in this system. These organizations submit applications for approval and approval is awarded to those who meet the criteria. Therefore, psychologists who attend activities offered by APA-approved sponsors can be assured that the organizations operate in compliance with the standards established and maintained by the APA CE Committee and Subcommittee on Continuing Education Sponsor Approval. As part of a two-category system of approval, Category I is awarded to organizations which offer formalized learning activities such as workshops, seminars and courses.

Until 1986, the APA CE program did not approve the individual CE activities of the organization. All sponsors were required to give CE documentation to those participants who successfully complete an activity and APA allowed individual participants to record their credits in an APA Registry. The registry was a centralized record-keeping system of credits earned from APA-approved sponsors. Recently, a Category II approval was developed and is awarded to organizations which have regularly scheduled meetings with sessions—such as symposia, forums, and poster sessions—but no evaluation or objectives component. Thus, individuals can also gain CE credit for attendance at professional meetings approved for Category II CE credit. However, individuals are advised to find out if their state recognizes attendance at professional meetings as meeting CE relicensure requirements, where such requirements are in effect.

A complete listing of activities offered by approved sponsors appears bi-monthly (beginning in January) in the "CE Calendar" section of the *APA Monitor*. Finally, the organizations approved by the APA to offer continuing education activities for psychologists are listed each year in the June issue of the *American Psychologist*.

Conventions

Attendance at national, regional, and state association meetings represents a less formal but nonetheless reasonable way to maintain one's awareness, if not actual understanding, of developments in the field. In addition to attendance at individual paper presentations, symposia, and poster sessions, convention workshops scheduled before or after the actual convention, or in some instances scheduled concurrently with other convention activities, provide excellent opportunities for learning. In instances of workshops, some form of documentation or CE credit for a particular state requirement may be available.

University Courses

Often the need for easily accessible postgraduate education has led professionals to seek out learning experiences in nonacademic settings. In some instances, time and cost factors have interfered with the traditional academic vehicle for learning. Universities, at times, have also been seen as less than flexible in responding to the needs of professionals. Nevertheless, universities are developing and implementing some creative alternatives that allow for the involvement of practitioners in postgraduate work. Even without these options, returning to re-take a course (originally taken during graduate work) as a refresher course or to learn about new service delivery approaches (e.g., consultation) should still remain one of the viable CE options for professionals. While some faculty may be accused of an ivory-tower existence, such criticism is hardly generalizable. What is being advocated here, then, is not a formal postgraduate program of study, although that notion has much to support it where development of a proficiency is desired. Rather, the suggestion is that university courses may at times be very appropriate CE activities to consider.

Change of Specialty

In 1976, APA Council of Representatives adopted a policy for psychologists wishing to change their specialty. Psychology departments were encouraged to develop individualized programs for such individuals holding the doctorate in psychology. Candidates were to meet all requirements for doctoral training in the new specialty, although credit for previously mastered, relevant coursework or requirements could be given. However, the internship or experience in a practicum setting was not considered adequate preparation. Programs offering change of specialty training were expected to make such declarations publicly and to award certificates confirming successful completion of the program. A later APA Council of Representatives resolution, approved at the January 22–24, 1982 meeting, reads as follows:

The American Psychological Association holds that respecialization education and training for psychologists possessing the doctoral degree should be conducted by those academic units in regionally accredited universities and professional schools currently offering doctoral training in the relevant specialty, and in conjunction with regularly organized internship agencies where appropriate. Respecialization for purposes of offering services in clinical, counseling, or school psychology should be linked to relevant APA approved programs. (Abeles, 1982, p. 656)

ACCOUNTABILITY

One clear responsibility of professionals involves the monitoring of their own work, so that systematic review can take place of the progress that is being made toward service delivery goals. The quality of the service depends on data to permit ongoing modifications to be made if they are indicated. Such an orientation also acts as a guide in the planning of professional development. Finally, information of this type is invaluable in helping consumers of the professional service to make informed decisions. In fact, the authors have noted Hogan's (1979) recommendation of a registration rather than licensure plan for professional credentialing (see chapter 2); registration included the annual submission of clinical services data, which would be in the public domain.

Accountability can take different forms. A formative and/or summative model can be followed (Scriven, 1967) and concentrated on a unit's service delivery program and/or the practices of the individual psychologist's functioning. The data can be used internally (as by the unit) or externally (as by the department in which the unit is housed or some superseding level). At its best, the evaluative process(es) can have a positive effect on client outcome and at its worst, can create serious morale problems. Consequently, these decision-making points need to be carefully considered in designing or evaluating an accountability plan. However, the intent of this section is not to deal with such issues, but to review the expectations set forth by the profession. Thus, the type of information that should be available, as well as some procedural matters, will be addressed.

Psychological Services Audit

Two documents form the APA policy regarding service delivery: Standards for Providers of Psychological Service (1977) and the 1981(c) Specialty Guidelines for the Delivery of Services (see chapter 3). Taken together, these materials provide the basis for evaluating the performance of individual psychological service providers as well as the psychological services unit responsible for the services. The statements not only can be used in determining the acceptable structure, budget, and staffing patterns in organizations, but can provide the foundation for a mutual understanding to be developed between provider and user. Finally, these statements can serve as a yardstick by which the community of users of such services can measure their quality.

Specifically, it is recommended that the psychological services unit have developed, in writing, a plan of operation and a set of procedures by which the services are offered as well as a documentation/information system (see Tables 5.1–5.3). This information should be available to employers and consumers and where appropriate, worked out in advance with the appropriate party. Thus, a program can be reviewed in terms of its goals and objectives along with the degree to which minimum standards for the specialty are being met.

Periodic, systematic, and effective evaluations of psychological services are expected to be conducted internally and when possible, under external auspices. The evaluation is expected to include an assessment of effectiveness, costs, continuity, availability, accessibility, and adequacy. It is also expected that such evaluations should not encumber providers or add unnecessarily to the expenses of clients or sanctioners.

It is important to note again that accountability constitutes one of the four principles that guided the development of the APA Standards (1977) document for psychological providers. The general parameters for the type of program information that should be available have been identified along with the targeted areas that should be evaluated periodically. The specifics of that plan are left open to be determined by the unit.

Peer Review

The notion that a professional's service plan for a client, goals of intervention strategies adopted, and assessed progress can be best evaluated by a body of that professional's peers seems to be a legitimate premise to adopt where questions arise in any of those service areas. In fact, such information would provide sufficient data to make judgments regarding questions related to treatment. As Theamon (1984) points out, standards and ethics rely on the initiative of clients and colleagues for any monitoring to be initiated. The peer review, quality assurance model makes collegial accountability a continuing presence in professional practice. Peer review models, therefore, extend quality assurance to the area of performance, where heretofore a monitoring of the professional adherence to a set of credentialing criteria was employed.

Currently, when psychological services treatment is supported by third-party payment (insurance companies, Civilian Health and Medical Program of the Uniformed Services [CHAMPUS]), a claim for reimbursement will have to be submitted at some point. Questions then may arise

Table 5.1. Psychological Services Unit, Plan of Operation

I. Description of the Psychological Services Unit
   A. Organization
      1. Nature and extent of services.
      2. Qualification of providers.
      3. Lines of responsibility.
      4. Level and extent of accountability for each staff member.
      5. Amount and nature of supervisory relationships.
      6. Financial costs, where appropriate.
      7. Benefits and possible risks, where appropriate.
      8. Modified when changes are made in the above.

   B. Objectives and Scope of Services—Policies
      1. Consistent with staff competencies and current psychological knowledge and practice.
      2. Discussed with staff and reviewed by appropriate administrators.
      3. Distributed to administrative staff and users when appropriate.
      4. Available on request.
      5. Reviewed annually by psychological services staff.

II. Delivery of Service Procedures
      1. Description of current methods, forms, case study and assessment procedures, estimated time lines, interventions and evaluation techniques related to objectives and goals.
      2. Communicated to users; staff sanctioners and local administrators.
      3. Reviewed annually by the unit.

III. Evaluation
      1. Regular evaluation of progress in achieving goals, to include assessment of effectiveness, efficiency, continuity, availability, accessibility, and adequacy.
      2. Plan determined by resources of unit.
      3. Conducted internally and externally when funds available.
      4. Evaluation plan reviewed periodically to determine cost effectiveness and feasibility.

Note. From "School Psychology Training and Practice: The APA Perspective," by W. B. Pryzwansky, in *Advances in School Psychology: Volume II* (p. 30), edited by T. R. Kratochwill, 1982, Hillsdale, NJ, Lawrence Erlbaum Assoc. Copyright 1982 by Lawrence Erlbaum Assoc. Adapted by permission.

Recommended in Specialty Guidelines (APA, 1981c).

regarding the necessity and appropriateness of the services provided by psychologists or the continuance of treatment. Health costs have skyrocketed and consumers seem to hear almost daily "horror" stories of professionals bilking the insurance industry and thereby contributing to personal insurance costs. Legitimate questions do arise and, therefore, the need for a professional review system that understands the professional's field and has the knowledge and experience to answer questions seems reasonable.

Table 5.2. Guidelines for Maintenance of Records and Information Consumer File

---

I. Documentation of Services Record
   1. Includes at minimum, identification data, date(s) of service, name of providers, type of service, significant actions taken, outcome at termination.
   2. Policy on maintenance and review of psychological records.
   3. System to protect confidentiality.

II. Information File
   1. Maintain information on human services available in the community.

Note. From "School Psychology Training and Practice: The APA Perspective," by W. B. Pryzwansky, in *Advances in School Psychology: Volume II* (p. 31), edited by T. R. Kratochwill, 1982, Hillsdale, NJ: Lawrence Erlbaum Assoc. Copyright 1982 by Lawrence Erlbaum Assoc. Adapted by permission.

Recommended in Specialty Guidelines (APA, 1981c).

American Psychological Association support for peer review is noted in the following from the APA (Tuma, 1971) statement entitled "Psychology and National Health Care":

> All professions participating in a national health plan should be directed to establish review mechanisms (or performance evaluations) that include not only peer review but active participation by persons representing the consumer. In situations where there are fiscal agents, they should also have representation when appropriate. (p. 1026)

As of 1984, the APA had contractual agreements with nine insurance carriers to provide peer review services. However, that effort has been reduced significantly; third-party payers often hire their own psycholo-

Table 5.3. Psychological Services Procedures

I. Plan of Services
   A. Include provisions for written consent, nature and rationale for assessment tools, objectives and procedures for implementing interventions, estimate of time when appropriate, intent to inform guardians of decisions that may ensue, opportunities for participatory decision making and appeal options.
   B. Notify unit of plan in writing and resolve any points of difference.
II. Obligations to User
   A. Promote freedom of choice and informed consent.
   B. Restrict services for professional reasons only.
   C. Make available information and provide opportunity for users to participate in decisions regarding issues as initiation, termination, continuation.
   D. Promote confidentiality.
   E. Facilitate establishment of a physical, organizational, and social environment that promotes optimal human functioning.

Note. From "School Psychology Training and Practice: The APA Perspective," by W. B. Pryzwansky, in *Advances in School Psychology: Volume II* (p. 31), edited by T. R. Kratochwill, 1982, Hillsdale, NJ: Lawrence Erlbaum Assoc. Copyright 1982 by Lawrence Erlbaum Assoc. Adapted by permission.

Recommended in Specialty Guidelines (APA, 1981c).

gists to serve as in-house evaluators of claims, use other professional associations, and/or reduce benefits for mental health treatment. In fact, APA's Subcommittee on Professional Services Review (SOPSR) has entered "a period of what some called 'maintenance' of the program . . ." (APA, 1986b, p. 6).

Through their Professional Services Review Office (OPSR), APA matched reviewers from the same geographic area as the providers. Their reports are considered advisory and the APA has no involvement in final decisions on payment of benefits. Currently, the APA has made a specific proposal to the insurance carriers that would refine its current procedures and would include education of the consumer about the process, frequency of reviews, confidentiality of records, lines of responsibility, costs, and legal issues. Similarly, OPSR hopes to address conflict-of-interest issues represented by in-house reviewers.

It is interesting to note that peer review is typically requested in a small percentage of cases. Approximately 1,000 cases have been processed by the APA peer review program in the period from 1979 until 1983 (Spence, Bennett, & Shapiro, 1984), with an average of fewer than 50 insurance claims per month.

State Professional Standards Review Committees (PSRCs)

PSRCs may exist within state psychological associations although liability concerns have affected their growth. They constitute a mechanism by which the consumer, the third-party payer, or the provider of psychological services could have questioned claims and practices investigated. These committees vary greatly in the level and range of their activities. The APA has published a procedures manual to provide uniformity among these committees on a national basis. Such uniformity may make this system attractive to insurers that are almost all interstate in their operations.

In addition, APA has published a *Peer Review Manual for Providers of Outpatient Psychological Services* (APA, 1983) which explains APA's peer review program and how the psychologist should respond to third-party requests for treatment reports. Treatment reports usually include statements of the client's current problems; goals of treatment; description of progress; and a description of the specific procedures, techniques, and strategies for obtaining the goals that were stated for the treatment. Questions regarding peer review can be directed to the state PSRC or the APA Peer Review Office.

Finally, to qualify as a peer reviewer, a psychologist must be licensed, hold a doctorate degree, have 2 years of experience in health service and 5 years of postdoctoral experience, and be involved currently in 10 hours minimum of direct service. Peer reviewers are chosen by the APA in cooperation with state PSRCs; about 60% of peer reviewers have submitted treatment reports themselves. A diversity of background, theoretical orientation, and current clinical involvement is represented.

SUGGESTED READINGS

Internship

Grace (1985) writes a thorough guide for the graduate student looking for an internship. The article includes references to objective resources, personal resources, and many practical suggestions. Outlined are different types of questions to consider from professional to personal, and some pitfalls to avoid. For example, if the internship looks too good to be true, it may not be true! And does Dr. Famous on the staff have any contact with the interns? On the other hand, Solway (1985) addresses the stressors on graduate students created by the transition from graduate school to a professional internship. Recommendations for how to deal with such concerns are presented.

A survey of both interns and directors of internship sites comparing their impressions of the intern's preparation for training yielded some interesting findings (Malou, Haas, & Farah, 1983). The need to coordinate university training with the internship site is discussed and the authors suggest that the beginning intern's needs should be assessed more thoroughly.

Finally, the information on postdoctoral internships remains fragmented and limited. Several surveys are underway to explore this topic and the reader is advised to monitor professional journals and trade newsletters for information when it becomes available. Similarly, a national conference is planned for 1987 which will tackle a wide range of issues related to the internship in psychology. Also, it may be interesting to note the 1983 National Academy of Sciences recommendation that federal programs for training in the behavioral science areas shift grant and fellowship awards from predominantly predoctoral training to predominantly postdoctoral training (Institute of Medicine, 1983). Furthermore, research training at the postdoctoral level was targeted as a way to bolster the nonclinical component of the behavioral sciences and meet the anticipated labor force demands in the 1990s.

Respecialization

Respecialization programs were surveyed by Stricker, Hull and Woodring (1984) in terms of the feasibility and success of such programs. Twenty-six programs were identified and both students and directors were sent questionnaires. The authors draw positive conclusions from their data and encourage the expansion of respecialization.

Accountability

While accountability for one's services should be promoted as expected professional practice, it must be done at a level that is consistent with the amount of resources available to support it. Similarly, conditions must exist that protect against the abuse of such evaluations and promote the quality of service and the professional's continued development. Theamon (1984) considers peer review as the next logical step in quality assurance mechanisms available to the profession. His article reviews that historical development and explores the effect on professional practice in terms of the issues of confidentiality, the nature of the mental health treatment report, the dilemma caused by differences in theoretical orientation of the provider versus the reviewer, and the relationship of benefit decisions to treatment. A specific detailed description and comparison of three national peer review programs covering a number of critical dimensions can be found in a chapter by Stricker (1983). In addition, Stricker and Cohen (1984) have summarized the research on the APA peer review project developed with CHAMPUS and discuss the implications of the system for provider, patient, and the profession. An example of a document-based peer review program developed for a psychology training clinic was recently presented by Cohen (1983). An interesting and informative comparison of work samples and simulations for examining psychological competence is found in Howard's article (1983). Finally, a peer review case appears in the 1981 Casebook for Providers of Psychological Services (APA, 1981a, pp. 682–684).

A proactive rationale and plan for the school psychologist to establish accountability was presented by Zins (1984). Accountability is viewed as a means to demonstrate effectiveness to others and as a means for the professional to evaluate his/her own objectives and improve service delivery. A problem-solving approach and a case example are presented. Jackson and Pryzwansky (in press) give an example of an audit-evaluation of a large school psychological services unit, utilizing the APA *Specialty Guidelines* as part of the undertaking. Some suggestions are made for adapting their approach to other school units.

Norcross and Stevenson (1984) studied how clinical training programs presently evaluate themselves, how valuable these evaluations are, and the obstacles to meaningful evaluation. They found a wide range of procedures being used, some of which were very creative. Regardless, most programs relied very heavily on subjective, informal, qualitative information. The authors make several recommendations for improving the evaluation process.

Biskin (1985) examines the relationship between a peer reviewer's theoretical orientation and the orientation of the provider, in regard to the quality of the service review. Psychodynamic and cognitive-behavioral orientations were observed in treating depression and anxiety. The orientations of the reviewers were behavioral, Gestalt, psychodynamic, rational-emotive, and Rogerian, among others.

Cohen's (1983) article presents an interesting approach to peer review. Graduate students in a psychology training clinic learned how to submit a case for peer review and received feedback from psychologists in the state. Cohen suggests that this approach both trains students in treatment documentation and provides supervision.

REFERENCES

Abeles, N. (1982). Proceedings of the American Psychological Association, Incorporated, for the year 1981. *American Psychologist, 37,* 632–666.

American Psychological Association. (1977). Standards for providers of psychological services. *American Psychologist, 32,* 495–505.

American Psychological Association. (1981a). Casebook for providers of psychological services. *American Psychologist, 36,* 682–685.

American Psychological Association. (1981b). Ethical principles of psychologists. *American Psychologist, 36,* 633–638.

American Psychological Association. (1981c). Specialty guidelines for the delivery of services. *American Psychologist, 36,* 639–681.

American Psychological Association. (1983). *Peer review manual for providers of outpatient psychological services, Version 1.1.* Washington, DC: Author.

American Psychological Association. (1986a). *Accreditation handbook* (rev. ed.). Washington, DC: Author.

American Psychological Association. (1986b, October). Peer review scaled back. *APA Monitor,* p. 6.

Association for Advancement of Behavior Therapy. (1981). *Graduate study in behavior therapy: Psychology internship program.* New York: Author.

Association for Advancement of Behavior Therapy. (1986). *1986 membership directory.* New York: Author.

Biskin, B. H. (1985). Peer reviewer evaluations and evaluations of peer reviewers: Effects of theoretical orientation. *Professional Psychology: Research and Practice, 16,* 671–680.

Cohen, L. H. (1983). Document-based peer review in a psychology training clinic: A preliminary report of a statewide program. *Professional Psychology: Research and Practice, 14,* 362–367.

Council for the National Register of Health Service Providers in Psychology. (1981). *Guidelines for defining supervised experience in an "organized health service training program."* Washington, DC: Author.

Council for the National Register of Health Service Providers in Psychology. (1985). *National register of health service providers in psychology.* Washington, DC: Author.

Grace, W. C. (1985). Evaluating a prospective clinical internship: Tips for the applicant. *Professional Psychology: Research and Practice, 16,* 475–480.

Hogan, D. B. (1979). *The regulation of psychotherapists* (Vol. 1.). Cambridge, MA: Ballinger.

Howard, A. (1983). Work samples and simulations in competency evaluations. *Professional Psychology: Research and Practice, 14,* 780–796.

Institute of Medicine, National Academy of Sciences: Committee on National Needs for Biomedical and Behavioral Research Personnel. (1983). *Personnel needs and training for biomedical and behavioral research.* Washington, DC: Institute of Medicine.

Jackson, J. H., & Pryzwansky, W. B. (in press). An audit-evaluation of a school psychological unit utilizing professional standards: An example. *Professional School Psychology.*

Malou, J., Haas, L. J., & Farah, M. J. (1983). Issues in the preparation of interns: Views of trainers and trainees. *Professional Psychology: Research and Practice, 14,* 624–631.

Norcross, J. C., & Stevenson, J. F. (1984). How shall we judge ourselves? Training evaluation in clinical psychology programs. *Professional Psychology: Research and Practice, 15,* 497–508.

Pryzwansky, W. B. (1982). School psychology training and practice: The APA perspective. In T. R. Kratochwill (Ed.), *Advances in school psychology: Vol. II* (pp. 19–39). Hillsdale, NJ: Lawrence Erlbaum Assoc.

Reilly, D. H., & Pryzwansky, W. B. (1973). A model of concurrent field experiences in school psychology training: The externship. *Journal of School Psychology, 11,* 168–171.

Scriven, M. (1967). The methodology of evaluation. In R. W. Tyler, R. M. Gagné, & M. Scriven (Eds.), *Perspectives of curriculum evaluation.* AERA Monograph Series on Curriculum Evaluation. Chicago: Rand McNally.

Solway, K. S. (1985). Transition from graduate school to internship: A potential crisis. *Professional Psychology: Research and Practice, 16,* 50–54.

Spence, J. T., Bennett, B., & Shapiro, A. E. (1984, August 10). Letter to APA membership on peer review. (Available from American Psychological Association.)

Stricker, G. (1983). Peer review systems in psychology. In B. D. Sales (Ed.), *The professional psychologist's handbook* (pp. 223–245). New York: Plenum Press.

Stricker, G., & Cohen, L. H. (1984). APA/CHAMPUS peer review project: Implications for research and practice. *Professional Psychology: Research and Practice, 15,* 96–108.

Stricker, G., Hull, J. W., & Woodring, J. (1984). Respecialization in clinical psychology. *Professional Psychology: Research and Practice, 15,* 210–217.

Theamon, M. (1984). The impact of peer review on professional practice. *American Psychologist, 39,* 406–414.

Tuma, M. (1971). Psychology and national health care. *American Psychologist, 26,* 1025–1026.

Tuma, M. (Ed.). (1984). *Directory of internship programs in clinical child and pediatric psychology* (4th ed.). Baton Rouge, LA: Louisiana State University.

Zins, J. E. (1984). A scientific problem-solving approach to developing accountability procedures for school psychologists. *Professional Psychology: Research and Practice, 15,* 56–66.

Chapter 6
Professional Organizations

> Americans of all ages, all conditions, and all dispositions constantly form associations. They have not only commercial and manufacturing companies, in which all take part, but associations of a thousand other kinds, religious, moral, serious, futile, general or restricted, enormous or diminutive. The Americans make associations to give entertainments, to found seminaries, to build inns, to construct churches, to diffuse books, to send missionaries to the antipodes; in this manner they found hospitals, prisons, and schools. If it is proposed to inculcate some truth or to foster some feeling by the encouragement of a great example, they form a society. Wherever at the head of some new undertaking you see the government in France, or a man of rank in England, in the United States you will be sure to find an association. (Alexis de Tocqueville, *Democracy in America*, 1835)

As noted in chapter 1, an important defining characteristic of professions is their organization of members in formal ways. Such entities, known as societies, academies, or associations, assist in further promulgating the profession, establishing its standards, and even promoting its scientific development. Their goals can be comprehensive and expansive then, or quite specific. Colgate (1983) makes the distinction between professional and trade associations in that the ultimate goal of trade associations is " . . . increased income from its product or service, the goals of professional societies are commonly considered to point more towards the expansion of knowledge or the establishment of professional standards" (p. 5). Scientific or learned societies are formed by individuals with a common background in a subject/discipline and promote operation of knowledge in that area. Colgate also notes that lobbying has become an important contemporary function of the organization. Reports are made to the membership on governmental developments that might affect them, and viewpoints of the members are presented to representatives in the federal government. Moore (1970) argued that the attributes of professionalism should be regarded as a scale rather than in a cluster; as such, the attributes would have values. Each scale would then have its own subset of scale values. According to Moore, the subscales of the organization attributes follow the order of recognizing a common occupational interest, and then establishing control to maintain standards of performance and finally, controlling access to the occupation. Moore perceives the utility of organizations in several ways; for example, they provide a formal means of communication among their constituents, represent professional organizations with various outside interests, as well as promote the profession through activities ranging from public relations to enforcing ethical codes.

Scientific societies started in Europe with the Renaissance, the first being the Academia Secretorum Naturae in Naples in 1560. The American Philosophical Society, which is the oldest American scientific society, was founded by Benjamin Franklin in 1743 (Colgate, 1983). The most recent edition of the *Encyclopedia of Associations* (Akey, 1983) contains 17,644 entries. Colgate (1983) reports that 2,300 professional and learned societies are listed among the 5,800 national trade and professional associations in that encyclopedia. The largest percentage of associations (30%) have their offices in Washington, DC. Approximately 45 psychology organizations can be identified, ranging from the large American Psychological Association to a number of small psychology organizations such as Society for Experimental Psychology, Society for Engineering Psychology, The American Psychology-Law Society and the Psychometric Society.

One intent of this chapter is to present the characteristics and structure of the more representative organizations that psychologists join, with special emphasis on the American Psychological Association (APA) because of its size and influence. Given the multitude of organizations, however, even the final choices may be considered arbitrary. In addition, significance of organizations for individual professionals will be addressed along with other pertinent questions. A list of organizations, with their addresses and phone numbers, can be found in Box 6.1 at the end of this chapter.

AMERICAN PSYCHOLOGICAL
ASSOCIATION (APA)

Considered the major psychology organization in the United States because of its size (58,000 members) and resources (the 1987 operating budget was about $25 million), the APA has a comprehensive set of objectives touching upon all facets of the psychology profession. The purpose of the APA, as described in their literature, is to advance psychology as a science and a profession, and as a means of promoting human welfare. APA's programs aim at disseminating psychological knowledge; promoting research; improving research methods and conditions; and developing the qualifications and competence of psychologists through standards of education, ethical conduct and professional practice. (APA, 1984, p. 1)

Since its founding in 1892 at a meeting convoked by G. Stanley Hall at Clark University, the APA has grown into a complicated organization representing the scientific and professional arms of psychology. The structure as it is known today came about in the years 1942–1945, when 12 organizations representing specialized interests in psychology reorganized with the APA. A rather elaborate governance structure and an equally complex central office operation now exist within the association. The former includes elected representatives of the membership who hold their terms for a prescribed period, while the latter are salaried administrative officials and staff selected by and responsible to the elective governing body. Given the size of the organization and its influence, the APA will be described in detail, beginning with membership criteria and then the governance structure and central office operation. However, it is important to recognize that the APA is currently (September 1986) in a state of some internal reorganization, particularly at the central office level; nevertheless, most of what is written will remain in effect in one form or another and probably in a discernable way. Of more importance is the fact that a drastic restructuring of the APA is being recommended which could result in dramatic changes; those changes are discussed in the last chapter.

Membership

The APA has two basic membership categories, Member and Associate, with other categories (Fellow; Dues Exempt) also recognized, along with an Affiliate status (Foreign Affiliate; High School Teacher Affiliate; Student Affiliate). The qualifications vary as expected with each of the categories, as do the cost of membership (1986 figures are used in this book), rights, and privileges. Also, member dues provide the APA with only 25% of its operating expenses. Each membership category is briefly described in the following numbered paragraphs.

1. The minimum standard for full membership is a doctoral degree based in part on a psychological dissertation, or other evidence of proficiency in psychological scholarship. The degree must also have been received from a program that is primarily psychological in content and conferred by a regionally accredited graduate or professional school. Annual dues are $110, although a sliding, reduced dues structure exists

for the first 3 years of membership with initial-year dues of $55. Members may vote and hold office.

2. Individuals with (a) a master's degree in psychology from a recognized graduate school who have successfully completed 1 full year of professional work in psychology or are engaged in work or graduate study that is primarily psychological in nature, or (b) have completed 2 years of graduate work in psychology at a recognized graduate school and are engaged in work or graduate work that is primarily psychological in nature, may apply for associate membership. Dues are $84, although first-year dues are $42. While initially associates may not vote or hold office in the association, after 5 consecutive years of membership they may vote.

3. The status of Fellow of APA is a titular one that recognizes unusual and outstanding contributions or performance of members in the field of psychology. Fellow nominees must have been members for 1 full year, hold a doctoral degree in psychology, and have had at least 5 years of experience beyond that degree. The nomination for consideration of such status must come from one of the APA divisions (of which the individual is a member) and be supported by evidence put forward by the division to support the "unusual and outstanding contribution." At least three Fellows of that division need to endorse the nominee. Following nomination by the division and evaluation by the APA Membership Committee, the names of those individuals recommended for election are forwarded to the APA Board of Directors for review and nomination to the Council of Representatives (C/R). Election by the C/R is required for Fellow status to be conferred. Individuals may hold Fellow status in several divisions, by meeting the procedures and criteria for such status in that division. Once the C/R has elected a member Fellow in a division, subsequent Fellow status in other divisions is conferred at the division level. At times, one hears the designation of "Old Fellow," which simply refers to the individual in one division who has been awarded such recognition in another division.

4. Dues Exempt status is open to members who have reached the age of 65 and have been members for 25 years. Also, members who have been adjudged to be permanently and totally disabled qualify for this membership category. Hardship cases, defined by available income of less than $7,500, have dues of $15.

5. Affiliates include (a) Foreign Affiliates, (b) High School Teacher Affiliates, and (c) Student Affiliates. The annual fee for the first two types of affiliates is $15, while the Student Affiliate's fee is $10. Subscriptions to any of the APA's journals or other publications are available at the special rate charged to members.

Membership Entitlements

American Psychological Association members are entitled to participate in a low-cost insurance program in several areas of coverage. Programs are tailored to the needs of psychologists. The following programs are available to members: professional liability; life insurance; medical protection; hospital indemnity; income protection; accident and travel; excess liability; office overhead; Keogh retirement plan; and student/school liability. The programs are tailored to the needs of psychologists, and are reviewed several times a year. The APA negotiates premium rates and refunds, and makes modifications as necessary.

The members also receive the official journal of the association, *American Psychologist* (which publishes empirical, theoretical, and practical articles), along with the official newspaper, *APA Monitor* (which reports news about psychology and psychologists along with listings of employment opportunities), and the consumer magazine *Psychology Today*. All publications are monthly and included as part of the membership dues.

It should be noted that the Council of Representatives (C/R) only meets twice a year and, therefore, applications for membership (upon which it votes) must be completed before the postal deadlines. Thus it is possible that 6 months may pass between time of application and acceptance of membership. Applicants for Associate or Member status must have applications completed either by August 1 for election effective the following January 1, or by February 1 for election effective the following July 1.

For further information and applications (specify the type of membership or affiliation desired) write to: Membership Office, APA, 1200 Seventeenth Street, N.W., Washington, D.C. 20036.

Governance Structure

Divisions

After becoming an APA member, an individual may apply for membership in one *or more* of the APA's 45 divisions. The divisions have their own standards for election to membership which tend to be more specialized than those of the APA. Divisional affiliation is not required by APA membership to be retained. The divisions are listed in Table 6.1.

As part of the major reorganization of the APA in 1945, divisions were created to recognize differences in interest among psychologists. A division may be established whenever 1% of the association petitions for it and the C/R approves. Division officers are elected according to the bylaws of the division at the time officers of the APA are elected; ballots are mailed to the membership on or about May 15th. Typically the president and president-elect serve for 1 year and the secretary/treasurer for 3

Table 6.1. Divisions of the American Psychological
Association

1. General Psychology
2. Teaching of Psychology
3. Experimental Psychology
5. Evaluation and Measurement
6. Physiological and Comparative Psychology
7. Developmental Psychology
8. The Society of Personality & Social Psychology—A
   Division of the APA
9. The Society for the Psychological Study of Social
   Issues—A Division of APA
10. Psychology and the Arts
12. Clinical Psychology
13. Consulting Psychology
14. The Society for Industrial & Organizational Psycho-
    logy, Inc.—A Division of the APA
15. Educational Psychology
16. School Psychology
17. Counseling Psychology
18. Psychologists in Public Service
19. Military Psychology
20. Adult Development and Aging
21. Applied Experimental and Engineering Psychologists
22. Rehabilitation Psychology
23. Consumer Psychology
24. Theoretical and Philosophical Psychology
25. Experimental Analysis of Behavior
26. History of Psychology
27. Community Psychology
28. Psychopharmacology
29. Psychotherapy
30. Psychological Hypnosis
31. State Psychological Association Affairs
32. Humanistic Psychology
33. Mental Retardation
34. Population and Environmental Psychology
35. Psychology of Women
36. PIRI—Psychologists Interested in Religious Issues
37. Child, Youth, and Family Services
38. Health Psychology
39. Psychoanalysis
40. Clinical Neuropsychology
41. Psychology and Law
42. Psychologists in Independent Practice
43. Division of Family Psychology
44. Society for the Study of Lesbian & Gay Issues
45. Society for the Psychological Study of Ethnic
    Minority Issues
46. Media Psychology
47. Exercise and Sports Psychology

Note. There are no Divisions 4 or 11.

years. The list of division officers appears each year in the June issue of the *American Psychologist*. The names of Fellows, Members, and Associates also appear in the annual *APA Membership Register* and the *Directory* of the association.

Divisions also are represented on the C/R according to the apportionment ballot results described in the next section. That apportionment is done annually so it is conceivable they may not serve a full term in some instances.

Council of Representatives (C/R)

The C/R is the body with legislative power over most business of the APA, and is made up of elected representatives from the divisions and state associations. The number of seats for both groups is determined by apportionment ballots sent to the membership each year. Individual members may allocate their 10 votes among divisions, state associations, or (in some cases) coalitions. A division or state association receives one council seat for each 1% of the allocated seats. The size of the council is approximately 115 members, with 76 representatives from divisions, 26 from state associations, and 9 from coalitions. The individual representatives are elected at the division or state association level. Finally, the APA Board of Directors are also members of the council.

The C/R is a major link between division and APA activities. The C/R's legislative year begins at the end of the *annual adjourned business meeting* in January (the beginning, incidentally, of C/R terms of office). The adjourned meeting is considered to be a continuation of the meeting held at the annual convention. The terms of APA officers, and members and chairs of boards and committees begin at the same time as those of the newly seated council members. The APA reimburses some expenses of council members so that they may attend these two meetings; the sponsoring division or state association may cover some of the rest. It is interesting to note that members of the C/R have formed coalitions and caucuses, representing groups with common concerns. Current groupings include the Coalition of Applied/Professional Psychologists, Public Interest Coalition, Women's Caucus, Scientist/Practitioner Coalition, Research/Academic Coalition, and the State Psychological Association Caucus. The C/R members are listed each year in the June issue of the *American Psychologist*. To be eligible to serve as a council representative one must be a member of the APA, a member of the group one represents (e.g., division), and serve as representative of only one voting unit. Representatives are ineligible for reelection for a 1-year period following 3 consecutive years of serving on the C/R.

The C/R also elects individuals who serve (a) on the APA's standing boards/committees and continuing committees, and (b) as representatives for organizations that report through the APA Board of Directors. Nominations are solicited from the membership (see the January–February *APA Monitor*), the divisions, state associations, and each board and committee. Approximately 1,200 nominations are received each year, with 100 names appearing on the ballot from which 45 selections are made. The APA Subcommittee on Nominations of the Board of Directors submits the list of candidates, selected according to stated criteria, to the APA Board of Directors, who approve the final ballot sent to the C/R.

Items for the C/R agenda come from the annual reports of divisions, items sent forward by APA Boards/Committees, and new business introduced by council representatives. Further, upon petition of 1% of APA members, business can be brought before the C/R.

Board of Directors

The APA Board of Directors serves as the administrative agent for the C/R, and has the authority to take actions necessary for the conduct of the association's affairs between council business meetings. The board of directors consists of the association officers and six other individuals. The elected officers are the president, president-elect, past president, recording secretary, and treasurer. The executive officer is also a member. The six other members are elected by and from those members who held seats on the C/R during the year immediately preceding the current year (they are elected for 3 years).

Policy and Planning Board (P&P)

Provision for the elected Policy and Planning Board, consisting of nine members, is in the APA Bylaws (APA, 1986a). It is mandated to make recommendations on current and long-term policy of the association and "extensions and restrictions of the functions of the association, its divisions, or state associations, that are consonant with the purpose of the association" (APA, 1986b, p. 626). It is *unique* among boards in that it can make recommendations directly (a) to the voting members of the APA, (b) to the APA Board of Directors, or (c) the C/R. Members are listed in the June issue of the *American Psychologist*.

Committee on Structure and Function of the Council

The APA Committee on Structure and Function of the Council is the only continuing committee that reports directly to the C/R. The mission of this six-member committee is to (a) receive, review, and initiate recommendations, suggestions, and complaints about council function and operations; and (b) give continuing attention to the development of procedures by which the council can be kept informed about the history and nature of problems or issues currently facing the APA. Members are listed in the June issue of the *American Psychologist*.

Boards and Committees

Table 6.2 lists six selected boards with the committees that report through them. Procedures for election to these boards/committees have been outlined earlier. Again, the names and terms of their members may be found by referring to the June issue of the *American Psychologist*.

Central Office

The program and business activities of the APA are coordinated at the association's central office in Washington, DC and nearby Arlington, Virginia. A paid staff headed by the executive officer is responsible for these activities. The major operating offices include the Governance Affairs, Office of Legislative Affairs, Office of Public Affairs, Office of Financial Affairs, Office of International Affairs, and the Convention Of-

Table 6.2. Committees of Selected APA Boards

Education and Training Board
Committees on (a) Graduate Education and Training, (b) Undergraduate Training, (c) Continuing Education, (d) Continuing Education Sponsor approval, (e) Psychology in the Secondary Schools, (f) Accreditation.

Publications and Communications Board
Council of Editors.

Board of Scientific Affairs
Committees on (a) Scientific Awards, (b) Research Support, (c) Protection of Human Subjects in Research, Animal Research, and Experimentation, (d) Psychological Tests and Assessment, (e) Testing Practices.

Board of Social and Ethical Responsibility for Psychology
Committees on (a) Women in Psychology, (b) Lesbian and Gay Concerns, (c) Psychology in the Public Interest Award, (d) Psychology and Handicaps, (e) Children, Youth, and Families.

Board of Ethnic Minority Affairs
Committees on (a) Ethnic Minority Human Resources Development, (b) Communications with Minority Constituents.

Board of Professional Affairs
Committees on (a) APA/State Association Relations, (b) Professional Standards, (c) Professional Practice.

fice. Thus, the coordination and service functions are widespread and interface with the membership, the governance structure, and the public. Research and operational responsibilities are handled by Central Office staff. In addition to coordinating the annual APA convention, the Central Office is the site of more than 100 meetings of the governance body. A brief description of these varied functions will follow.

The APA Governance Affairs office coordinates and directs a wide-ranging set of activities in the areas of accreditation of training programs, the peer review process (CHAMPUS project, see next chapter), educational affairs, ethics, ethnic minority affairs, minorities fellowship program, professional affairs, scientific affairs, social and ethical responsibility, state associations program, women's program.

The APA's Office of Legislative Affairs helps to formulate and implement federal policy and legislative activities of the association. In addition to keeping the membership and governance structure informed on national policies through monitoring and analysis of proposed legislation, they develop advocacy positions and represent the organization in government circles. This office works with coalitions of outside organizations on common legislative issues. Two components involved are (a) human resources research, which surveys psychology's national labor force and training system, and (b) coordinating the work of two grassroots networks in the areas of research support and health and services support.

The APA's Public Affairs Offices "works with television, radio, and print media to demonstrate the contributions psychologists make to society and to improve public understanding of psychology's broad scope and application." (APA, 1984, p. 8) They are responsible for the APA Convention and Meeting Services Office and the APA Public Relations Program. The Public Information Office is the interface between the general public and media about the APA and the work done by psychologists. They distribute news releases, provide background information for reporters to prepare stories, and also are available to members of the press covering the APA's annual convention. A National Media Awards program is also conducted through this office. The International Affairs office facilitates contact between the APA and those colleagues and students abroad who desire professional ties and information about psychology in the United States. Similarly, any involvement of the APA in international meetings and with issues is coordinated by this office.

Publications

To fulfill the objective of pushing and distributing knowledge about psychology, the APA Office of Communications is responsible for the following areas: Psych INFO, publications, marketing, advertising sales, publishing support, and the *APA Monitor*. Twenty-seven periodicals plus a variety of books, brochures, and pamphlets are available from the APA.

As noted earlier, the *American Psychologist* is published monthly; the APA dues include a subscription to this journal. In addition to the scientific and professional articles that appear therein, the journal is important for the regularly published information that is included. For example, the June issue serves as the organization's archival issue. Each June issue contains the names of elected officers of the organization, board and committee members, as well as subcommittees and task forces. In addition, officers of each state psychological association are included, along with the secretaries and addresses for state and provincial boards and agencies for the statutory licensure or certification of psychologists. The proceedings of the APA Council for Representatives, along with the treasurer's and executive officer's yearly reports are also included therein. Major policy statements of the organization such as Ethical Principles of Psychologists usually appear initially in this month's issue. The March issue lists the APA Awards for the year, including a citation for the individual recipients, biography, and bibliography. The awards are for:

1. Distinguished Scientific Contributions
2. Distinguished Scientific Awards for the Applications of Psychology
3. Awards for Distinguished Profession Contributions
4. Award for Distinguished Contributions to Psychology in the Public Interest
5. Distinguished Scientific Awards for an Early Career Contribution to Psychology

Beginning with each April issue, through July, the *American Psychologist* provides detailed information about the upcoming APA Convention, including preregistration application and advanced hotel registration materials. The December issue lists APA-accredited doctoral training programs in clinical, counseling, and school psychology, along with accredited predoctoral internship training programs; a supplement to that listing appears in the June issue.

In addition to the *American Psychologist*, the official newspaper, the *APA Monitor*, is published monthly and sent to members as part of their subscription dues. It features coverage of legislative developments, editorials, news, and notes about members. In addition to that material, a current listing of employment opportunities is included.

The journals and periodicals published by the APA in addition to the *American Psychologist*, *APA Monitor*, and *Psychology Today* include the following:

Behavioral Neuroscience   *Journal of Experimental Psychology:*
Contemporary Psychology   *General*

Developmental Psychology
Journal of Abnormal Psychology
Journal of Applied Psychology
Journal of Comparative Psychology
Journal of Consulting and Clinical Psychology
Journal of Counseling Psychology
Journal of Educational Psychology
Journal of Experimental Psychology: Animal Behavior Processes

Journal of Experimental Psychology: Human Perception and Performance
Journal of Experimental Psychology: Learning, Memory and Cognition
Journal of Personality and Social Psychology
Professional Psychology: Research and Practice
Psychological Abstracts
Psychological Bulletin
Psychological Documents
Psychological Review

All are available to APA members at a discount. Some of these journals are published with divisions and, therefore, may be available as part of the divisions assessment. Clearly, *Psychological Bulletin* (evaluative reviews), *Psychological Documents* (abstracts), and *Psychological Review* (theoretical papers) serve as reference materials. In addition, *PsychScan* is a quarterly publication that helps professionals and students keep up to date in the areas of applied psychology, clinical psychology, developmental psychology, and learning disabilities/mental retardation. The material included in *PsychScan* is designed for researchers and based on abstracts from special subscriber-selected journals. *PsychInfo* is a family of interrelated information services providing access to the literature in psychology.

The APA also publishes an annual membership *Register*, as well as a detailed *Directory* on an irregular basis. The *Publication Manual* is the guide to preparing manuscripts for publication in APA and related journals. Public information materials are also available, such as the booklet detailing applied functions entitled *Psychology as a Health Care Profession*. Career information can be found in a booklet entitled *Careers in Psychology*. For undergraduates, several excellent publications are available. For example, (a) *The Psychology Major: Training and Employment Strategies*; (b) *Graduate Study in Psychology and Associated Fields* (a comprehensive survey of more than 600 graduate programs (see chapter 1); (c) *Preparing for Graduate Study: Not for Seniors Only* (a how-to sourcebook); and (d) *Library Use: A Handbook for Psychology* (a how-to handbook). For any of these materials one needs to write the APA Order Department, 1400 North Uhl St., Arlington, VA 22201.

Annual Convention

The annual APA Convention is held in late August with more than 10,000 members in attendance. The location is different each year, and the dates of the upcoming six conventions and locations can be found by referring to the Calendar of each issue of the *American Psychologist*. Similar information regarding regional, state, and international psychological meetings as well as psychological workshops, conferences, and related association meetings are also included.

One of the largest conventions in the United States and the world's largest meeting for psychologists, the APA week-long program features more than 3,000 presentations in the form of symposia, lectures, invited addresses, workshops, and other forums. Of special note is the Master Lecture Series on Psychology, which consists of 2-hour lectures dealing with a different area of psychology each year. The lectures are taped for distribution and also are available in book form. The G. Stanley Hall Lecture Series consists of five 2-hour lectures designed to update the teaching of introductory psychology; they are also available in book form. Each division is allotted convention time for business meetings and for the presentation of papers relevant to their interests. A call for papers is distributed to the membership in January with directions for proposing papers for consideration. In addition to the above emphasis, exhibits, films, and a placement service are also a part of the opportunities provided.

Advocacy

In addition to the present organizational offices, the APA Council of Representatives established the Interim Advisory Committee for Professional Development in January 1986. This committee will work to establish a permanent Office of Professional Development to generate and allocate funds to advance the professional practice of psychology at the state and federal levels. Among current proposed activities, the office intends to survey state psychological associations to identify issues of concern and to develop and implement professional psychology's position on changes in the health care system. Thus, services to state associations and marketing objectives have been established. A special assessment of $50 was charged to APA members in 1986, and may be the beginning of a differentiated dues structure for the APA in subsequent years.

Finally, the APA Council of Representatives has set up the Psychology Defense Fund to finance special projects and legislative actions at the state level. It does not overlap with federal legislative activities of the Association for the Advancement of Psychology (AAP—see below). The fund is separate from the APA budget and supported by individual contributions as well as contributions of APA divisions, state affiliates, and other groups. Examples of the awards they have made include grants to psychologists in suits over confidential or ethics issues, a research project to review statutes, and court decisions on the legal status of psychology, state by state.

Restructuring of APA

By now, the size and complexity of the APA should be obvious. However, with this growth has naturally come a variety of subdisciplines and special interest groups. The tensions existing in psychology's early beginnings (see the Introduction chapter) have not only become magnified, but are now intertwined with an even more complicated set of agendas promoted by a variety of constituencies among the membership. As a result, the APA has increasingly found itself ineffectual in doing business. Consequently, in confronting this challenge the APA Council tried to divide its work between two bodies, or forums, as they were called. Basically, the forums included researchers and academicians in one group and practitioners in the second. The notion that was followed was simple in design, that is, each group/forum would conduct business relevant to its respective interests. A number of factors arose to defeat this initial attempt to reorganize. At the 1985 APA Convention, a task force set up to study APA structure made recommendations of a rather sweeping nature. At the time of this writing, no decision has been made regarding their proposals. However, given the changes that were proposed, those recommendations are presented for review in chapter 7, where future perspectives on the profession are discussed.

THE AMERICAN
PSYCHOANALYTIC ASSOCIATION

The American Psychoanalytic Association was founded in 1911 and currently has a membership of about 3,000 analysts. It also includes 26 accredited training institutes and 35 affiliate psychoanalytic societies throughout the United States. Since its inception, it has been a member of the International Psychoanalytic Association, the official representative of worldwide psychoanalysts.

One of the main functions of the American Psychoanalytic Association is scientific. It keeps members informed by providing forums for the exchange of new ideas and discoveries in areas such as practice, theory, and research. It holds two annual national meetings, and publishes the *Journal of the American Psychoanalytic Association*. Founded in 1953, this journal is noted for articles on all aspects of psychoanalysis, as well as articles relevant to other areas of mental health and the behavioral sciences, including the application of psychoanalysis to other fields.

A major responsibility of the Association is that of creating and maintaining high professional standards. A training institute may be granted membership in the Association and, periodically, the educational program at each member institute is re-evaluated to assure that these requisite standards are maintained. Programs involve 6 to 10 years of training beyond the entry degree. In addition, the Association evaluates graduates from approved institutes who wish to become full, certified members.

AMERICAN PSYCHOLOGICAL FOUNDATION (APF)

A nonprofit organization, the American Psychological Foundation (APF) was created to advance the science and the profession of psychology. Donations, which support the foundation, help extend the benefits of psychology to the public.

A board of trustees, including past presidents and prominent members of the APA, control and manage the foundation and award the contributions carefully in each of the following areas:

Gifted Children. The largest bequest currently administered is the Esher Katz Rosa Fund, which is granted by the trustees after careful evaluation of proposals relative to the advancement and application of knowledge about gifted children.

Gold Medal, Teaching, and Media Awards. The Gold Medal is the major APF award given at the APA convention, and is given to an American psychologist in recognition of a long, continued record of scientific and scholarly achievement. The Distinguished Teaching Award is made to an individual who has made outstanding contributions to education in the field of psychology. Five national media awards were also conferred in the following areas: (a) books/monographs; (b) newspaper reporting; (c) magazine writing; (d) television/film; and (e) radio.

Journals for the Blind. Recorded Psychological Journals, a nonprofit organization, is partially supported by the APF and prepares and distributes tapes of psychological journals to visually impaired psychology students.

Foreign Grants. Grants of APA journal subscriptions are made to a limited number of foreign psychologists who were trained in American and Canadian universities and now reside in their native lands.

Congressional Fellowship. A Congressional Science Fellowship in the area of child psychology is sponsored in which the recipient works as a special legislative assistant on the staff of a Congressional committee or Congressperson.

Archival Grants. One goal of the APF is to preserve relevant archives in order to keep records, documents, and other research material accessible, and to promote the preservation of historic documents and their use by scholars.

THE ASSOCIATION FOR ADVANCEMENT OF BEHAVIOR THERAPY (AABT)

Founded in 1966, the Association for Advancement of Behavior Therapy (AABT) is basically an interest group, and is active in "1. encouraging the development of the conceptual and scientific basis of behavior therapy as an empirical approach to applied problems; 2. facilitating the appropriate utilizations and growth of behavior therapy as a professional activity; and 3. serving as a resource and information center for matters related to behavior therapy" (AABT, 1984, p. v). In addition to the AABT Board of Directors (president, past president, president-elect, secretary-treasurer, and three representatives-at-large), there are five coordinators with the responsibility respectively for education affairs, membership affairs, convention affairs, professional affairs and publications. The six-member staff includes an executive director. Over 30 special interest groups (SIGs) are currently active and cover a diversity of interests such as specific behavior change techniques, focal target problems and populations, particular work settings, central theoretical concerns, and salient change agent issues. Almost all distribute a newsletter and conduct educational activities.

The Educational Affairs Office of the AABT offers a broad range of professional consultations, as well as peer review services such as assembling briefs and depositions in legal proceedings involving behavior modification procedures and programs. The AABT Professional Affairs office monitors state and legislative activity that may have an impact on behavior therapy (BT) and make information available to government policymakers. Similar functions are pursued vis à vis other mental health organizations and insurance carriers.

Publications of the AABT include the magazine/newsletter *The Behavior Therapist*, published 10 times per year and distributed as part of the membership fee. It includes current information on the field, book reviews, employment listings, and so on. The major journal of the association, *Behaviour Therapy*, is devoted to the publication of original experimental or clinical research that advances the theory and practice of BT. It is available to members at a discount. (*Behavioral Assessment*, a journal that deals with assessment as well as research/methodological issues, was formerly an AABT publication, but is now published solely by Pergamon Press.)

Membership in the AABT is at the full, associate, or student level. Full membership is open to all persons who agree with the purposes and objectives of the organization and are professionals in good standing in the American Psychological Association or American Psychiatric Association, or else are: (a) practicing behavior clinicians, (b) engaged in research or activities pertinent to the "development and advancement" of BT, or (c) "interested in acquiring professional knowledge and competence in some aspect of the behavior therapies with a view toward eventual participation" (AABT, 1986, p. vii). Individuals who do not meet the membership criteria but whose credentials are otherwise acceptable to the membership are eligible for associate membership. Student membership is open to students at the bachelor's, master's, or doctoral level. As of 1984, full and associate membership dues are $50 with a one-time $20 initiation fee. Student membership is $15 per year.

An annual convention is held which includes poster sessions, symposia, invited addresses, workshops, institutes, and fundamentals courses. While the AABT does not have continuing education (CE) requirements, CE credits are available for the fundamentals courses, preconvention institutes, and the workshops.

Finally, the AABT geographical affiliate groups engage in activities determined by their membership. Almost all of these groups hold meetings and distribute newsletters.

ASSOCIATION FOR THE ADVANCEMENT OF PSYCHOLOGY (AAP)

Originally founded in 1974 by the APA's Council of Representatives, the Association for the Advancement of Psychology (AAP) has functioned as an independent political advocacy organization for all psychologists. It was supported by individual membership dues and APA contributions. However, in February 1986, it was agreed that "all public policy information gathering, professional legislative lobbying and interactions with federal agencies being done by AAP and the then Office of National Policy Studies of APA, should be amalgamated into a single APA office" (Voorde, 1986, p. 710). As a result, the APA Office of National Policy Studies (now the Office of Legislative Affairs) was restructured to accommodate this merger of resources.

The AAP has also been reorganized into a separate membership political action organization designed to meet the needs of psychologists. This objective will be pursued partly through development of a former AAP committee, Psychologists for Legislative Action Now (PLAN), as a political action group. Voluntary contributions will be the basis of PLAN's efforts to demonstrate to congressional members their concerns and maximize legislative effectiveness through political action.

ASSOCIATION FOR BEHAVIOR ANALYSIS (ABA)

An international organization, the Association for Behavior Analysis (ABA) grew out of the Midwestern Association of Behavioral Analysis, which had been organized to establish a separate identity for the behavioral analysis group of the larger psychological community. A major purpose is to

> provide a forum for the discussion of issues and the dissemination of information pertinent to the interests of the membership by means of an annual convention. It is an interdisciplinary group of professionals, paraprofessionals, and students interested in the experimental, theoretical and applied analysis of behavior, (ABA, 1985, p. i)

The ABA is organized around an executive council standing committee, select committee, and special interest groups. The executive council includes the president, past presidents, president elect, secretary/treasurer, four council members, two affiliate representatives, and two honorary council members. The standing committees are affiliate, certification, education and evaluation, international development, membership, and membership recruitment. There is a convention staff.

Membership is limited to one class of members and determined by a minimum of a master's degree in psychology or a related field and demonstrated competence in either the experimental or applied analysis of behavior (demonstrated by a minimum of a year's supervised work in either area, and a graduate project, thesis, or dissertation in one of the areas as well). Applicants who do not meet those criteria must demonstrate their competency in behavioral analysis by submitting evidence of at least two years of supervised experience or of having made significant contributions to knowledge in behavioral assessment by research publications or other means. There is also a student affiliate class of participants. As of 1984, initial membership was $26 for full membership and $12 for students, with renewal rising to $45 respectively. Sustaining, supporting, and emeritus status is recognized through a varying membership rate. The *ABA Newsletter* is sent to the membership.

An annual convention is held, which includes a business meeting. Invited addresses, papers, poster sessions, pre-convention institutes, seminars, symposia, and workshops make up the program. The ABA is supported by the APA to sponsor CE programs in psychology, which is done through the workshops. A placement service is also offered along with exhibits.

Finally, this organization sponsors certification as a behavior analyst (see chapter 1).

ASSOCIATION OF BLACK PSYCHOLOGISTS (ABP)

Founded in 1968 by black psychologists from across the country, the Association of Black Psychologists' (ABP's) goal is to actively address the problems and expected needs of black psychologists and the black community. The ABP's objectives are based on the needs and experience of black people, including advancement of the psychological well-being of black people in America and developing internal support systems for black psychologists and students of psychology.

Membership is open to all persons, professional students and others, who are interested in advancing the association goals. The fees range from $90 for professional or associate to $30 for student; the institutional fee is $100. Affiliation support membership requires an additional $100.

The association's newsletter, *Journal of Black Psychology,* voting privileges, and convention discounts are included with membership.

BRITISH PSYCHOLOGICAL SOCIETY

The British Psychological Society was founded in 1901 ". . . to promote the advancement of the study of psychology and its applications, and to maintain high standards of professional education and conduct" (BPA, p. 1). Its organization is complex, divided into 10 sections—Medical Psychology and Psychotherapy, Educational, Occupational, Social, Mathematical, Statistical and Computing, Developmental, Cognitive, Counseling, Psychobiology, and History and Philosophy; and also five divisions—the Division of Educational and Child Psychology, the Scottish Division of Educational and Child Psychology, the Division of Clinical Psychology, the Division of Criminology and Legal Psychology, and the Division of Occupational Psychology. There are also numerous committees, working parties, and several regional offices in Great Britain.

Training and practice of psychologists in Great Britain is somewhat different than in the United States, and this difference is reflected in the requirements for British Psychological Society membership. Full membership status is afforded to persons holding a university of polytechnic degree with psychology as the main subject. This degree is comparable to an advanced degree in the United States. In addition, one may qualify for membership by holding postgraduate qualifications, commensurate qualifications, or by passing an examination. For psychologists outside of the United Kingdom, a doctoral degree or satisfactory results on the society's qualifying examination are required. All applicants must also have the endorsement of two members. As with other organizations, associate fellow, student, and subscriber memberships are available. Members of overseas psychological societies may apply for foreign affiliateship. Costs for membership range from 7 pounds for students to 30 pounds for full members.

The society publishes seven journals. Membership includes two monthly newsletters which cover the society's announcements and position vacancies.

There is an annual conference held in early April and an additional London Conference in December. The different regional offices and sections also hold conferences and produce newsletters.

CANADIAN PSYCHOLOGICAL ASSOCIATION

The Canadian Psychological Association (CPA) represents the professional and scientific interests of all psychologists in Canada. Among its purposes are to promote both the research and application of psychology to provide leadership in establishing national standards and ethics, and to promote unity and a sense of identity among the diverse interests and geographical differences of Canadian psychologists. In addition, the association provides assistance to the government and other organizations concerned with social and national problems such as education and health.

The CPA is organized into two divisions: Experimental and Applied. The CPA Experimental Division, in promoting the interests of experimental psychologists, coordinates the experimental presentations at the association's annual convention. Also, it seeks to enhance research funding in Canada and provides information on visiting psychologists in Canada. Similar to the Experimental Division, the Applied Division is responsible for the activities related to the applied interests at the convention. This latter division represents the applied and professional needs of psychologists.

In addition to the two divisions, there are 17 sections (as of October 1982) within the CPA, composed of psychologists with common interests in the following areas: Brain and Behaviour; Canadian Psychologists for Social Responsibility; Community Psychology; Educational Psychology; Environmental Psychology; Criminal Justice Systems; Developmental Psychology; Health Psychologists; Industrial/Organizational; International and Cross-Cultural Psychology; Programme Evaluation; Psychological Gerontology; Psychology of Fitness; Psychopharmacology; Social Psychology; Teaching of Psychology; and Women and Psychology.

To be a member of the CPA, one must have a master's or doctoral degree in psychology or the equivalent thereof, and be a resident of Canada or the United States. In most circumstances, two sponsors must endorse an application for membership. The APA and CPA have reciprocal agreements for membership. An APA member may join the CPA for one half of the CPA dues, and the same arrangement exists for CPA members to join the APA. In addition, there are student memberships for graduate and undergraduate students, foreign affiliate memberships, and special affiliate memberships for persons who are actively interested in psychology but who are not psychologists. The cost of dues (in Canadian dollars) is $85.00 for a member, $35.00 for foreign and special affiliates, and $25.00 for student affiliates. Fees for members cover subscriptions for two journals: *Canadian Psychology*, and a choice of either the *Canadian Journal of Psychology* or the *Canadian Journal of Behavioral Science*. The third journal may be subscribed to for $15. In addition, all members and affiliates receive the quarterly newsletter, *Highlights*. Publications are in both French and English.

In addition to the publication of three quarterly journals, the CPA holds annual meetings and presents an annual award for "Distinguished Contributions to Canadian Psychology as a Science" and "Distinguished Contributions to Canadian Psychology as a Profession."

THE HUMAN FACTORS SOCIETY

The Human Factors Society is the largest society in the field of ergonomics. It is ". . . the one focus for the professional exchange of information on scientific, engineering, business, and career developments in human factors . . . " (Human Factors Society, 1985).

Structured to depend mostly on volunteer work from its members, the society holds an open meeting with a choice of candidates for office. There are approximately 20 local chapters and several technical groups that promote special interests ranging from computer systems to the aging.

While approximately half of the 4,000 members are psychologists, membership includes a wide range of professions. Members are required to have a bachelor's degree and 3 years of experience in human factors work, or advanced graduate work in lieu of 2 of the 3 year's experience. Membership decisions are made by a committee which may waive requirements for exceptional candidates. There are also associate and student memberships available. Fees range from $15 for a student to $35 plus a $10 application fee for a member. Sustaining membership is offered to individuals or corporations who wish to contribute a determined amount of money to the organization (minimum of $100).

The organization meets as an international body in the fall to allow members to present research developments and provide a forum for discussion of important issues.

Several publications are offered by the society, including the journal *Human Factors*, the *HFS Bulletin*, and the *HFS Directory and Yearbook*, all of which are free to members. There are also videotapes and films available for members to borrow.

Awards are made annually to recognize outstanding achievement in the field. Representation before Congressional committee is also provided to promote the interests of human factors professionals.

PSYCHONOMIC SOCIETY

The objective of the Psychonomic Society is to "promote the communication of scientific research in psychology and allied sciences" (The Psychonomic Society, 1982). Members are persons holding the doctorate who are qualified to conduct and to supervise scientific research in psychology or allied sciences. They must have published significant research. Recommendation for membership is initiated by one of the members, with election conducted by the governing board. Associate membership status is available to individuals who have been in the field of psychology or allied sciences for a maximum of 5 years. Associates must also hold the doctorate.

A governing board supervises the general affairs of the society. The board consists of 12 members and the ex-officio secretary-treasurer; terms are for 6 years. The board elects a chairman and the secretary-treasurer. Each year the membership at large nominates persons for the board. The names of the six persons receiving the greatest number of nominations make up the ballot for that year.

The society publishes the following journals: *Bulletin of the Psychonomic Society; Animal Learning and Behavior; Physiological Psychology; Memory and Cognition; Perception and Psychophysics; Behavior Research Methods;* and *Instruments & Computers*. An annual scientific meeting is held with members presenting papers or sponsoring nonmember presentations. The annual business meeting is also held at this time.

SOCIETY OF BEHAVIORAL MEDICINE

A relatively new organization, the Society of Behavioral Medicine was begun in 1978. It is an interdisciplinary group whose focus is the relationship of behavior to health and health care. Most of the members are psychologists and physicians, but persons from other disciplines are encouraged to join. There are approximately 1,500 members, and it is anticipated that the organization will continue to grow.

Membership dues are $50 annually (1985). Membership includes subscriptions to two journals, a membership directory, and discounts on monographs and registration fees. *Annals of Behavioral Medicine*, a review journal, and *Behavioral Medicine Abstracts* represent the journals published by the organization.

SOCIETY FOR RESEARCH IN CHILD DEVELOPMENT

Since its founding in 1933, the Society for Research in Child Development has functioned to support and advance research in the scientific study of child development. There are approximately 4,000 members who are actively engaged in research or otherwise supporting the purposes of the organization.

The society is governed by a council of 13 members. These include four officers—president, president-elect, past president, and secretary; six elected members; and three members appointed by the council. Length of term is staggered and varied among the council members.

Membership fees are $75 per year (1985). A student membership is available for up to 5 years for $35 a year, and includes reduced costs for other services as well. Members over 65 who have belonged to the society for at least 15 years are eligible for emeritus status at no cost.

Three journals are published by the society. These are *Child Development, Child Development Abstracts and Bibliography*, and *Monographs of the Society for Research in Child Development*. In addition, there is a newsletter, a membership directory, and a review series. Conferences are also held.

INTERNATIONAL ORGANIZATIONS

The International Association of Applied Psychology (IAAP)

The largest international psychology organization, the International Association of Applied Psychology (IAAP) has 90 countries represented among its membership. Founded over 60 years ago (1920), its objective is to increase communication among the world's psychologists. In serving psychologists both in and out of academia, the IAAP strives to put psychologists in touch with one another so that they can share findings and views and avoid duplication of work. The officers include a president, vice president, past president, and general secretary-treasurer. There are currently seven divisions which provide newsletters, activities, and networks of contracts for psychologists doing applied research. The divisions are as follows: Organizational Psychology; Psychology and National Development; Psychological Assessment; Environmental Psychology; Educational, Instructional, and School Psychology; Clinical and Community Psychology; and Applied Gerontology.

There are two types of membership in the IAAP. Full members must be members of a national psychological society (dues are $25.00). The criteria for associate membership include a degree that contains a substantial proportion of psychology and employment in psychological work (dues are $23.50). The dues include a subscription to the IAAP publication, *International Review of Applied Psychology*, which is published in English and French. The *Review* devotes whole issues to particular topics. The association also organizes regular international conferences; members are given cost-saving discounts to make it easier to attend the meetings. The IAAP is considering developing a computer databank that will contain information about members, new research, and previous publications.

International Society for Developmental Psychobiology

In 1967, the International Society for Developmental Psychobiology was begun to promote "research into the relationship between behavioral and biological aspects of the developing organism at all levels of organization" (International Society for Psychobiology, 1986). The society has been associated with the AAAS and the Society for Neuroscience and is now a member of the Federation of the Behavioral, Psychological and Cognitive Sciences. There are nearly 300 members in this organization; its primary function is to provide a forum for sharing research through an annual convention and also by publishing a journal, *Developmental Psychobiology*. The officers in the society include a president, secretary/treasurer, past president, president-elect, program coordinator, representative to the federation, and three board members.

In order to be a member, an advanced degree (PhD, EdD, MD) is required as well as at least two publications on topics related to psychobiology. Students engaged in this line of research are also eligible for membership. Dues are $37 annually and include subscription to the society's journal and membership in the Federation of Behavioral, Cognitive and Psychological Sciences. Also published are a newsletter, membership directory, and a program and proceedings of the annual meeting.

SHARE

A program of hospitality for psychologists who travel internationally, SHARE (Sharing Home and Round the World Experience) is co-sponsored and co-financed by ten international and national psychological societies. Formed in 1973, they provide lists of registered hosts in countries where psychologists plan to travel. There are more than 200 such registered hosts on all continents who are interested in promoting professional and cultural exchange. These lists are available to members of co-sponsoring organizations, that is, the International Association of Applied Psychology, the Internation Council of Psychologists, the Inter-American Society of Psychology, the National Association of School Psychologists, and the APA Divisions of School Psychology and APA Division of Humanistic Psychology. SHARE advances psychology by providing opportunities for members to make contacts in the course of international travel with colleagues of similar psychological interests. Some psychologists offer visits or tours of local facilities; others offer one-night home stays.

TRAINING PROGRAM
ASSOCIATIONS

Council of Graduate Departments of Psychology (COGDOP)

The Council of Graduate Departments of Psychology is an association of chairs of departments of psychology or their equivalents (e.g., departments or schools with a current APA-accredited program). Their objectives include (a) the promotion of the development of psychology by providing forums for discussion of education, training, and research; and (b) establishment of a mechanism to interact with and make recommendations to various levels of APA governance and central office operations, government agencies, foundations, and other organizations. The executive board consists of six elected representatives. Their annual meeting is scheduled for the winter, and a second meeting is scheduled annually concurrent with the APA convention.

Specialty Training Councils

There are three councils representing the psychology specialties of clinical (Council of University Directors of Clinical Psychology), counseling (Council of Counseling Psychology Training Programs), and school (Council of Directors of School Psychology Programs). The program representative for each of the councils is the director/chair/coordinator. Their annual meetings are usually held at the same time as the APA convention. In addition, a mid-winter meeting is scheduled; at this time the three councils may also hold meetings together with APA staff and interact around common issues.

SOME ISSUES

Do Organizations Matter?

The value of organizations to their respective professions as well as individual members has been both prized as well as maligned by professionals. Certainly, the opportunities organizational membership presents for professional and personal exchange seem to be an obvious advantage; in current jargon they stimulate "networking" experiences. Such regular interactions with one's colleagues can be valuable in terms of professional rejuvenation. Sharing of ideas, both in formal and informal contexts, should take place at the meetings/conventions of the associations. The newsletters and journals of the organization also provide information regarding current developments in the specialities of the profession. At the same time, many of the guild responsibilities are more than the self-protectionism some would argue. Promotion of scientific, educational, and applied standards facilitates the integrity of the profession, while contributing to its evolution. However, association activities require monetary resources that are primarily derived from membership dues; thus, the individual professional interested in such goals becomes obliged to join the organization.

Organizations do engage in a variety of activities, particularly the larger their constituencies become. The professional, therefore, needs to assess what the organization does for the profession and not simply the direct benefit that is received. If the conclusion is that the profession requires representation, membership is not an unreasonable obligation.

Often, the letters-to-the-editor sections of organization newsletters contain public notice of individuals who have terminated their membership because of a particular action or lack of responsiveness of the organization to an issue. Organizations, like our society, must serve a pluralistic membership. The APA is one such example wherein various specialties are represented; also, given its size, members of various political persuasions can be found. It would seem then, that single-issue decisions cannot fairly be used as the criterion for a decision to terminate membership in an organization.

Aside from the general question of organizational membership, some choices obviously need to be made among a plethora of association options. National versus regional and/or state choices sometimes represent the most obvious competing interests. Where issues can take on dimensions unique to a state, then a powerful state organization is obviously necessary. A national group can be a valuable, formidable ally in that example, and serve as a buffer to prevent a parochial view from dominating an issue. On the other hand, national associations' resources may truly never be expected to be matched by states, particularly the small states, in population numbers. Likewise, the national organization can forge a unity among the professionals while serving to eliminate the waste of time, money, and energy accompanying activities that "reinvent the wheel." Yet, if more federal power (and decision making) is shifted to the states in the coming years, then a different alignment of state organizations to national organizations may have to evolve.

The generic versus specialty issue (see chapter 1) is reflected in this question as well. Should psychologists judge the organization by what it does for his/her specialty, or even whether it deals with applied versus scientific concerns? On the other hand, are the two so intertwined that efforts done on behalf of one automatically and inevitably benefit the other? Are the needs and priorities of each camp better served by their own group? Must there be one overarching organization? In fact, these questions and others are currently being faced by the APA. Witness the efforts to experiment with two houses of the APA's Council of Representatives as one example.

Another concern that has been voiced by some is that organizations have become closed groups, run by the same people (organizational "groupies") who are inaccessible except where their agendas are concerned. The larger the organization, and the more limited one's mentorship in relation to professional organizations, the greater the likelihood of such alienation developing. Ironically, organizations subsist on volunteer help, and very often bemoan the reality of the low percentage of the membership that expresses interest in becoming involved at the committee level. Generally speaking, degree of involvement is limited only by the member's interest and time commitment.

Arguments also abound that organizations can become out of touch with the membership and therefore preoccupied with the goal of self-perpetuation. While such concerns are possible, the solution is all too obvious for that situation to exist over a long period of time. More likely it is the frustration over the slowness with which some organizations respond that is behind such a charge. While a legitimate issue, the potential for sound policy to develop under considered review, insulated from the Zeitgeist, may be the most important service that an organization can offer a profession.

SUGGESTED READINGS

Because there is no U.S. center for recording information about associations, two directories must be utilized. The *Encyclopedia of Associations* (Akey, 1983) categorizes associations under 17 headings ranging from trade, business, and commercial associations to Greek-letter organizations. Available in most libraries, 18 items of information are noted regarding the associations, including address, phone number, purpose, number of members, and so on. Similarly, the *National Trade and Professional Associations of the United States* (Colgate, 1983) provides a comparable range of information. In addition, the latter publication presents a useful introduction on the evaluation and purposes of associations, particularly their role in lobbying and promotion of political action committees.

McClellan (1985) has written a historical account of scientific societies in the 18th century, a time when such societies grew exponentially and were quite significant until the French revolutionary era. The author gives a brief review of the history of all of the major societies and many smaller ones. He also covers the organization, publications, sources of support, and so on. In addition, a substantial bibliography is provided.

One of the more recent views of APA status as an organization was written by two of its central staff (Kilburg & Pallak, 1978). The role of the administrative officer in the APA Central Office is discussed by Zaro and Kilburg (1984). In addition to presenting the ups and downs of those positions, advice is presented on how to prepare for and secure this type of position.

For those interested in policy advocacy and the legislative process, the 1983 November issue (Volume 38, Number 11) of the *American Psychologist* contains five articles dealing with various aspects of that experience (pp. 1206–1231).

State associations would seem to have an important role in the promotion of ethics and standards, particularly when it comes to serving as a resource to the profession (Pryzwansky & Wenger, 1979).

Through surveying 319 psychotherapists in three different associations—APA Division 29 (Psychotherapy), APA Division 32 (Humanistic), and the AABT—Norcross and Wogan (1983) compared psychologists along the dimensions of personal characteristics, types of training, professional activities, and theoretical issues. In most areas there were differences between psychologists in different associations. One conclusion of the article is that there is no single organization that represents psychologists engaged in psychotherapy.

Tryon (1983) reports the results of a survey of private practitioners asked to list the journals they found most useful. The author rank ordered the responses (113 different journals were mentioned by 139 practitioners) of the top 10 journals used. Even the most popular, *American Psychologist*, was listed by only 29% of the respondents. The article provides information on the types of commonly used journals and their readers. As many of the journals are published by professional organizations, this article may be relevant to anyone wanting to know more about the organizations.

Pros and cons of the APA's advocacy role are presented and examples of APA advocacy positions are discussed in a recent article by Robinson (1984). Robinson argues from a philosophical viewpoint that advocacy positions have not been ethically sound. This article is somewhat esoteric and geared to professionals interested in philosophical issues in organizations.

Box 6.1. Professional Organizations

Addresses	Phone
American Psychoanalytic Association 1 East 57th Street New York, NY 10022	(212) 752-0450
American Psychological Association 1200 Seventeenth Street, N.W. Washington, DC 20036	(202) 955-7600
American Psychological Foundation 1200 Seventeenth Street, N.W. Washington, DC 20036	
Association for Advancement of Behavior Therapy 15 West 36th Street New York, NY 10018	(212) 682-0065
Association for the Advancement of Psychology Suite 200 1200 Seventeenth Street, N.W. Washington, DC 20036	(202) 466-5757
Association for Behavior Analysis Department of Psychology Western Michigan University Kalamazoo, MI 49008	(616) 383-1629

Box 6.1. Continued

The Association of Black Psychologists
P.O. Box 2929
Washington, DC 20013   (202) 289-3663

The British Psychological Society
St. Andrews House
48 Princess Road East
Leicester, England LEI 7DR

Canadian Psychological Association
558 King Edward Avenue
Ottawa, Ontario KIN 7N6
Canada

Human Factors Society
Box 1369
Santa Monica, CA 90406   (213) 394-1811

The International Association of Applied
    Psychology
Applications can be solicited from:
Dr. Peter Werssenberg
Faculty of Business Studies
Rutgers University
Camden, NJ 08102
        or
Prof. dr. Ch. J. de Wolff
Psychology Laboratory
Montessorilaan 3
6500 HE Nijmegen
HOLLAND

International Society for Developmental Psychobiology
(Contact JoAnne Weinberg)
Department of Anatomy
University of British Columbia
Vancouver, British Columbia
Canada V6T 1W5   (303) 394-7212

Psychonomic Society
Psychology Department
University of Minnesota
Minneapolis, MN 55455   (612) 373-3430

                                                        (*continued*)

PAAP-K

Box 6.1. Continued

SHARE Chairperson
Janell Holle
4217 Whitsett Avenue #1
Studio City, CA 91604

Society of Behavioral Medicine
P.O. Box 8530
University Station
Knoxville, TN 37996   (615) 974-5164

Society for Research in Child Development
Institute of Human Development
Tolman Hall
University of California
Berkeley, CA 94720   (415) 642-6401

REFERENCES

Akey, D. S. (Ed.). (1983). *Encyclopedia of associations* (17th ed., Vols. 1–2). Detroit, MI: Gale Research Company.

American Psychological Association. (1984). *The American Psychological Association*. Washington, DC: Author.

American Psychological Association. (1986a). *Bylaws of the American Psychological Association*. Washington, DC: Author.

American Psychological Association. (1986b). Five-year report of the policy and planning board: 1985. *American Psychologist, 41*, 626–632.

Association for Advancement of Behavior Therapy. (1984). By-laws of the Association for Advancement of Behavior Therapy. *1984 Membership Directory*. New York: Author.

Association for Behavior Analysis. (1985). *Eleventh annual convention program*. Kalamazoo, MI: Author.

British Psychological Association. *General information*. Leicester, England: Author.

Colgate, C., Jr. (Ed.). (1983). *National trade and professional associations of the U.S.* (18th annual ed.). Washington, DC: Columbia Books, Inc.

Human Factors Society. (1985). *The Human Factors Society should be your professional society*. Santa Monica, CA: Author.

International Society for Developmental Psychology. (1986). *Application for membership*. Denver, CO: Author.

Kilburg, R. R., & Pallak, M. S. (1978). A professional's guide to the American Psychological Association. In B. D. Sales (Ed.), *The professional psychologist's handbook* (pp. 157–184). New York: Plenum Press.

McClellan, III, J. E. (1985). *Science reorganized: Scientific societies in the eighteenth century*. New York: Columbia University Press.

Moore, W. E. (1970). *The Professions: Roles and rules*. New York: Russell Sage Foundation.

Norcross, J. C., & Wogan, M. (1983). American psychotherapists of diverse persuasions: Characteristics, theories, practices, and clients. *Professional Psychology: Research and Practice, 14*, 529–539.

Pryzwansky, W. B., & Wenger, R. D. (1979). The role of state school psychology organizations in the promotion of professional ethics. *Psychology in the Schools, 16*, 540–543.

Robinson, D. N. (1984). Ethics and advocacy. *American Psychologist, 39*, 787–793.

The Psychonomic Society. (1982). *By-laws of the Psychonomic Society, Inc.* El Paso, TX: Author.

Tryon, G. S. (1983). Professional publications of most use to full-time private practitioners. *Professional Psychology: Research and Practice, 14*, 549–553.

Voorde, C. (1986). Association for the advancement of psychology. *American Psychologist, 41*, 709–711.

Zaro, J. S., & Kilburg, R. R. (1984). Managing the business of psychology: Administrative officers at the APA Central Office. *Professional Psychology: Research and Practice, 15*, 723–729.

Chapter 7
New Horizons

This chapter deals with several emerging trends in the professional area that the practitioner should note. These trends are evolving from both inside and outside the profession. Three trends involve issues within the applied arm of psychology. In the first instance, the discussion really involves professional emphasis rather than any conflict. Many psychologists, for personal and professional reasons, feel that the profession should be active in influencing public policy, shaping legislation, and generally displaying a more active community orientation. Increasingly, then, the perspective of psychologists is broadening, as evidenced by the desire to have an impact on social and public policy. Also, attention is being directed to the need to provide a support system for psychologists as they face personal problems. This development is briefly discussed. The third internal issue is potentially more serious in terms of its affecting the field in a dramatic fashion. A current proposal for reorganization of the APA reflects the fact that psychology is at a crossroads in its history, similar to the one it faced in the early 1900s. The outcome could influence the profession in a most dramatic way.

At the same time, external developments also have begun to affect professional practice in potentially significant ways. Computer technology holds a great deal of promise for improving the efficiency, if not effectiveness, of practice. However, given the computer field's current stage of development, considerable concern about a number of professional issues have begun to surface in the literature. Similarly, as practice trends are often shaped by the legislature and economic considerations, the service delivery model is slowly being reorganized. The trends in the insurance industry appear to be moving psychology toward group practices such as health maintenance organizations. Finally, the impact of current employment trends is discussed in relationship to future needs.

PUBLIC POLICY

Psychology as a profession still remains largely unknown to the general public. For example, less than 25% of the American public can distinguish between a psychologist and a psychiatrist just in terms of the former holding a PhD and the latter an MD (Yankelovich, Skelly, & White, 1980). From approximately the same time as that report was made (1980), psychology has moved increasingly in the direction of shaping public policy.

This trend has stemmed interestingly from two divergent viewpoints. The first is related directly to guild issues facing the profession. If, indeed, psychologists remain unknown to the general public, then insurance carriers, the local, state, and federal agencies that maintain service delivery, and elected officials will form policies that may inhibit the practice of professional psychologists. Therefore, public policy advocacy or political activism are vital to the growth of psychological practice. While applied interests have become distinct within the profession, outside the discipline a number of steps have been taken toward professionalism. A specialized body of knowledge has been defined, training programs established, and legal recognition and skills in this form of licensure/certification laws secured.

The opposite viewpoint has been a result of a number of professional psychologists' belief that the profession has moved too far in pursuing guild issues. In practice, this concern might include overcharging of clients, using professional associates to eliminate competition, perpetuating inequitable social situations for clients, and generally placing their own welfare ahead of those clients and society as a whole. Essentially, as the profession matures, so does the weight of professional responsibility.

Social Perspective

The public policy movement within the psychology profession is also, for the most part, not consistent with the background and training of psychologists. To view individuals' psychological problems from a preventive context contrasts with the emphasis of some psychology training programs. This section will discuss public policy first from a political and professional organization format, and second from a political activism and practical perspective for the practicing psychologist.

In 1974, the Association for the Advancement of Psychology was incorporated as a national lobbying organization. Its purpose was to:

> Promote human welfare through the advancement of the science and profession of psychology by the promotion of the interest of all psychology; by

the representation of psychology before public and governmental bodies, by seeking out and contributing to the passage of important social and psychological issues in current legislation and to advocate to the legislature, judicial, executive branches of government the ethical and scientific views of the American psychological community. (Association for the Advancement of Psychology, 1977, p. 1)

Additionally, at the state level, most psychological associations have organized committees, task forces, and communication networks, which have proven effective in influencing legislation and administrative policies at the state level.

At the national level, psychologists have visibly contributed to public policy through participation in various national advising commissions. Additionally, there are four Bush Policy Centers, and several other centers attached to academic institutions, which have generated policy. By and large, these efforts, while extensive, have gone largely unrecognized by the public as well as the "reward" system within the profession.

A number of divisions within the APA have sporadically dealt with political policy issues, but usually on a crisis basis. Efforts in terms of systematic or active involvement are limited by change in elected officials, geographical distance, limited meetings, and fiscal resources. The APA Division of Health Psychology (Division 38) probably has, at least more recently, been the most active in federal policymaking.

The commitment of the American Psychological Association in the last decade toward public policy formation has been extensive. The *American Psychologist* has devoted sections to the shaping of public policy in such areas as child and adolescent health services, gerontology, AIDS, and numerous areas of health psychology. In response to the recent increase in insurance rates, public policy advocacy for applied psychology will increase significantly; it is hoped that the result will be greater visibility for the profession and changes for the betterment of society.

Implication For the Psychologist

The practicing psychologist with a public interest should find a diversity of activities that are more wide-ranging and far-reaching than in traditional practice. During the 1960s and 1970s, psychologists tended to respond to changing social needs by developing new techniques (e.g., drug counseling, emergency hotlines), by modifying old ones (e.g., nonbiased testing), and learning the culture and language of new and neglected client groups (Simon, 1983). As a result, psychologists with a patient advocacy viewpoint developed practices that met the needs of clients within a social context rather than rigidly adhering to prior training and traditional values of practice.

Essentially, psychologists are already seeing the need to function as client advocates, based upon a commitment to service. As a result, the psychologists in these situations shift from a traditional role to a social role. This shift entails working with clients when necessary at a very practical level, for example, in assisting the client in dealing with the social bureaucracy in terms of a complaint or hearing. This role also calls for active participation in social reforms on a community level. From a conceptual point of view, social action can be seen as a means of reducing psychological problems through the application of professional skills to community problems. Increasingly, psychologists, as another example, are serving on local mental health or other social policymaking boards. From even another point of view, psychologists, consistent with the Ethical Principles of Psychologists (APA, 1981) which clearly specifies that psychologists may willingly contribute a portion of their work with little or no financial return, provide some services without fee to individuals or social causes. It is essentially this provision that distinguishes psychology as a humanitarian profession (Goode, 1960).

Another perspective involving benefits to the practitioner is that the action of involving oneself as a professional in large arenas in everyday practice is an excellent method for battling burnout. Burnout, in effect, leaves the professional feeling uncaring, cynical, and sometimes angry, leading toward an indifferent feeling about work. Too much of one thing, such as endless hours of therapy, leads to an emotional drain which affects many professionals. Maslach (1976) described the need to limit contact hours and make use of "time outs" where other activities can be substituted. Support groups and physical exercise are also very helpful. While not an answer for this problem, involvement in national, state, and local causes, through professional associations or otherwise, helps the practitioner retain a sense of perspective and balance.

SUPPORT FOR DISTRESSED PSYCHOLOGISTS

Every profession, just as every segment of our society, has individuals who undergo stress that results in mental health or personal problems and that will significantly interfere with their capacity to offer quality services. The types of problems most often cited involve alcoholism, drug related problems, job burnout, and sexual misconduct. The psychology profession, ironically, seems to lag behind other professions in offering an organized support system for dealing with these problems to its members (Nathan, Thoreson, & Kilburg, 1983). In 1981, the APA Board of Professional Affairs appointed a committee to examine the history of and current needs caused by these stress-related problems, in order to formulate a proposal suggesting ways in which an organization could approach the professional-in-distress with some assistance. As part of that effort, the APA will be publishing an edited book on this topic to educate the field and public on the various aspects of stress-related problems.

To provide additional support, colleagues and families could also be provided with information on ways of dealing with professions who manifest a need for help in this area. Information is needed to assist in training those individuals who might be involved in helping and managing the problems. In general, however, there is no current national support system and few programs on the state level for psychologists displaying such stress-related syndromes. An international program, entitled "Psychologists Helping Psychologists" (Turkington, 1986), does systematically address this issue.

THE REORGANIZATION OF AMERICAN PSYCHOLOGY

As was briefly mentioned in chapter 6, the APA is in the throes of a soul-searching mission to maintain the scientist and practitioner interests within a single organization. It has been pointed out that not only are the proportions of psychologists being trained in traditional academic/research subfields decreasing, but smaller proportions of these individuals are joining the APA and state psychological associations. Of equal concern is the fact that larger proportions are leaving the APA (APA, 1985). In 1985, the APA also reported that the picture is better in the applied areas, where clinical (71%), industrial/organizational (66%), and school psychology (50%) 1981 graduates still become APA members. If psychology's dual stance as a profession and a science is being compromised and these trends continue, "psychology's future standing as a science is in jeopardy" (APA, 1985, p. iii). Some would claim that the outcome of those deliberations could have a dramatic impact on the discipline and its professional arm in particular. The long-term effects of a separation are unknown, and whether each could survive without the other is debatable; and perhaps more critical than the survival query is the health of each area of emphasis without the other. The science of psychology certainly benefits from a strong positive opinion from the public, which is influenced in large measure by direct contact with the practitioner. By comparison, the profession itself relies on the credibility of its scientific foundation and the relationship with its basic science.

It has been argued by some that for all practical purposes, the split between scientist and practitioner has occurred. In fact, scientists would seem to have multiple "vendor" organizations serving their needs, as reflected in the professional organizations chapter (chapter 6) of this book. Those organizations, and others like the American Educational Research Organization, cater to the specific research interests of psychologists, and offer relatively small forums for the sharing of research data, a priority for this group. The professional psychologist would seem to have fewer options in terms of vendors (the state organization excluded) and requires a single organization that can provide vigorous leadership and responsiveness to political and legal developments. Professionals, therefore, seek a power broker or advocate for their interests, while researchers are interested in the promotion of scientific endeavors.

The APA Task Force on the Structure of APA is currently (May 1986) proposing a reorganizational structure involving two assemblies. One assembly will represent *scientific and academic psychology*, while the other will represent *psychologists in health and human services*. The basis of this suggestion represents a model that strives to serve the complexity of interests in the APA in a unified manner while retaining the uniqueness of the constituencies within the organization. The task force has examined the "identity" thrust of both the practitioner and scientist in terms of the matrix presented in Figure 7.1. This figure reflects the goal of the basic science adherents, which is promotion of knowledge. It is often because of those discoveries that a public policy will result. For example, in the medical area, the discovery of the cause of an affliction is likely to lead to a policy for inoculation. Yet knowledge remains the primary objective of the scientist, rather than the alleviation of physical, societal, or psychological problems. By contrast, the professional is interested in providing the best service (practice) for a problem, based on an incomplete database. The professional seeks relevant data through applied research undertakings that can have an impact on the effectiveness of practice. In essence, the applied research–practice continuum represents the Boulder model of training, that is, the scientist-practitioner. At the

Figure 7.1. The relationship of science to practice.

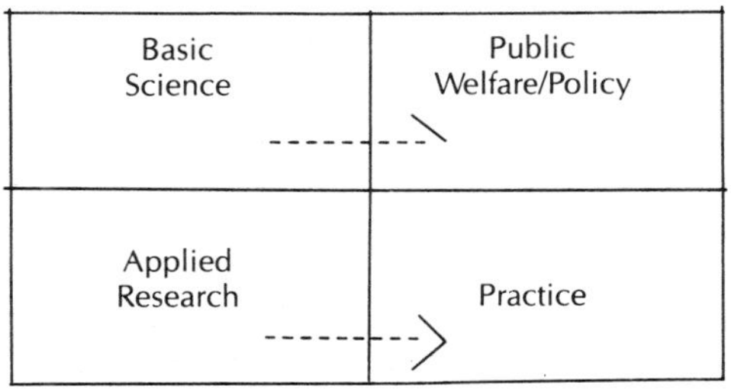

same time, the professional is interested in basic research, in terms of how it can influence applied research, relate to practice, and influence public policy. Clearly, the scientist wants to be separated from practice, in terms of goals and priorities, while the professional seeks to promote applied research and public policy, while looking to basic science as its foundation in the way a physician looks to chemistry, with immunology serving as an applied research arm.

Although the proposal is for a reorganization of the APA into two separate, incorporated assemblies, the APA will continue as an umbrella organization, with APA-wide boards and committees and a board of trustees. The proposal plan is now under discussion by various groups within the APA. If it were to be eventually accepted in its proposed or modified form, there will undoubtedly be several years of transition.

COMPUTER TECHNOLOGY

Developments in the computer industry have been explosive over the last decade. This phenomenon is due mainly to the development of the microchip, which integrates a rapidly growing number of components onto a single circuit. In terms of psychology, an initial application has involved the use of computers for psychological assessment (Schwartz, 1984). The computers offer, through on-line administration, the advantage of accurate scoring and immediate feedback via test graphics and printed reports. The superior computation and organizational power of computers can offer exciting possibilities for psychological practice. Indeed, computers will continue to expand in terms of capabilities and the complexity of systems.

Computers also offer the potential for improving clinical decisions. However, Young (1982) points out this may well be perceived as a threat to the exercise of clinical judgments by psychologists which, in turn, can produce counter-resistance on the part of clinicians.

Currently, there are approximately seven companies marketing computer hardware and software related to psychological testing. The following paper and pencil tests are available for computer use (Ryabik, Olson, & Klein, 1984, p. 31):

1. Minnesota Multiphasic Personality Inventory
2. Million Clinical Multiaxial Inventory
3. Strong-Campbell Interest Inventory
4. Kent Infant Development Scale
5. Otis Intelligence Test
6. Wahlen Physical Symptoms Inventory
7. Quick Word Test

8. Test of Abstract Concept Learning
9. Taylor-Johnson Temperament Analysis
10. Shipley Institute of Living Scale
11. Psychotic Inpatient Profile
12. Sixteen Personality Factors Inventory
13. Edward Personal Preference Schedule
14. Rorschach
15. Beck Depression and Hopelessness Scale
16. Lauria Neuropsychological Test Battery

This list is only a partial compilation of assessment programs, with new programs, such as the Wechsler Scales for Children and Adults, being developed continually by major companies. A major concern has developed relative to the ethical and legal issues presented by the above programs in the literature (Matzarro, 1983, 1986; Ryabik, Olson, & Klein, 1984). Several states, notably Colorado, Kansas, and Ohio, among others, have developed guidelines for implementing their use in practice. Within the APA, the Committee on Professional Standards (COPS) and the Committee on Psychological Tests and Assessment (CPTA) have jointly developed a draft of *Guidelines for Computer-Based Tests and Interpretation* (APA, 1986). These guidelines are designed to assist psychologists in applying computer-based assessments competently and in the best interests of clients. They are also designed to aid test developers in establishing and maintaining the quality of the new product. This document has gone through a number of drafts, with the January 1986 publication the most recent at this writing. Numerous issues and concerns are addressed through the principles, some of which involve the responsibility, competence, and careful monitoring of the assessment. The issues for developers underscore the need for psychometric properties of the program to meet basic standards for tests. Additionally, the issue of validity of interpretation and classification is discussed. It appears these statements are still in guideline form and probably subject to further revision.

In particular, Matzarro (1986) is concerned about the thousands of untrained physicians (and psychologists) who have purchased microcomputer interpretations of psychological tests. He points out that the use of such interpretations is quite different from the broader process of psychological assessment. Additionally, he warns that computerized testing can lead to impersonal testing in contrast to mature psychological assessment. Two consequences are foreseen: (a) third-party payers will deny payment for services for computerized tests unless these tests' responsible clinical use can be documented; and (b) considerable embarrassment can ensue for the profession when such results are the sole basis for courtroom testimony. The need for professionals' appropriate training in psychological assessment, as a basic foundation before the use of computer programs is implemented, cannot be emphasized strongly enough.

This conclusion is especially true when dealing with "canned" or automated psychological interpretations of test results. Most programs yield a single lengthy clinical narrative which takes the appearance of being "valid." Butcher (1978), relative to the MMPI computer analysis system, has pointed out that the clinical reports are not a substitute for clinical judgment as they fail to take into account other demographic data. Additionally, he feels the system is often not updated, and as yet, the validity of the narrative has not been updated. For the MMPI, Green (1982) cautions the use of automated scoring services. Based on his analysis, Green (1982) feels that the computer clinical interpretations of the MMPI have improved considerably; however, he still recommends caution regarding most such services.

While computers offer fast decision making, graphics, and report writing, they also can improve the efficiency of psychological testing. However, Skinner and Pakula (1986) raise a number of professional questions relative to computer assessment beyond the psychometric and reporting issues. For instance, what about client impact, and what types of clients will respond to a computerized assessment? What about staff acceptance, a problem that has developed in medical settings? Computers must provide rapid computation and can be helpful in many clinical judgments, especially concerning diagnosis and treatment planning. However, computerized programs are only as good as the validity of the instrument utilized.

From a positive perspective, Reynolds, McNamara, Marion, and Tobin (1985) have pointed out a number of uses of computers for psychologists. They have found that computer techniques are especially helpful in physiological monitoring, biofeedback, interviewing and history taking, assisting in diagnosis through assessment, and with self-help programs. It seems that the use of computers and software is still in the infancy stage; in the meantime, there is considerable concern about ethical and legal issues. Psychologists should be aware they are legally responsible for any computerized testing done with their clients. Knowledge about the validity of the program, assessment procedures in general, coupled with discretion in the selection and use of programs are important points for consideration. Despite the concerns expressed, it is generally believed that most of the problems can be overcome through research and that this tool holds exciting possibilities for the profession.

CHANGES IN SERVICE DELIVERY

The idea of marketing services, responding to consumer need while appealing to business and industry, has become a recent and important phenomenon for psychologists to address. Changes in government funding of health care and the increasing role of industry and business in alternative health care programs are already affecting service delivery of mental health professionals. Not only must all mental health professionals reconsider their traditional forms of service delivery, but psychologists also need to create markets for their specialized services, distinct from psychiatry or social work.

Traditionally, psychologists and other mental health professionals have provided clinical services to their clients in a fee-for-service model. Services have been paid for either by the client, insurance companies, or government resources. Within such a model, the individual practitioner has usually functioned autonomously as a "cottage industry." Clients were secured through the practitioner's establishment of a referral network and his or her reputation of responsibility and competence. Few constraints threatened the independence of the psychologist. Clients were free to choose the professional they wished, and some reimbursement was provided by insurance companies to licensed professionals. Fees were competitive and largely dictated by what the market would bear, that is, what the consumer was willing to pay and the limits of reimbursement from third-party reimbursers. At the same time, there were few, if any, mechanisms in place to monitor the quality of professional service to the consumer. Until recently, this model has been accepted as the modus operandi of practice. While some professionals may be able to continue service delivery as an independent practitioner under such a model, it is no longer feasible for psychologists to assume that this model of service delivery will be the most viable one for themselves personally, or for the profession in general.

As the philosophy and priorities of government funding have changed and the federal deficit has become of paramount concern, health care delivery has been influenced in significant ways. Health care costs in the United States have grown dramatically in the last 10 years and now account for over 11% of the gross national product (Uyeda & Moldawsky, 1986). Both the public at large and the government appear to be concerned about the rising costs.

At the same time that government and the public are looking for ways to reduce health care costs, other demographic changes are taking place that also affect the profession economically. The number of physicians and mental health professionals is growing, and an oversupply of providers is anticipated in the near future. Thus, a supply and demand issue is emerging.

While many psychologists may be resistant to change in how they manage their practice economically (as well as being naive and uninterested in business management), it is becoming crucial that psychologists become aware of and respond to the economic changes that are currently taking place in the health care industry. In response to these needs, the APA's Board of Professional Affairs began to address service delivery issues in a 1982 symposium (Kilburg, 1982). As a next step, the Task Force on Marketing and Promotion of Psychological Services (TF–MAPPS) was established to educate psychologists about the marketplace trends and to motivate them to shape and participate in the evolving changes. Many alternatives for practice may be available in the future for the psychologist, including the fee-for-service model, yet it behooves psychologists to be aware of the overall shifts in control of the health care system from the provider to government, business, and industry.

In an attempt to levy more control over health care spending, the government has put into place a significant change in funding acute hospital care for Medicare patients. The traditional fee-for-service model is no longer applicable; rather than services being paid on a retrospective system, they are now paid on a prospective payment system. Total reimbursement is therefore determined before the service is rendered rather than after service delivery. Fees are based on a list of 467 diagnosis-related groups; this plan is referred to as DRG. Patients are grouped by what organ is involved in the treatment (e.g., cardiac arrest, viral meningitis), and payment is based on the average cost of such treatment in the past. The intent of this model is to provide incentives for increasing efficiency by making providers more cost conscious.

While DRGs are presently not applied to most mental health services, there is doubt that this exemption will continue indefinitely (Binner, 1986). Some may argue, still, that DRGs only affect Medicare patients and therefore have little relation to their practice. Medicaid, Blue Cross/Blue Shield, and other private plans, however, tend to model their coverage and reimbursement structure on Medicare policy (Uyeda & Moldawsky, 1986). The impact of the DRG for the health care professional, therefore, cannot be ignored.

In addition to DRGs affecting the health care system, other delivery system changes have appeared in the private sector. These systems include health maintenance organizations (HMOs) and preferred provider organizations (PPOs).

Health maintenance organizations have been in existence for over 50 years, but have only recently become popular. An HMO functions as a prepaid model so that people know their health care expenses in advance. The patients pay one set fee and, in return, are eligible to receive all services that are covered by their particular HMO. There are three types of HMOs: staff, group, and individual practice association (IPA). In the *staff/group* models, providers of professional services contract with the HMO to provide care. Usually, there is a central facility for the *staff* model; overhead is paid by the HMO and providers are salaried employees. In the group practice model, a provider group contracts with the HMO for prepaid service delivery. By contrast, independent practice associations are made up of individual providers who work out of their own offices and set aside a percentage of their practice to see HMO patients. When working for an HMO, IPA providers are not paid by the number of patients seen or the types of services provided. It is interesting to note that federally controlled HMOs limit mental health services to 20 visits per patient.

Another alternative health care service that is growing in popularity is the preferred provider organization (PPO). The PPO is a limited group of practitioners who provide service to a specific community. Fees are negotiated by a fee schedule or relative value system and are discounted. Consumers pay lower deductibles and insurance payments for PPO services, yet maintain the option to use non-PPO providers at higher costs. Services are extensively reviewed toward the aim of lowering health care costs in the long run. PPOs are usually administered by a board of directors. While the services cost less, the provider has patients, and claims are processed rapidly. The difference between HMOs and PPOs are that, for the latter, costs are reduced by discounting the fee for service. Health maintenance organizations are controlled by capitation, that is, fees and services are predetermined regardless of individual need or utilization.

For both HMOs and PPOs, there are many issues that could be potentially detrimental to psychology. The only mandated providers of HMOs are physicians, although psychologists are allowed to participate in an HMO. There are no federal laws and few state laws controlling PPOs and physicians may exclude psychologists. According to the Employee Retirement Income Security Act of 1974 (ERISA, 1974), HMOs, PPOs, and self-insured companies are all exempt from state controls. Thus, freedom of choice laws which require third party payers to reimburse for psychological services may not apply to HMOs and PPOs. Finally, some have questioned whether quality of service is also sacrificed in such service delivery models. Expensive but needed tests are not cost-effective, and thus may be discouraged. Mental health services may not reflect the individual's needs; either a patient may have to forego services or a provider may ethically have to continue services without compensation.

In addition to alternative service delivery models, the types of services being offered are also changing. Health care and mental health have become more integrated and lifestyle issues have been linked to physical health. For industry, the cost benefits of preventive care are becoming more visible. Employee assistance programs (EAPs) have been demonstrated both to have directly reduced health care costs and to have increased productivity. While there are many variations on how an EAP may operate, generally an EAP has an education and counseling component. Examples of the variety of programs offered are stress management, exploration of single parenting issues, and prevention of job burnout and alcoholism. Services may vary from large group lectures to individual counseling, with the goal of directing the individual to act and think in more productive, healthy ways (Goldman et al., 1984).

With the structure and power base of health care changing, the competition between mental health professionals growing, and the consumer responding to economic ramifications, psychologists need to be knowledgeable about these changes as well as more acutely aware of the need to develop marketing strategies and managerial acumen.

Marketing psychological services can follow the same general principles as the marketing of any product. The basic goal of a marketing strategy is to anticipate and satisfy the needs of the client, while at the same time meeting the goals of the provider. The provider needs to assess his/her own resources, as well as identify the clients he/she wishes to serve. Assessing resources is a comprehensive exercise which could include the social, political, economic, and legal climate, as well as examining personal and professional issues. Once the resources and appropriate populations have been identified, marketing variables commonly referred to as the four P's—product, place, promotion, and price—need to be examined. "Product" refers to defining what the client will get for the service. "Place" includes where the product will be available. The promotion strategy, the third "P," is how the client will be influenced to partake of the services. Primarily, in psychology, this task may be viewed as a means of educating the population about the service, and the strategies for achieving that objective may include networking, advertising, or public speaking. Finally, price must be considered, both in terms of financial costs and also emotional, social, and physical costs to the consumer.

As a final step in marketing, the process must be evaluated and flexible enough to be changed as needed. If psychology is to remain a viable profession, providing unique and needed services to society, then it must remain responsive to the needs of the society. Marketing is a tool by which the profession can remain economically viable as well as socially responsible. There are many advantages and disadvantages to the changing trends in health care and governmental policies; the professional psychologist must be informed of these changes so that the profession can influence future policy and contribute in the most effective way to the mental health needs of individuals.

EMPLOYMENT TRENDS IN PSYCHOLOGY

The number of doctorates in psychology in the early 1970s was soaring, according to APA studies on employment that have been conducted since 1981. At the same time, academic positions have decreased, with the consequence being that most doctoral graduates find employment in nonacademic settings (Stapp & Fulcher, 1982).

More recently, the number of doctoral recipients has leveled off and the employment market also has stabilized. Most graduates are able to find jobs related to their training and the percentage that find academic jobs has stopped declining.

Stapp, Fulcher, and Wicherski (1984) also report some interesting trends. First, the number of doctorates awarded to women has risen from 17.5% of total doctorates in 1960, to 23.5% in 1970 to 47.5% in 1983. An additional finding has been that women are more likely to be employed part-time; how this trend will affect employment patterns is open to question. Second, there has been a distinct change relative to a reduction of federal support for graduate programs. Predoctoral research training has been drastically reduced by the National Institutes of Health (NIH). As research funding has decreased, membership in the clinical psychology subfields (e.g., clinical, counseling) has continued to grow. It appears that research funding in particular may be a problem for the profession in the immediate future. Third, there does seem to be a change—graduate programs relative to applied research are being emphasized, in conjunction with career role preparation for nonacademic settings. The main issue for the profession is whether psychology can expand into new movements before the growth and demand for health care providers becomes saturated. Over 5,000 psychologists are licensed each year, which suggests we will have, most likely, 50,000 additional psychologists in the U.S. employment market in the next 10 years. While major shifts are unlikely in the next several years, it is hoped that training and graduate programs will allow for the expansion of the profession.

In order to expand, psychology must continually search the market to keep pace with the needs for society. Increasingly, for example, psychology has linked itself with Medicare through health psychology practice. Philosophically, this requires a shift in thinking toward body-mind relationships. Increasingly, psychologists have been involved in dealing with stress, behavioral actions in illness, and pain management techniques. Working in medical settings, they will perform psychological assessment and employ cognitive-behavioral treatment techniques.

The major point is the expansion of settings, populations, and techniques, illustrating the process by which psychology has adapted itself to the marketplace. As a profession, we have been able to sell ourselves as having a distinct product to offer people that is different from medicine.

Unfortunately, the proportion of women entering the academic/research areas has not grown; this fact is of more concern when it is noted that the number of males in these areas is declining. It may well be that employment needs and marketing linkages will propel psychology, especially in the next decade. Group practice, for example, like HMOs and PPOs, will support the individual practitioner. Greater diversity of practice (e.g., business and industry) will prevail. New programs and products for the consumer will emerge as psychology will continue to evolve in exciting directions.

SUMMARY

So, we have explored the promises and perils that are part of any prognostication. Is our glass half full or half empty? Certainly, when we look back at our development and achievements, it is only the pathological pessimist who would not see a bright future. It will undoubtedly be a future of changes, as all futures are, but it should offer expanded opportunities for psychology to make its impact.

SUGGESTED READINGS

Cummings (1986) has demonstrated, in a most provocative manner, that psychology must develop strategies responsive to the current cost-containment climate in health care delivery. He presents a model in which all schools of psychology and psychotherapy are blended into one practice offering "brief, intermittent" targeted therapy throughout the life cycle. He argues that this type of PPO will help psychologists to be in control of their own mental health delivery, offer quality services, and compete effectively with HMOs.

Turkin and Frank (1985) discuss the implications and professional compromises that psychologists face in an HMO setting. Working in any organization presents different issues from those in private practice, particularly where professional autonomy is involved, but these authors see unique opportunities as well. Liese's (1986) survey of physicians' perceptions of problems having the largest psychological component and what specialties should be consulted yields some interesting findings.

An introduction to marketing planning starts with the identification of the initial key steps that need to be made. Winston (1983) delineates 10 steps that should be considered in writing a marketing plan for a group practice.

Employment trends in psychology might best be reviewed through a series of articles in the *American Psychologist*. The reader is advised to begin with the Stapp et al. (1984) article (a survey of employment of doctoral recipients in psychology from 1981 through 1982). Stapp, Tucker, and VandenBos (1985) also provide an extremely comprehensive analysis of employment patterns within the field of psychology, including degree levels, employment status and settings, and professional activities.

Two recent articles dealing with the topic of computer technology provide excellent overviews for professional issues from contrasting points of view. Skinner and Pakula (1986) provide an overview of assessment issues within a cautionary and conservative framework. Reynolds et al. (1985) discuss in detail the positive and proven uses of computers in a broad range of clinical services. Additionally, both articles provide a comprehensive list of references for further reading and research.

Psychologists interested in the burnout issue, which was briefly mentioned in this chapter, should refer to the Farber and Heifetz (1982) study of burnout of psychotherapists. The article provides an interesting perspective on client load, personal issues, and methods for dealing with over-stress resulting from providing therapeutic services.

REFERENCES

American Psychological Association. (1981). Ethical principles of psychologists. *American Psychologist, 36*, 633–638.

American Psychological Association. (1985). *The changing face of psychology.* Committee on Employment. Washington, DC: Author.

American Psychological Association. (1986). *Guidelines for computer-based tests and interpretations.* Committee on Professional Standards and Committee on Psychological Tests and Assessment. Washington, DC: Author.

Association for the Advancement of Psychology. (1977). *Bylaws of the American Association for the Advancement of Psychology.* Washington, DC: Author.

Binner, P. R. (1986). DRG's and the administration of mental health services. *American Psychologist, 41*, 64–69.

Butcher, J. N. (1978). Automated MMPI interpretative systems. In O. K. Buros (Ed.), *Eighth mental measurements yearbook* (pp. 942–945). Highland Park, IL: Gryphon Press.

Cummings, N. A. (1986). The dismantling of our health care system. *American Psychologist, 41*, 426–431.

Employee Retirement Income Security Act of 1974. Pub. L. No. 93–406, 88 Stat. 829 (1974).

Farber, B. A., & Heifetz, L. J. (1982). The process and dimension of burnout in psychotherapists. *Professional Psychology, 13*, 293–301.

Goldman, R. L., Reyes, J. G., Young, G. T., Barsamian, S., Thomas, A., & Thuss, M. (1984). Marketing employer assistance programs to industry. In W. J. Winston (Ed.),

Marketing for mental health services (pp. 91–98). New York: Haworth Press.

Goode, W. J. (1960). Encroachment, charlatanism, and the emerging profession: Psychology, sociology, and medicine. *American Sociological Review, 25*, 902–914.

Green, C. J. (1982). The diagnostic accuracy and utility of MMPI and MCMI computer-interpretation reports. *Journal of Personality Assessment, 46*, 359–365.

Kilburg, R. R. (Chair). (1982, August). Marketing psychological services. Symposium conducted at the meeting of the American Psychological Association. *Ninetieth Annual Convention Program*, p. 135.

Liese, B. S. (1986). Physicians' perception of the role of psychology in medicine. *Professional Psychology: Research and Practice, 17*, 276–277.

Maslach, C. (1976). Burned-out. *Human Behavior, 7*, 16–22.

Matzarro, J. D. (1983). Computerized psychological testing. *Science, 221*, 323.

Matzarro, J. D. (1986). Computerized psychological test interpretations. *American Psychologist, 41*, 14–24.

Nathan, P., Thoreson, R., & Kilburg, R. (1983, November). *Board of Professional Affairs Steering Committee on distressed psychologists: Draft report.* Washington, DC: American Psychological Association.

Reynolds, R. V. C., McNamara, J. R., Marion, R. J., & Tobin, D. L. (1985). Computerized service delivery in clinical psychology. *Professional Psychology: Research and Practice, 16*, 339–353.

Ryabik, J., Olson, K. R., & Klein, D. M. (1984). Ethical issues in computerized psychological assessment. *Professional Practice of Psychology, 5*, 31–39.

Schwartz, M. D. (1984). *Using computers in clinical practice.* New York: Haworth Press.

Simon, G. (1983). Psychology, professional practice, and the public interest. In B. Sales (Ed.), *The professional psychologist's handbook.* New York: Plenum.

Skinner, H. A., & Pakula, A. (1986). Challenge of computers in psychological assessment. *Professional Psychology: Research and Practice, 17*, 44–50.

Stapp, J., & Fulcher, R. (1982). The employment of 1979 and 1980 doctorate recipients in psychology. *American Psychologist, 37*, 1159–1185.

Stapp, J., Fulcher, R., & Wicherski, M. (1984). The employment of 1981-1982 doctorate recipients in psychology. *American Psychologist, 39*, 1408–1423.

Stapp, J., Tucker, A. M., & VandenBos, G. R. (1985). Census of psychological personnel: 1983. *American Psychologist, 40*, 1317–1351.

Turkin, S. R., & Frank, G. W. (1985). The changing role of psychologists in health maintenance organizations. *American Psychologist, 40*, 1125–1130.

Turkington, C. (1986, November). Impaired psychologists. *APA Monitor, 17*, 10.

Uyeda, M. D., & Moldawsky, S. (1986). Prospective payment and psychological services: What difference does it make? Psychologists aren't in Medicare anyway! *American Psychologist, 41*, 60–63.

Winston, W. J. (1983). Marketing planning for group practices. In W. J. Winston (Ed.), *Marketing for mental health services* (pp. 13–22). New York: Haworth Press.

Yankelovich, Skelly, & White, Inc. (1980). [Unpublished study of the American Psychiatric Association Joint Commission on Public Affairs]. (Available from the American Psychiatric Association, 1700 18th Street N.W., Washington, DC 20009.)

Young, D. W. (1982). A survey of decision aids for clinicians. *British Journal, 285*, 1332–1336.

Appendix
Ethical Principles of Psychologists

PREAMBLE

Psychologists respect the dignity and worth of the individual and strive for the preservation and protection of fundamental human rights. They are committed to increasing knowledge of human behavior and of people's understanding of themselves and others and to the utilization of such knowledge for the promotion of human welfare. While pursuing these objectives, they make every effort to protect the welfare of those who seek their services and of the research participants that may be the object of study. They use their skills only for purposes consistent with these values and do not knowingly permit their misuse by others. While demanding for themselves freedom of inquiry and communication, psychologists accept the responsibility this freedom requires: competence, objectivity in the application of skills, and concern for the best interests of clients, colleagues, students, research participants, and society. In the pursuit of these ideals, psychologists subscribe to principles in the following areas: 1. Responsibility, 2. Competence, 3. Moral and Legal Standards, 4. Public Statements, 5. Confidentiality, 6. Welfare of the Consumer, 7. Professional Relationships, 8. Assessment Techniques, 9. Research With Human Participants, and 10. Care and Use of Animals.

Acceptance of membership in the American Psychological Association commits the member to adherence to these principles.

Psychologists cooperate with duly constituted committees of the American Psychological Association, in particular, the Committee on Scientific and Professional Ethics and Conduct, by responding to inquiries promptly and completely. Members also respond promptly and completely to inquiries from duly constituted state association ethics committees and professional standards review committees.

Note: Reprinted with permission from the American Psychological Association, copyright 1981 by the American Psychological Association.

Principle 1: RESPONSIBILITY

In providing services, psychologists maintain the highest standards of their profession. They accept responsibility for the consequences of their acts and make every effort to ensure that their services are used appropriately.

a. As scientists, psychologists accept responsibility for the selection of their research topics and the methods used in investigation, analysis, and reporting. They plan their research in ways to minimize the possibility that their findings will be misleading. They provide thorough discussion of the limitations of their data, especially where their work touches on social policy or might be construed to the detriment of persons in specific age, sex, ethnic, socioeconomic, or other social groups. In publishing reports of their work, they never suppress disconfirming data, and they acknowledge the existence of alternative hypotheses and explanations of their findings. Psychologists take credit only for work they have actually done.

b. Psychologists clarify in advance with all appropriate persons and agencies the expectations for sharing and utilizing research data. They avoid relationships that may limit their objectivity or create a conflict of interest. Interference with the milieu in which data are collected is kept to a minimum.

c. Psychologists have the responsibility to attempt to prevent distortion, misuse, or suppression of psychological findings by the institution or agency of which they are employees.

d. As members of governmental or other organizational bodies, psychologists remain accountable as individuals to the highest standards of their profession.

e. As teachers, psychologists recognize their primary obligation to help others acquire knowledge and skill. They maintain high standards of scholarship by presenting psychological information objectively, fully and accurately.

f. As practitioners, psychologists know that they bear a heavy social responsibility because their recommendations and professional actions may alter the lives of others. They are alert to personal, social, organizational, financial, or political situations and pressures that might lead to misuse of their influence.

Principle 2: COMPETENCE

The maintenance of high standards of competence is a responsibility shared by all psychologists in the interest of the public and the profession as a whole. Psychologists recognize the boundaries of their competence and the limitations of their techniques. They only provide services and only use techniques for which they are qualified by training and experience. In those areas in which recognized standards do not yet exist, psychologists take whatever precautions are necessary to protect the welfare of their clients. They maintain knowledge of current scientific and professional information related to the services they render.

a. Psychologists accurately represent their competence, education, training, and experience. They claim as evidence of educational qualifications only those degrees obtained from institutions acceptable under the Bylaws and Rules of Council of the American Psychological Association.

b. As teachers, psychologists perform their duties on the basis of careful preparation so that their instruction is accurate, current, and scholarly.

c. Psychologists recognize the need for continuing education and are open to new procedures and changes in expectations and values over time.

d. Psychologists recognize differences among people, such as those that may be associated with age, sex, socioeconomic, and ethnic backgrounds. When necessary, they obtain training, experience, or counsel to assure competent service or research relating to such persons.

e. Psychologists responsible for decisions involving individuals or policies based on test results have an understanding of psychological or educational measurement, validation problems, and test research.

f. Psychologists recognize that personal problems and conflicts may interfere with professional effectiveness. Accordingly, they refrain from undertaking any activity in which their personal problems are likely to lead to inadequate performance or harm to a client, colleague, student, or research participant. If engaged in such activity when they become aware of their personal problems, they seek competent professional assistance to determine whether they should suspend, terminate, or limit the scope of their professional and/or scientific activities.

Principle 3: MORAL AND LEGAL STANDARDS

Psychologists' moral and ethical standards of behavior are a personal matter to the same degree as they are for any other citizen, except as these may compromise the fulfillment of their professional responsibilities or reduce the public trust in psychology and psychologists. Regarding their own behavior, psychologists are sensitive to prevailing community standards and to the possible impact that conformity to or deviation from these standards may have upon the quality of their performance as psychologists. Psychologists are also aware of the possible impact of their public behavior upon the ability of colleagues to perform their professional duties.

a. As teachers, psychologists are aware of the fact that their personal values may affect the selection and presentation of instructional materials. When dealing with topics that may give offense, they recognize and respect the diverse attitudes that students may have toward such materials.

b. As employees or employers, psychologists do not engage in or condone practices that are inhumane or that result in illegal or unjustifiable actions. Such practices include, but are not limited to, those based on considerations of race, handicap, age, gender, sexual preference, religion, or national origin in hiring, promotion, or training.

c. In their professional roles, psychologists avoid any action that will violate or diminish the legal and civil rights of clients or of others who may be affected by their actions.

d. As practitioners and researchers, psychologists act in accord with Association standards and guidelines related to practice and to the conduct of research with human beings and animals. In the ordinary course of events, psychologists adhere to relevant governmental laws and institutional regulations. When federal, state, provincial, organizational, or institutional laws, regulations, or practices are in conflict with Association standards and guidelines, psychologists make known their commitment to Association standards and guidelines and, wherever possible, work toward a resolution of the conflict. Both practitioners and researchers are concerned with the development of such legal and quasi-legal regulations as best serve the public interest, and they work toward changing existing regulations that are not beneficial to the public interest.

Principle 4: PUBLIC STATEMENTS

Public statements, announcements of services, advertising, and promotional activities of psychologists serve the purpose of helping the public make informed judgments and choices. Psychologists represent accurately and objectively their professional qualifications, affiliations, and functions, as well as those of the institutions or organizations with which they or the statements may be associated. In public statements providing psychological information or professional opinions or providing information about the availability of psychological products, publications, and services, psychologists base their statements on scientifically acceptable psychological findings and techniques with full recognition of the limits and uncertainties of such evidence.

a. When announcing or advertising professional services, psychologists may list the following information to describe the provider and services provided: name, highest relevant academic degree earned from a regionally accredited institution, date, type, and level of certification or licensure, diplomate status, APA membership status, address, telephone number, office hours, a brief listing of the type of psychological services offered, an appropriate presentation of fee information, foreign languages spoken, and policy with regard to third-party payments. Additional relevant or important consumer information may be included if not prohibited by other sections of these Ethical Principles.

b. In announcing or advertising the availability of psychological products, publications, or services, psychologists do not present their affiliation with any organization in a manner that falsely implies sponsorship or certification by that organization. In particular and for example, psychologists do not state APA membership or fellow status in a way to suggest that such status implies specialized professional competence or qualifications. Public statements include, but are not limited to, communication by means of periodical, book, list, directory, television, radio, or motion picture. They do not contain (i) a false, fraudulent, misleading, deceptive, or unfair statement; (ii) a misinterpretation of fact or a statement likely to mislead or deceive because in context it makes only a partial disclosure of relevant facts; (iii) a testimonial from a patient regarding the quality of a psychologists' services or products; (iv) a statement intended or likely to create false or unjustified expectations of favorable results; (v) a statement implying unusual, unique, or one-of-a-kind abilities; (vi) a statement intended or likely to appeal to a client's fears, anxieties, or emotions concerning the possible results of failure to obtain the offered services; (vii) a statement concerning the comparative desirability of offered services; (viii) a statement of direct solicitation of individual clients.

c. Psychologists do not compensate or give anything of value to a representative of the press, radio, television, or other communication medium in anticipation of or in return for professional publicity in a news item. A paid advertisement must be identified as such, unless it is apparent from the context that it is a paid advertisement. If communicated to the public by use of radio or television, an advertisement is prerecorded and approved for broadcast by the psychologist, and a recording of the actual transmission is retained by the psychologist.

d. Announcements or advertisements of "personal growth groups," clinics, and agencies give a clear statement of purpose and a clear description of the experiences to be provided. The education, training, and experience of the staff members are appropriately specified.

e. Psychologists associated with the development or promotion of psychological devices, books, or other products offered for commercial sale make reasonable efforts to ensure that announcements and advertisements are presented in a professional, scientifically acceptable, and factually informative manner.

f. Psychologists do not participate for personal gain in commercial announcements or advertisements recommending to the public the purchase or use of proprietary or single-source products or services when that participation is based solely upon their identification as psychologists.

g. Psychologists present the science of psychology and offer their services, products, and publications fairly and accurately, avoiding misrepresentation through sensationalism, exaggeration, or superficiality. Psychologists are guided by the primary obligation to aid the public in developing informed judgments, opinions, and choices.

h. As teachers, psychologists ensure that statements in catalogs and course outlines are accurate and not misleading, particularly in terms of subject matter to be covered, bases for evaluating progress, and the nature of course experiences. Announcements, brochures, or advertisements describing workshops, seminars, or other educational programs accurately describe the audience for which the program is intended as well as eligibility requirements, educational objectives, and nature of the materials to be covered. These announcements also accurately represent the education, training, and experience of the psychologists presenting the programs and any fees involved.

i. Public announcements or advertisements soliciting research participants in which clinical services or other professional services are offered as an inducement make clear the nature of the services as well as the costs and other obligations to be accepted by participants in the research.

j. A psychologist accepts the obligation to correct others who represent the psychologist's professional qualifications, or associations with products or services, in a manner incompatible with these guidelines.

k. Individual diagnostic and therapeutic services are provided only in the context of a professional psychological relationship. When personal advice is given by means of public lectures or demonstrations, newspaper or magazine articles, radio or television programs, mail, or similar media, the psychologist utilizes the most current relevant data and exercises the highest level of professional judgment.

l. Products that are described or presented by means of public lectures or demonstrations, newspaper or magazine articles, radio or television programs, or similar media meet the same recognized standards as exist for products used in the context of a professional relationship.

Principle 5: CONFIDENTIALITY

Psychologists have a primary obligation to respect the confidentiality of information obtained from persons in the course of their work as psychologists. They reveal such information to others only with the consent of the person or the person's legal representative, except in those unusual circumstances in which not to do so would result in clear danger to the person or to others. Where appropriate, psychologists inform their clients of the legal limits of confidentiality.

a. Information obtained in clinical or consulting relationships, or evaluative data concerning children, students, employees, and others, is discussed only for professional purposes and only with persons clearly concerned with the case. Written and oral reports present only data germane to the purposes of the evaluation, and every effort is made to avoid undue invasion of privacy.

b. Psychologists who present personal information obtained during the course of professional work in writings, lectures, or other public forums either obtain adequate prior consent to do so or adequately disguise all identifying information.

c. Psychologists make provisions for maintaining confidentiality in the storage and disposal of records.

d. When working with minors or other persons who are unable to give voluntary, informed consent, psychologists take special care to protect these persons' best interests.

Principle 6: WELFARE OF
THE CONSUMER

Psychologists respect the integrity and protect the welfare of the people and groups with whom they work. When conflicts of interest arise between clients and psychologists' employing institutions, psychologists clarify the nature and direction of their loyalties and responsibilities and keep all parties informed of their commitments. Psychologists fully inform consumers as to the purpose and nature of an evaluative, treatment, educational, or training procedure, and they freely acknowledge that clients, students, or participants in research have freedom of choice with regard to participation.

a. Psychologists are continually cognizant of their own needs and of their potentially influential position vis-à-vis persons such as clients, students, and subordinates. They avoid exploiting the trust and dependency of such persons. Psychologists make every effort to avoid dual relationships that could impair their professional judgment or increase the risk of exploitation. Examples of such dual relationships include, but are not limited to, research with and treatment of employees, students, supervisees, close friends, or relatives. Sexual intimacies with clients are unethical.

b. When a psychologist agrees to provide services to a client at the request of a third party, the psychologist assumes the responsibility of clarifying the nature of the relationships to all parties concerned.

c. Where the demands of an organization require psychologists to violate these Ethical Principles, psychologists clarify the nature of the conflict between the demands and these principles. They inform all parties of psychologists' ethical responsibilities and take appropriate action.

d. Psychologists make advance financial arrangements that safeguard the best interests of and are clearly understood by their clients. They neither give nor receive any remuneration for referring clients for professional services. They contribute a portion of their services to work for which they receive little or no financial return.

e. Psychologists terminate a clinical or consulting relationship when it is reasonably clear that the consumer is not benefiting from it. They offer to help the consumer locate alternative sources of assistance.

Principle 7: PROFESSIONAL RELATIONSHIPS

Psychologists act with due regard for the needs, special competencies, and obligations of their colleagues in psychology and other professions. They respect the prerogatives and obligations of the institutions or organizations with which these other colleagues are associated.

a. Psychologists understand the areas of competence of related professions. They make full use of all the professional, technical, and administrative resources that serve the best interests of consumers. The absence of formal relationships with other professional workers does not relieve psychologists of the responsibility of securing for their clients the best possible professional service, nor does it relieve them of the obligation to exercise foresight, diligence, and tact in obtaining the complementary or alternative assistance needed by clients.

b. Psychologists know and take into account the traditions and practices of other professional groups with whom they work and cooperate fully with such groups. If a person is receiving similar services from another professional, psychologists do not offer their own services directly to such a person. If a psychologist is contacted by a person who is already receiving similar services from another professional, the psychologist carefully considers that professional relationship and proceeds with caution and sensitivity to the therapeutic issues as well as the client's welfare. The psychologist discusses these issues with the client so as to minimize the risk of confusion and conflict.

c. Psychologists who employ or supervise other professionals or professionals in training accept the obligation to facilitate the further professional development of these individuals. They provide appropriate working conditions, timely evaluations, constructive consultation, and experience opportunities.

d. Psychologists do not exploit their professional relationships with clients, supervisees, students, employees, or research participants sexually or otherwise. Psychologists do not condone or engage in sexual harassment. Sexual harassment is defined as deliberate or repeated comments, gestures, or physical contacts of a sexual nature that are unwanted by the recipient.

e. In conducting research in institutions or organizations, psychologists secure appropriate authorization to conduct such research. They are aware of their obligations to future research workers and ensure that host institutions receive adequate information about the research and proper acknowledgment of their contributions.

f. Publication credit is assigned to those who have contributed to a publication in proportion to their professional contributions. Major contributions of a professional character made by several persons to a common project are recognized by joint authorship, with the individual who made the principal contribution listed first. Minor contributions of a professional character and extensive clerical or similar nonprofessional assistance may be acknowledged in footnotes or in an introductory statement. Acknowledgment through specific citations is made for unpublished as well as published material that has directly influenced the research or writing. Psychologists who compile and edit material of others for publication publish the material in the name of the originating group, if appropriate, with their own name appearing as chairperson or editor. All contributors are to be acknowledged and named.

g. When psychologists know of an ethical violation by another psychologist, and it seems appropiate, they informally attempt to resolve the issue by bringing the behavior to the attention of the psychologist. If the misconduct is of a minor nature and/or appears to be due to lack of sensitivity, knowledge, or experience, such an informal solution is usually appropriate. Such informal corrective efforts are made with sensitivity to any rights to confidentiality involved. If the violation does not seem amenable to an informal solution, or is of a more serious nature, psychologists bring it to the attention of the appropriate local, state, and/or national committee on professional ethics and conduct.

Principle 8: ASSESSMENT TECHNIQUES

In the development, publication, and utilization of psychological assessment techniques, psychologists make every effort to promote the welfare and best interests of the client. They guard against the misuse of assessment results. They respect the client's right to know the results, the interpretations made, and the bases for their conclusions and recommendations. Psychologists make every effort to maintain the security of tests and other assessment techniques within limits of legal mandates. They strive to ensure the appropriate use of assessment techniques by others.

a. In using assessment techniques, psychologists respect the right of clients to have full explanations of the nature and purpose of the techniques in language the clients can understand, unless an explicit exception to this right has been agreed upon in advance. When the explanations are to be provided by others, psychologists establish procedures for ensuring the adequacy of these explanations.

b. Psychologists responsible for the development and standardization of psychological tests and other assessment techniques utilize established scientific procedures and observe the relevant APA standards.

c. In reporting assessment results, psychologists indicate any reservations that exist regarding validity or reliability because of the circumstances of the assessment or the inappropriateness of the norms for the person tested. Psychologists strive to ensure that the results of assessments and their interpretations are not misused by others.

d. Psychologists recognize that assessment results may become obsolete. They make every effort to avoid and prevent the misuse of obsolete measures.

e. Psychologists offering scoring and interpretation services are able to produce appropriate evidence for the validity of the programs and procedures used in arriving at interpretations. The public offering of an automated interpretation service is considered a professional-to-professional consultation. Psychologists make every effort to avoid misuse of assessment reports.

f. Psychologists do not encourage or promote the use of psychological assessment techniques by inappropriately trained or otherwise unqualified persons through teaching, sponsorship, or supervision.

Principle 9: RESEARCH WITH HUMAN PARTICIPANTS

The decision to undertake research rests upon a considered judgment by the individual psychologist about how best to contribute to psychological science and human welfare. Having made the decision to conduct research, the psychologist considers alternative directions in which research energies and resources might be invested. On the basis of this consideration, the psychologist carries out the investigation with respect and concern for the dignity and welfare of the people who participate and with cognizance of federal and state regulations and professional standards governing the conduct of research with human participants.

a. In planning a study, the investigator has the responsibility to make a careful evaluation of its ethical acceptability. To the extent that the weighing of scientific and human values suggests a compromise of any principle, the investigator incurs a correspondingly serious obligation to seek ethical advice and to observe stringent safeguards to protect the rights of human participants.

b. Considering whether a participant in a planned study will be a "subject at risk" or a "subject at minimal risk," according to recognized standards, is of primary ethical concern to the investigator.

c. The investigator always retains the responsibility for ensuring ethical practice in research. The investigator is also responsible for the ethical treatment of research participants by collaborators, assistants, students, and employees, all of whom, however, incur similar obligations.

d. Except in minimal-risk research, the investigator establishes a clear and fair agreement with research participants, prior to their participation, that clarifies the obligations and responsibilities of each. The investigator has the obligation to honor all promises and commitments included in that agreement. The investigator informs the participants of all aspects of the research that might reasonably be expected to influence willingness to participate and explains all other aspects of the research about which the participants inquire. Failure to make full disclosure prior to obtaining informed consent requires additional safeguards to protect the welfare and dignity of the research participants. Research with children or with participants who have impairments that would limit understanding and/or communication requires special safeguarding procedures.

e. Methodological requirements of a study may make the use of concealment or deception necessary. Before conducting such a study, the investigator has a special responsibility to (i) determine whether the use of such techniques is justified by the study's prospective scientific, educational, or applied value; (ii) determine whether alternative procedures are available that do not use concealment or deception; and (iii) ensure that the participants are provided with sufficient explanation as soon as possible.

f. The investigator respects the individual's freedom to decline to participate in or to withdraw from the research at any time. The obligation to protect this freedom requires careful thought and consideration when the investigator is in a position of authority or influence over the participant. Such positions of authority include, but are not limited to, situations in which research participation is required as part of employment or in which the participant is a student, client, or employee of the investigator.

g. The investigator protects the participant from physical and mental discomfort, harm, and danger that may arise from research procedures. If risks of such consequences exist, the investigator informs the participant of that fact. Research procedures likely to cause serious or lasting

harm to a participant are not used unless the failure to use these procedures might expose the participant to risk of greater harm, or unless the
research has great potential benefit and fully informed and voluntary
consent is obtained from each participant. The participant should be
informed of procedures for contacting the investigator within a reasonable time period following participation should stress, potential harm, or
related questions or concerns arise.

h. After the data are collected, the investigator provides the participant with information about the nature of the study and attempts to
remove any misconceptions that may have arisen. Where scientific or
humane values justify delaying or withholding this information, the
investigator incurs a special responsibility to monitor the research and to
ensure that there are no damaging consequences for the participant.

i. Where research procedures result in undesirable consequences for
the individual participant, the investigator has the responsibility to de-
tect and remove or correct these consequences, including long-term effects.

j. Information obtained about a research participant during the course
of an investigation is confidential unless otherwise agreed upon in advance. When the possibility exists that others may obtain access to such
information, this possibility, together with the plans for protecting confidentiality, is explained to the participant as part of the procedure for
obtaining informed consent.

Principle 10: CARE AND USE
OF ANIMALS

*An investigator of animal behavior strives to advance understanding of basic
behavioral principles and/or to contribute to the improvement of human health
and welfare. In seeking these ends, the investigator ensures the welfare of animals and treats them humanely. Laws and regulations notwithstanding, an
animal's immediate protection depends upon the scientist's own conscience.*

a. The acquisition, care, use, and disposal of all animals are in compliance with current federal, state or provincial, and local laws and regulations.

b. A psychologist trained in research methods and experienced in the
care of laboratory animals closely supervises all procedures involving
animals and is responsible for ensuring appropriate consideration of
their comfort, health, and humane treatment.

c. Psychologists ensure that all individuals using animals under their
supervision have received explicit instruction in experimental methods
and in the care, maintenance, and handling of the species being used.

Responsibilities and activities of individuals participating in a research project are consistent with their respective competencies.

d. Psychologists make every effort to minimize discomfort, illness, and pain of animals. A procedure subjecting animals to pain, stress, or privation is used only when an alternative procedure is unavailable and the goal is justified by its prospective scientific, educational, or applied value. Surgical procedures are performed under appropriate anesthesia; techniques to avoid infection and minimize pain are followed during and after surgery.

e. When it is appropriate that the animal's life be terminated, it is done rapidly and painlessly.

Author Index

Subject Index

About the Authors

Walter B. Pryzwansky is Professor and Chair of the Division of Organizational and Psychological Studies in the School of Education, University of North Carolina at Chapel Hill. His teaching responsibilities are in the university's APA-approved graduate training program in School Psychology, for which he has served as coordinator; prior to his academic appointment, he was a psychologist with the Devereux Foundation. He earned his doctorate from Teachers College, Columbia University in 1969. Currently President of the APA's Division of School Psychology, he has also been active in the North Carolina Psychology Association and North Carolina School Psychology Association, and served as chair of the North Carolina State Board of Examiners. He is an APA Fellow and ABPP Diplomate in School Psychology. A member of the editorial board of several journals, his research and writings have been in the areas of consultation, professional issues and practice, and learning disabilities.

Robert N. Wendt (PhD, The University of Wisconsin–Madison) is a Professor in the Department of Counselor and Human Services Education, the University of Toledo, and is Director of the School Psychology Training Program. He also teaches courses in marital and family therapy. Professor Wendt holds a diplomate in Marital and Family Therapy from the American Board of Family Psychology; in addition to his private clinical practice, he is director of a clinical research program with family therapy for families experiencing cancer, at St. Vincent Medical Center in Toledo. His most recent publications have appeared in *Professional Practice in Psychology* (where he is an editorial consultant), *Psychology in the Schools*, and *Elder Abuse: Perspectives on an Emergency Crisis*, in which he co-authored a chapter. Dr. Wendt is Past President and still an active member of the Ohio State Board of Psychology. In addition, he is active both as a workshop presenter and as a participant in local, state, and national psychological organizations.

Psychology Practitioner Guidebooks

Editors

Arnold P. Goldstein, Syracuse University
Leonard Krasner, Stanford University & SUNY at Stony Brook
Sol L. Garfield, Washington University